Seamless Teamwork

Using Microsoft® SharePoint®
Technologies to Collaborate,
Innovate, and Drive Business
in New Ways

MICHAEL SAMPSON

PUBLISHED BY
Microsoft Press
A Division of Microsoft Corporation
One Microsoft Way
Redmond, Washington 98052-6399

Library of Congress Control Number: 2008935424

Printed and bound in the United States of America.

1 2 3 4 5 6 7 8 9   QWT   3 2 1 0 9 8

Distributed in Canada by H.B. Fenn and Company Ltd.

A CIP catalogue record for this book is available from the British Library.

Microsoft Press books are available through booksellers and distributors worldwide. For further information about international editions, contact your local Microsoft Corporation office or contact Microsoft Press International directly at fax (425) 936-7329. Visit our Web site at www.microsoft.com/mspress. Send comments to mspinput@microsoft.com.

Microsoft, Microsoft Press, Access, Excel, Groove, Internet Explorer, OneNote, Outlook, PowerPoint, SharePoint, Windows, Windows Live, and Windows Vista are either registered trademarks or trademarks of the Microsoft group of companies. Other product and company names mentioned herein may be the trademarks of their respective owners.

The example companies, organizations, products, domain names, e-mail addresses, logos, people, places, and events depicted herein are fictitious. No association with any real company, organization, product, domain name, e-mail address, logo, person, place, or event is intended or should be inferred.

Acquisitions Editor: Juliana Aldous Atkinson
Developmental Editor: Sandra Haynes
Project Editor: Kathleen Atkins
Editorial Production: Online Training Solutions, Inc.
Technical Reviewer: Bob Hogan; Technical Review services provided by Content Master, a member of CM Group, Ltd.
Cover: Tom Draper Design

Body Part No. X14-14007

To my parents, Kingsley and Barbara Sampson, for their early formative influences, especially modeling the love of words and good books.

—MICHAEL SAMPSON

About the Author

Michael Sampson is a leading expert on improving the performance capability of virtual teams. He is an Industry Analyst and Independent Consultant, and speaks at conferences around the world. He is the President of The Michael Sampson Company in New Zealand.

As an Industry Analyst, Michael helps end-user organizations understand the collaboration landscape, through independent analysis and briefings. As an Independent Consultant, Michael provides impartial counsel and advisory services to clients wanting to improve the capability of people and teams to work with others through collaboration technology. Michael writes the "Working with People You Can't Be With" blog, at *www.michaelsampson.net*.

Michael holds a Master of Commerce with first class honors in telecommunications-based IT, from the University of Canterbury in New Zealand. He is currently working on his doctorate in collaborative applications and virtual teams.

Michael lives in New Zealand with his glorious wife, Katrina, and eight children: David, Matthew, Philip, Daniel, Timothy, Susanna, Jonathan, and Elizabeth. No, there were no multiple births, and at the time of writing this, their oldest child is 12. How's that for a busy household!

Acknowledgments

IT SEEMS ALMOST PASSÉ to write that a book is a team effort, especially because there is only one name on the front cover of this one. I have read many previous book introductions, and the authors of those books are always calling out their thanks to a long list of people. For me, I have previously given mental assent to the idea that a book is a team effort, but having now written one and lived through the process as an author, I absolutely and unreservedly know it in my heart to be true. This book would not be in your hands if it were not for the diligent work and effort of many people.

First and foremost, thanks to Katrina and our children—David, Matthew, Philip, Daniel, Timothy, Susanna, Jonathan, and Elizabeth. Although writing this book was always "just part of my work day," there were costs in other areas as I got it out of my system. It always brought a smile to my face when one of the boys would ask, "Is your book finished yet?" And with them able to read this paragraph now, the answer must finally be "Yes!" Thank you for understanding that Dad had to get this done. And to David, who suggested that I should dedicate the book "To all those who buy this book and don't finish reading it because it is so boring," thanks for all your fun and great ideas. Keep them coming!

Marc Orchant played an early pivotal role in encouraging me to take my research on the effective use of SharePoint and make a book out of it. I was speaking with Marc about this book in late November 2007, and thanked him for the role he had played in getting it going. He issued me with a huge challenge for the book; he wanted to be able to say that he knew me when I was merely a "collaboration guru," whereas after the book was out I would be the "worldwide expert in SharePoint." That was typical Marc—huge vision, and a way of expanding the horizons of those who were his friends. Marc suffered a major heart attack four days later, and died a week after that. I didn't get a chance to speak with him again, but in all of my writing, consulting, and teaching about SharePoint, I have tried to be true to his challenge to me. Thanks, Marc, but I still miss you.

Eric Mack, a long time friend and professional colleague, was relentless in offering his help and insight as I worked through the contents of this book. Thanks for looking out for me, and asking how it was going. It meant more than I can say, Eric! Eric blogs at *www.ericmackonline.com*.

Neil Salkind from The Salkind Agency was my agent for this book, and he gave valuable directions as I navigated through the passage of writing this book. My thanks to Neil and the members of his team—Katrina and Heather in particular.

Juliana Aldous Atkinson was the first contact I met at Microsoft Press, and the Product Planner there who championed my book proposal through the Microsoft Press Editorial Board. (I was on vacation in a small house on the coast of New Zealand when she told me that the Board had signed off.) Juliana was also the one who received my original proposal for a book about SharePoint, and encouraged me to think broader and deeper than I originally planned. That was such a helpful push-back early in the process. This book bears her indelible imprint. My thanks.

Sandra Haynes was my Development Editor at Microsoft Press, and helped me survive the process through regular phone calls and marked-up chapters when I needed them. Thank you, Sandra.

The team at Online Training Solutions, Inc. (OTSI), was fantastic at taking my so-called "completed" manuscript and getting it to a final state—copyediting, graphics enhancing, and so on. It was a real delight to work directly with members of the OTSI team—Joan Preppernau, Jean Trenary, Kathy Krause, Jaime Odell, Terence Maikels, Debbie Berman, Jan Bednarczuk, and Lisa Van Every—and to observe the contributions of a whole cadre of others at OTSI who worked in the background. My thanks to each person.

The technical reviewer, Bob Hogan, likewise gave valuable feedback during the final stages. I really appreciated the way Bob approached his review, and his feedback was always right on the mark.

Chandima Kulathilake (*www.chandima.net*), a SharePoint MVP and consultant in New Zealand, deserves a medal for his patience with me. Questions like "Why doesn't SharePoint work like X?" popped up on his Windows Live Messenger more than once! Thank you, Chan, for helping me to understand some of the technical matters I needed to get my head around. And thank you especially for coming to my rescue with a deployment of SharePoint Enterprise near the end of writing when I was down to the wire. You worked over a weekend for me, building an in-house test environment for me to use for this book, and for my workshops—you proved yourself a true friend. Thank you.

Peter Drucker, the great management sage, once wrote something to the effect that "There has to be more to your work than just writing books—they have to make an impact." I hope this work lives up to his edict.

Contents

What do you think of this book? We want to hear from you!

Microsoft is interested in hearing your feedback so we can continually improve our books and learning resources for you. To participate in a brief online survey, please visit:

microsoft.com/learning/booksurvey

Introduction

An Analyst Writing a Book on SharePoint?

MY DAY JOB IS running an industry analyst firm. Industry analysts look at what is happening with vendors and products at the level of the industry as a whole, instead of being worried about the messiness of individual situations. Analysts look for trends.

One of the trends I have been watching is the emergence of Microsoft SharePoint as a major force in multiple industries. The collaboration strategy of Microsoft in the late 1990s was centered on Microsoft Exchange Server, but with the dawn of a new millennium, Microsoft started to position SharePoint to take a far greater role. As the years have passed and the versions of SharePoint have ticked over, SharePoint has become increasingly central to the collaboration strategy of Microsoft, and indeed to many conversations about collaboration in organizations today.

The final frontier of the ascendency of SharePoint is for it to take a central role in the work of individuals and teams in day-to-day organizational life. This book outlines a way to make that happen. The focal question is this: How can a team make the best use of SharePoint for team collaboration? Or saying that in a slightly different way, how can a team use all of the capabilities in SharePoint to work effectively with others they can't be with, to enhance team collaboration, and to drive business forward?

Seamless Teamwork is not written for my normal clients—the CIOs and IT decision makers in organizations. It is written for the business managers, team leaders, and end users in organizations who have been told by IT to use SharePoint. They haven't necessarily had a say in the matter, but for various business, regulatory, and technical reasons, change is in the air. Therefore, this book outlines a way of making the best of SharePoint for individuals and teams.

Overview

This book is about a revolution in the way that people work together in business teams. For at least a decade, people have relied on Microsoft Office Outlook as the mainstay of their communication, collaboration, and coordination activities. E-mail messages are sent to team members to request information, to share a document or slide deck, and to start the brainstorming of a concept. Meetings are scheduled through the Outlook Calendar, with free and busy times flagged for ease of scheduling, and with calendar invites moving seamlessly between people by e-mail. Tasks are managed within Outlook, allowing people to create a sense of order in their lives.

But Outlook isn't enough, and in saying that, the criticism is leveled at e-mail in general. The wild success of e-mail—of which Outlook is a leading example— is a huge problem. Nearly everyone uses e-mail at work (90 percent), and nearly everyone uses e-mail every time they communicate with others using electronic tools (95 percent). This is trending downward, however, as some people switch to instant messaging for a portion of their business communication activities. And yet, e-mail is not suitable for many of the tasks we put it to. Our use of it for team collaboration creates more problems than it solves.

Consider, for example, the pain caused by the use of Outlook by business work teams in their activities:

- Judy attaches a draft document to an Outlook message and sends it for review to five people on the team. Five modified editions are sent back, leaving Judy the mess of getting a new edition prepared.

- Discussions by e-mail about a pending decision are all over the place as team members sometimes respond to everyone on the original list, or other times respond to just a couple. Team members also respond to different e-mail messages in the thread, which pushes the flow of thoughts out of kilter. Each person on the team has to sort out for themselves what was said to whom in response to what, if they can be bothered going to the hassle.

- Adam joins a team halfway into a project. Others on the team have to forward Adam any e-mail messages, documents, and task assignments that have piled up. What Adam receives depends on how well the other team members have retained their earlier joint activities.

- Each member on the team sorts and organizes the e-mail messages, documents, and other electronic team artifacts in his or her own nuanced ways. When seeking clarity over the third message in her list, Judy is almost guaranteed to fail if she asks Adam about the third message in his list. Each will have a different third message.

- E-mail messages are stored in Outlook folders, various editions of documents are stored with e-mail messages in some situations and in Windows Explorer folders in others, upcoming scheduled meetings are in Outlook Calendar folders, and current task assignments are stored in Outlook task folders, with no integration between them, and no way for Judy, Adam, or other people on the team to get a single consolidated view about what is going on within the project according to their set of records, let alone based on a shared set. Their project materials are stored all over the place, and each person has to keep his or her own mental view of what is going on.

It's actually a wonder that teams using e-mail get anything done!

The Better Way

Seamless Teamwork explores a better way for work teams to communicate, collaborate, and coordinate their activities through SharePoint, a recent addition to the Microsoft product line. This use of SharePoint is instead of Outlook in certain situations and in addition to Outlook in others. Actually, it's in addition to a number of other products in the Microsoft product line—products such as OneNote, SharedView, Groove, Windows Live Messenger, and more.

Seamless Teamwork is organized around the idea of someone getting a new project to lead at their place of work, something that everyone reading this book should be able to relate to or aspire to.

Chapter 1, "The New Project," sets the stage for the rest of the book, introducing Roger and the project (Project Delta) that he has been asked to lead by using SharePoint. As you'll see, Roger represents an average project manager tasked with running a normal business project by using SharePoint, and the situations and decision points he faces will also look familiar. The chapter investigates the reasons for this use of SharePoint rather than continued reliance on e-mail, and it also addresses the issue of travel to accomplish teamwork.

Chapter 2, "Managing the Project and Finding a Team," introduces "The Five Phases Project Life Cycle Model" that applies to many business projects, and which is used as the organizing framework for the approach in *Seamless Teamwork*. The chapter provides a high-level overview of what's involved in each of the five phases, providing necessary context for the remainder of the book. Chapter 2 also looks at how a project leader can use the My Site capabilities of SharePoint to locate great people for team projects.

Chapter 3, "Setting Up SharePoint," is aimed at the person charged with setting up the structures in SharePoint, for effective collaboration, and outlines a three-site approach to supporting team collaboration projects. Not everyone will have to do the work in this chapter, but for the person who does, it provides step-by-step instructions about the tools from SharePoint to use in each of the three sites. This approach is also designed with an eye to the longer term, for when the project is finished and for what happens then.

Chapter 4, "Team, Meet SharePoint," is for the project team members themselves, and introduces them to the SharePoint site structure set up for their work in Chapter 3. It lays the foundation for effective teamwork by using SharePoint, and outlines how to keep team members involved in a project, even when they have many projects swirling around at any one time. The chapter also looks at the options for working with SharePoint team information when team members are not connected to the network.

The five chapters from Chapter 5, "Creating a Shared Vision," to Chapter 9, "Concluding the Project," each takes one of the five phases of the team project life cycle model and talks through the common events and activities in each phase, and addresses how and where SharePoint can be used to support these activities. For example, at some point, a document has to be written by the team that encapsulates their thinking and recommendations for moving the project forward. Chapter 7, "Analyzing the Options," addresses this under the "Coauthoring a Document" topic, and describes different ways of doing so by using SharePoint.

To conclude *Seamless Teamwork*, Chapter 10, "Winning in the Market," provides a brief snippet into what happened for Roger and Project Delta a year after the team finished their work. And it hints that, sometimes, working with others through SharePoint can lead to more than better business decisions!

Although Chapter 10 concludes the printed edition of *Seamless Teamwork*, there are two additional chapters available for readers. Chapter 11, "How to Use the Sponsors and Stakeholders Site," takes the ideas of the Sponsors and Stakeholders site, as discussed and configured in Chapter 3, and talks about how to use it. Chapter 12, "Beyond Seamless Teamwork," addresses the wider governance issues of using SharePoint for collaboration within an enterprise context. Chapters 11 and 12 are only available online. See *www.seamlessteamwork.com* for downloading instructions. Use the coupon code "IHAVETHEBOOK" to get both for no charge.

Finally, in a book of this nature, it is impossible to cover every eventuality, every situation, and every approach. What I hope you will get out of it is a vision of how you can apply the capabilities of SharePoint to the work of your team, rather than a prescription of what you need to do at each and every point of a teaming process. Embrace the ideas that work for you, and ignore the ones that don't.

Who This Book Is For

This book is for everyone in an organization that uses SharePoint as part of their day-to-day collaborative work. I'm thinking of business managers, team members, information workers, and generally, anyone who has work to get done with others through the use of SharePoint.

Seamless Teamwork is not written for IT professionals looking to administer SharePoint or design applications for SharePoint—you need to buy a different book to deal with those issues. But it can still help IT professionals in ways that all of those other technical and geek-speak books cannot. It shows SharePoint within the world of the user rather than the hum of the data center.

For end users, a companion reference to *Seamless Teamwork* is *Microsoft Windows SharePoint Services 3.0 Step by Step*, by Olga Londer, Bill English, Todd Bleeker, and Penelope Coventry (Microsoft Press, 2007). Where *Seamless Teamwork* takes the team and its work as the organizing principle, and then looks at how to use SharePoint to facilitate that work, this *Step by Step* book approaches it from the opposite direction. There are benefits to both approaches, so these two books are highly complementary.

So, read this book, bring its principles and ideas to life in your projects with SharePoint, and learn how to get the best out of what has been made available from Microsoft, and in the process reach the business, professional, and personal goals that you embrace.

Michael Sampson, michael@michaelsampson.net
The Michael Sampson Company Limited
September 2008

Foreword

SINCE THE TURN OF THE MILLENNIUM, online workspaces have become de rigueur for teams. Typically, a team comes together for its first meeting—whether face to face or by conference call—and proceeds to talk about how it will share documents, track progress, and keep up to date when they're no longer in one another's presence. For most teams, these conversations go no further than mentioning what technology they'll employ. "Use SharePoint," one team member might say. "Let's have weekly conference calls," says another, and off they go to do their work.

This is not best practice. Technology alone does not produce results for teams. They also need good sociology, which is why Jeff Stamps's and my motto has been, "90% people, 10% technology." Michael Sampson, the tireless analyst of collaboration, clearly adheres to this principle and provides SharePoint users with a must-read manual for teaming.

Rather than offering a simple how-to, which is the theme of most technology books, Michael has the insight and knowledge to show readers how to work— what they need to think about from a behavioral perspective to make "seamless teamwork" possible.

Michael practices what he espouses. He lives outside of Christchurch, New Zealand, not even in his small country's third-largest city. To connect to the larger global community of thinkers and practitioners concerned about virtual teams and collaboration, he must use the very best approaches to teamwork. I had the chance to visit his home office not long ago and saw the order he has created in the midst of the pandemonium of a house with eight home-schooled children. Mind maps, folksonomies for his knowledge management system, walls and walls of bookshelves, and several computer monitors facilitate his tracking trends in technology and teamwork. His widely read blog, "Working with People You Can't Be With," keeps up with both the technology and sociology of teamwork.

Put Michael's ideas into practice and you'll have a much more successful team.

Jessica Lipnack, CEO, NetAge, and coauthor with Jeff Stamps of many books, including Virtual Teams, The Age of the Network, *and* Networking

CHAPTER 1

The New Project

Projects and People

WORKING ON PROJECTS and working with other people are the two consistent hallmarks of corporate life for information workers today.

Projects are how we structure the work that we engage in—from the breakdown of lofty corporate strategy statements into programs of work to the tasks and activities that we actually do.

The second hallmark of corporate life is working with other people. Other people are essential to the success of our projects because life is too complex for us to do everything and know everything ourselves. They are essential because projects that we work on can have significant effects on other people, and it bodes badly for our projects if we overlook their concerns.

Seamless Teamwork brings these two hallmarks of corporate life together, as it explores working on projects with other people while using Microsoft SharePoint technologies. To that end, meet Roger. Roger is in his mid-30s, is on the corporate fast-track, and is about to be asked to lead an important company project using Microsoft SharePoint, a new tool from Microsoft that the IT department has just installed at his firm.

Let's become a fly on his office wall ...

Roger Gets Project Delta

Roger Lengel's thoughts were still racing at top speed as he flicked off his computer and got up from his desk to leave the office on Monday night. Tomorrow promised to be a pivotal day in his year, if not his entire career! He had been called into a big meeting earlier that day with some of the company bigwigs to talk about "Project Delta," a new company-wide initiative to drive growth in overseas markets. It hadn't been stated upfront why he was wanted in the meeting, but it slowly dawned on Roger as the meeting progressed that the senior executives wanted him to lead Project Delta. He had always played second fiddle to someone else on recent company projects, but this time it promised to be different. This time, he's on his own, and he's in charge. It's a great opportunity to make his mark and prove himself to the management team.

As he slumped into the seat on the train for his 20-minute commute back to his apartment, Roger reflected on the past five years of his career. At the age of 30, he had felt that he had stagnated and wasn't learning anything new, or contributing what he knew he was capable of contributing, so he had exited the corporate scene for a couple of years to put himself through an MBA program at a top business school. He had graduated near the top of the class and had accepted a job offer at Fourth Coffee, a U.S.–based coffee chain that was considering expanding into international markets.

Tuesday morning found Roger up bright and early, even earlier than usual. He skipped breakfast at the apartment, but grabbed a bagel and his regular coffee as he got off the train. He bounded into the office, powered up his computer, and saw the e-mail message that he had been expecting. It was from Kelly Rollin, his boss at Fourth Coffee.

Dear Roger,

You did great in yesterday's meeting with Martin, Janet, Tommy, and Darren. This e-mail message is to confirm what was verbally discussed, that you are project lead on Project Delta. It is critical to the future of our company that you get this right, and we all have full confidence in you to do so. You wouldn't have been tapped to do this otherwise.

A couple of pointers: You will need to assemble a team of people from across the firm to be involved, and given the emphasis of Project Delta on international expansion, I don't need to remind you to pull in some good people from our overseas offices. The implication, of course, is that you'll be leading a virtual team— you won't be able to work in person with all of the people on the team, but you'll still need to ensure that all of the work that gets done is done effectively.

Secondly, I think this is a great project for running through SharePoint. I have spoken to Gareth Chan in IT, and he will be setting up a new Project Delta site for you. Please make sure that you use SharePoint in the most effective way possible; it shouldn't merely be a file repository.

Let me know if there's anything I can do to assist. Happy to run interference for you where and if necessary.

Go get 'em!

Kelly Rollin, Manager, International Markets

What Now?

Roger's head was spinning as he finished reading Kelly's message, and he momentarily stood to gaze out the window. After yesterday's meeting, he was pretty sure the project was in the bag, but SharePoint? What's that all about? He'd seen SharePoint mentioned in the monthly IT newsletter, but had always thought that it was for "someone else." And now he was being asked to lead a project for the first time and run the project effectively using SharePoint to boot. "I'll do my best, on both counts," he said out loud to himself, and then turned to sit back at his computer. There was now much to do.

Why Can't We Just Use Outlook?

What's the big deal about using SharePoint rather than e-mail for a team project? Given that everyone already has e-mail, and knows how to use it, why should teams learn and embrace something else? Below are a number of reasons for using SharePoint.

E-Mail Doesn't Always Get Through

With the tremendous growth in spam over the past few years, organizations and Internet Service Providers (ISPs) have been forced to filter and block messages that could be spam. This is a best-efforts approach to block messages that look suspect, and the algorithms used to do the blocking are constantly being updated. But it is not perfect, and messages that are valid can be tagged as spam and blocked from being delivered. The person who sent the message doesn't know that the intended recipient didn't get his e-mail message, and the intended recipient doesn't know that she hasn't received something she should have.

Thus the use of e-mail leads to great possibilities of miscommunication and unintended silence ("Why hasn't she responded to me yet?").

Attachments Don't Always Get Through

Documents and files can be the bearer of viruses and other malicious code that do bad things to individual computers and even entire computer networks. Some organizations take a very stringent approach to dealing with attached documents and files from people outside of the organization, and while they permit the message to go through, attachments with certain file extensions may be stripped off. Thus, what was seen as being an easy way to share information becomes a headache.

E-Mail Is Bad for Information Management

Using an e-mail message to send an attachment to other members of the project team creates many copies of the attachment. Where you previously had only a single copy of a document, now you have many more. You have a second copy stored in your e-mail Sent folder, and each person who you sent it to now has his or her own copy.

This is problematic when looked at from a business perspective and a technical one. The business problem is that you are never quite sure which document is the most recent edition; when you want to refer to the document that you were sent, is it the latest? Unless you interrupt yourself and the original author, you are never quite sure. The technical problem is the increase in server storage required to store all of the duplicated copies. Because e-mail creates a copy of the attachment for each person, your IT department has to supply and support 5 times, 10 times, or 50 times the storage space to cope.

Both of these bode badly for information management.

SharePoint Is Easier to Hand Over to New People, or to Bring New People into the Project Team

It is easier to induct new people into the team when SharePoint is being used as the place for working on the project. Each additional person merely needs to be given access privileges to the team site, and all of the information related to the project is immediately accessible. All of the discussions, all of the documents, all of the current tasks and meetings—it's all there.

When e-mail is used as the place for working on the project, someone has to go through the historical messages and forward a copy on to the newcomer, and also find all of the current documents and send them or provide access to a shared storage location. This takes time, the nominated person is unlikely to do it perfectly, and after the e-mail messages are forwarded, the metadata about time and date received becomes lost; thus the newcomer has to manually recreate the historical message flow.

E-Mail Creates Unnecessary Communication

E-mail results in unnecessary communication being created and sent. For example, consider Matthew and Nancy, two of the members on a project team at their organization. Everyone on the project team has embraced a common project outcome, and various tasks and activities have been distributed among the members on the team. They are, however, using e-mail to facilitate interaction. Let's look at how Matthew and Nancy use e-mail to get their work done.

Matthew, Tuesday @5.18pm ... Nancy, hi. I'm working on my next deliverable for our project, and need the latest version of your document pls. Is it good to go, and if so, can you please send it to me? Thanks much, M.

Nancy, Wednesday @8.32am ... Matthew, here it is. There are still some areas to fix up and some finishing touches to apply, but the essence of the document won't change. Please advise if you have any questions. All the best, Nancy.

Matthew, Wednesday @9.14am ... Nancy, this is great. Thanks much. M.

If the project team had been using a SharePoint team site, none of this interaction would have been required for Matthew to get the document. He would merely have gone to the project workspace, looked for Nancy's document, and opened it up. Two messages in Nancy's Inbox and one in Matthew's Inbox would thus have been entirely eliminated. Also, with the interaction being run by e-mail, Matthew's work is constrained by the responsiveness or lack thereof by Nancy; he can't get on with his work until she has sent the document. If it was in the team site, he could get it immediately and keep working.

E-Mail Creates Confusion in the Flow of Conversation

When a team holds a conversation by e-mail, each person has to work through the messages in the conversation and note which ones add something and which ones merely reiterate what someone else has previously said. If Roger, Gregory, and Nancy send messages back and forth multiple times in any given day, but Matthew only checks e-mail every couple of days and then works through each message in succession, confusion in the flow of conversation will result. Matters that the other three considered closed because they had already dealt with them will be reopened as Matthew goes through the points and counterpoints. Because e-mail provides a store-and-forward method of sharing information, and thus gives individual people the power to check e-mail and respond when they want to, unless the team works in a similar way, holding conversations by e-mail will quickly deprecate into chaos. (Remember, too, that an e-mail client displays the messages that you receive about a conversation in a different place than those you send within a conversation, making the correlation between what you said and what others said more difficult than it needs to be).

E-Mail Is Easier in the Moment, but SharePoint Is Better Over the Life of the Project

E-mail has a lot going for it ... it's quick, it's easy, and we all know how to compose a message and send it on. But in embracing e-mail for teamwork, we seem to be saying that we want to minimize the energy we expend for communicating up front, and that we don't care about the remaining energy that we need to expend to overcome the above problems in using e-mail effectively. SharePoint does take more time in the upfront part ... you have to browse to the right place and you have to do things a bit differently than what you are used to, but the gain over the life of the project is huge. Everything is in one place, and in the right place. Others can be inducted into the team with minimal effort. The work of the team is visible to the other people who it should be visible to.

Some of the Things You Can Do in SharePoint, You Wouldn't Try to Do in E-Mail

The final reason that it's time for people to start using SharePoint for team collaboration is that some of the things you can do in SharePoint, you would never try to do in e-mail. Take the creation of a customer presentation as an example. Today we work in a very sequential way, because that's the way e-mail and file attachments enable us to work. One person drafts the deck in Microsoft Office PowerPoint and then sends it out to 3 or 4 or 10 other people to get their feedback and input. They duly add comments and slides in various places, and then each person sends the revised slide deck back to the originator.

But there is another way to create a customer presentation deck, although it depends on the possibilities opened by a SharePoint way of doing things, rather than a Microsoft Office Outlook e-mail style. In essence, a SharePoint *wiki* (a wiki is generally a Web page that can be edited by anyone) page is created so that everyone from wherever they are can view the common page and enter the input they have on the content of the deck in the early formative and brainstorming parts of the process. Each person can see the formative ideas that others have entered, and can use those as the starting point for their own additions and extrapolations. Or they can jump in with new ideas on different sections. After the content is agreed upon in the wiki, someone gets the job of turning the ideas into a slide deck for the customer. You wouldn't try to do this in e-mail, or if you did, you'd never want to again.

Why Can't We All Just Work in the Same Place?

By asking Roger to use SharePoint to run the project, is Kelly ruling out travel? Not at all. But let's face the facts here. Roger is working with a team of people who work in different countries, and have lives outside of this project. Many of them, like many of the people who you work with, have family members to care for and nurture. It is entirely infeasible to expect everyone to get into a plane and travel to one place, and work together in person until the whole project is completed. It's not going to happen. In the same way, many people are actively engaged in multiple projects at the same time, and they just can't devote 100 percent of their attention or time to a single project. Again, it's not going to happen.

So we come to the reality of work: people are juggling multiple projects, they have multiple priorities, and they are working with different groups of people ... all at the same time. Travel for the purpose of getting team or group work done cannot be embraced as the primary method of collaborative work. It has a place, but it doesn't and shouldn't have a primary place in the work practices and processes of teamwork. The team members individually and jointly need to accept the limited availability of travel, and work together as effectively as possible using the communication and collaboration tools they have at their disposal. When we want to, we can get a lot of things done without being in the same place as the people we are working with.

There will be times in the life of Roger's project, and in ones that you are involved in, where travel to be together is not only needed but is highly desirable. Many people suggest holding an in-person meeting at the very beginning of the project, particularly when there are people who haven't worked together before. Being together provides concentrated time to get off on the right foot, to learn how the other people think and work, to start developing trust in the others, and to actually get some work done together. Sticky issues like the scope of the project, developing a shared purpose or outcome for the project, and similar processes that require lots of rapid interaction and back-and-forth dialogue to come to a common place can be ideal fodder for an in-person meeting. Another way of saying it is that the strategic decision making of the team is highly amenable to interactive sessions, and if you don't know the other people, then an all-hands-on-deck in-person interactive session is appropriate. This means that the operational, "getting the agreed work done" processes can be done by each member back at his or her individual place of work.

So Why Do We Work in Teams Anyway?

Teamwork—combining strengths with other people, working with others toward a common objective—is a natural and normal part of business life. Many projects are too large or too complex for one person to deliver alone, so they must combine their efforts with the efforts of others. Thus, it is a bit funny to talk about what drives teamwork, when it is such an integral part of daily work in business. It is about as insightful as saying that a computer needs a power supply in order to work.

Nonetheless, it is helpful to stand on the brink of our action and the activity swirling around us and ask why we choose to do things in a certain way. Why do we, or those above us in organizations, choose to use teams as an organizing paradigm for work? What are the thinking frameworks that have arisen to this being considered "normal"? Why do we need teams? Why can't we just work as individuals? What good are teams for organizations today?

Teams are good for organizations in four areas (see Figure 1-1):

- They increase strength.

- They increase speed, or time-to-market.

- They increase breadth.

- They increase acceptance.

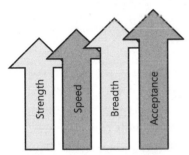

FIGURE 1-1 Teams offer four types of increased power to organizations.

Teams Increase Strength

When people work together on a project, the strength brought to bear on the work is increased in three key ways:

- Greater strength by using the knowledge of internal and external experts

- Greater strength by taking advantage of complementary competencies

- Greater power by combining the strengths of individuals

People who become experts through ongoing learning and experience are called upon to share their knowledge with people working on various teams. They may be within the business or an external consultant.

When organizations identify and focus on their core competencies, and seek to build specific and unique strength in the marketplace through working only within their core, they partner with other firms to offer complementary competencies.

Some people are really good at some things, and really bad at others. This is not a judgment on their expertise or knowledge, but an observation on their style and preferences. One person is able to see the big picture and lay out a path for getting from here to there, but they are terrible at the details. A second person is less able to see the big picture, but has tremendous ability to handle all of the scheduling details required to deliver the overall project on time and budget. A third person can sense when people in the group are at loggerheads in their views, and with grace and aplomb is able to draw each out and find a place of commonality and agreement between the previously warring factions. People of one kind need people of the other kinds close at hand and ready to help.

Teams Increase Speed

Teams can get the job done much faster than an individual working alone is able to do. There are two aspects to this:

- Greater speed by dividing the complexity
- Greater speed by collapsing elapsed time

Some projects are so complex, and have so many interlocking requirements, that although one person could get it done, it would take years or decades of his life to do so, and by which time the market opportunity would have closed and any hope for a return on his effort would have disappeared. Therefore, teams of people attack the complexity and deliver the desired outcome in weeks or months rather than years or decades.

Some projects are not so much complex—where the knowledge required to get them done is specialized and in short supply—but are instead large, and as such, are expected to take a long time to deliver. Again, there is little doubt that a diligent individual could do all of the work and see the project delivered eventually, but "eventually" is too long a timeframe for almost everything these days. And so multiple people are brought together to work on a team to attack the project and see it finished sooner rather than later.

Teams Increase Breadth

Breadth and perspective are valuable commodities in organizations, and when people work on teams, breadth is increased. Consider three aspects of this:

- Gaining a wider perspective
- Addressing customer needs more effectively
- Collating the ideas of many

Teams enable organizations to secure a wider perspective on pressing problems and opportunities. Different people bring different past experiences, different cultural mandates, and different points of reference to bear on these problems and opportunities, and the combination of their efforts can often lead to the detection of issues that a smaller, more homogeneous group would miss.

A diverse marketplace is best served by organizations that have eyes to see the diversity, and once seen, to factor in the different perspectives to their planning activities. Thus, teams staffed with people who bring different ideas and different tastes to the table, and who are able to adequately represent the different constituencies in their planning and design work, have a much greater chance of winning in the marketplace than those organizations that take the opposite route.

Teams are used to better capture and synthesize the ideas of many people within the organization and within its customer and partner ecosystem. Because we view and interpret the world through the framework of our worldview, we as individuals are not that great at understanding statements from others that fall outside of our worldview. So we need other people to actively work alongside us to interpret such statements, to give guidance on the underlying drivers of those statements, and to help ensure that the consequential decisions we make about such statements are valid.

Teams Increase Acceptance

Finally, teams can increase the acceptance of recommendations and pending changes by other people that someone working alone would struggle to achieve. There are three ways of thinking about increased acceptance:

- Securing buy-in within the organization
- Turning show stoppers into allies
- Minimizing the risks of loose cannons

Teamwork is driven by the need to secure buy-in from other people, groups, and departments within the organization. Initiatives that are cooked up in isolation from other teams and groups and are then imposed by fiat on an unsuspecting audience normally meet with a resounding rejection. And in many cases, rightly so. A leader is ineffective in implementing a vision if they haven't gone through the process of seeking early feedback on "drafts" and through involving stakeholders during the formative moments in the life of a vision. The same applies to the work of teams. Whether they are exploring changes to work practices, new market opportunities, revisions to products and services or other recommendations that impact the work and lives of people, those people need to be consulted, included, and sought for feedback and input.

"Keep your friends close, and your enemies closer" is a phrase of wisdom that applies well to work teams. If the work that you are doing on the team can be stymied and shot down by another group, or even by an influential person working alone, then it is essential to get their involvement or representation on the team as soon as possible.

Organizations need teams to rein in some individuals, who, left to their own devices would wreak havoc in organizational life. By using a team to get an initiative through, rather than a single individual, the risk of stupidity is greatly reduced, because if handled appropriately, one person is not able to dominate the decision process. Others on the team will be able to give credibility to the valuable ideas espoused by all individuals, while suppressing the stupid ones.

WORKING WITH PEOPLE FROM OTHER CULTURES IN SHAREPOINT

Working with people whom you can't be with in person raises the great possibility that you will be working with people from a different nationality and culture to you. And even for many of us within organizations, with the ease of mobility between countries, with the great attraction for people to travel and see the world, the likelihood is very high that you will be working with people from other nationalities and cultures even within the same office building.

How does SharePoint help and hinder cross-cultural communication?

On the helping side, SharePoint has a role to play in forcing everyone to rely on a common language: the written word. When you talk with people from other cultures on the phone, it can be very difficult to understand their accent and their way of speaking. Unless you work with the other people all the time, you will find yourself straining to hear and translate what they are saying, and this investment of greater cognitive resources in understanding the other people takes away from your ability to be fully present in your discussions. Or it means that the conversation takes longer because you have to listen extra-hard and then speak clearly yourself! If you can't understand them, then it is fairly certain that they, too, will not be able to understand you.

With SharePoint, the written word becomes the main way for communicating with the other people on your team. Everyone has to write out their thoughts, and because their thoughts are written out in a permanent location, anyone can go back and review what was written. If you want to know what a team member said in the last "conversation," go back and look it up in SharePoint. It should be there, in one of the lists. If you read something that someone else has said, and you don't understand what they are trying to say, or if they have written it in a way that could be interpreted in many different ways, then ask for clarification.

SharePoint can also help by making it clear what you do have in common with other people on your team. If everyone on the team is sharing the contextual information on the project, as is discussed in Chapter 4, "Team, Meet SharePoint," regarding the use of the team blog, then little snippets of information will be shared over time that help the others on the team understand who else is there. And for those who have filled out their profile in their SharePoint My Site, whenever you visit their profile page, you can see what they are interested in, and more than that, if the In Common With You Web Part has been enabled on their My Site, you will be told the areas of commonality. Building up a picture of common interests and areas helps mitigate against all of the areas of dissimilarity that you will have with many team members in any setting. So play to your common areas, and use these to overcome the natural challenges that you and everyone else will face with cross-cultural communication.

SharePoint can equally make cross-cultural communication more difficult—it's not the silver bullet! For some people, based on a cultural background that emphasizes talking things out, being forced to transact most of their interaction through the written word will make them feel devalued. They will feel like they are not being heard, because they are not allowed to speak.

How do you handle this? You handle it by being upfront, and asking people about their preferred ways of communication and interaction. If someone says that they will need to talk interactively more, then you will need to create time to listen. And on their side, if text-based communication is best for you, they will have to look to your interests and preferred way of working, and seek to help you. With a little bit of give-and-take, and a lot of willingness to make it work, you'll get there!

Is SharePoint Just for Managing Team Projects?

Roger and the team will be using SharePoint for managing the team collaboration activity on Project Delta. But "collaborating around" information is just one of the many ends that people in organizations need. Six areas are shown in Figure 1-2, and all of these can be supported by SharePoint.

FIGURE 1-2 SharePoint is useful for many information-related processes.

Accessing Information

People need a way to access business information of relevance to them and their work. Some examples include:

- Contact details for customers and suppliers.

- The part numbers for a new customer order.

- Previous contracts for customers in a particular industry.

- The latest intelligence on competitor moves.

- Industry snapshots about a new area the firm is looking at expanding into.

- Corporate policies for new employees.

- The latest news and events from the marketplace.

- Trend information about market growth in key areas.

- The names of people who worked on a particular business project three years ago.

The list is seemingly unending, and SharePoint can be used to provide access to many—if not all—of the items on the list through its portal capabilities.

Using Information for Decision Making

Information has utility in the context of decision making, and in order to make good decisions, good information is needed. Let's look at some common scenarios:

- You have to decide how much you will charge a new client for your products. You look at the current price list, as well as the discount schedule offered to previous clients in order to make your decision.

- You have to decide which of three new markets offers the best next place for international expansion. You look at market sizing information for the past five years, read numerous reports on anticipated growth in each of the markets, and review whether current business partners have existing operations in each market.

- You have to decide on a price increase for your main product line. You look at past sales volumes, competitor pricing strategies, market projections, and econometric analyses to make your decision.

The Business Intelligence capabilities of SharePoint assist with decision making tasks.

Publishing and Managing Information

Organizations need to make information available to a plethora of people and groups. In some cases, the information is used for subsequent decision making, and at other times the information is used for contextual awareness of what's going on. For example:

- Employees need to know what is going on within the organization, and keep abreast of the thinking of senior management.

- Customers need to know about the products and services offered by the organization, and learn about how they can maximize their use of such offerings.

- Partners need to know about partnering opportunities, so they can maximize their involvement.

- An organization with multiple offices needs a way of sharing its documents with its entire staff, regardless of geographical location.

- Team members need access to the working drafts of documents in their team project, and to be assured that when they start editing a document, that no one else will be able to overwrite their efforts.

- Staff members need to be certain that the information they are accessing represents the latest available information on offer. No one likes it when they start working on outdated information, only to find a more recent (and quite different!) recommendation actually exists.

- The actions and promises of other people in the organization toward customers and suppliers need to be available to be reviewed. These definitive statements—terms and conditions of sale, business contracts, and the like—must be protected to ensure that they are not changed after the fact.

- Information gets out of date, and some pieces of information get out of date much faster than others. The owners of particular pieces of information need to be reminded to check back and update the information that they have previously created.

SharePoint supports and enables these processes around publishing and managing information, through its document management, Web content management, and records management features.

Enforcing Structure on Information

Lots of ad hoc and unstructured information is created in organizations—documents, e-mail messages, meeting minutes—and there is also very structured information that is captured and stored in transactional databases. However, there is also a middle ground, around the day-to-day operating processes of the organization. These processes can be made more efficient and reliable when some degree of standardization is enforced. Consider the following examples:

- A customer wants a new loan at a bank. When the customer applies, she is asked to fill out a form that asks for certain information to be entered in particular fields. The bank is thereby guaranteed that all of the information it needs to collect for someone to make a lending decision is captured upfront.

- A team wants a new collaboration space for an upcoming project, but no one in the team is permitted to create the site directly. Instead, a team member fills out a form on the intranet specifying what the team wants the new site for, and after the request has been approved, the site is automatically created in accordance with their directions.

- Soldiers on the front line of action need additional supplies to win against the enemy. They fill out a form to describe their needs, and all of the forms from across the army are analyzed together for assigning priority.

- A new case is opened, and the process of managing the case involves securing client approval to certain documents, and once those are obtained, a set process has to be followed. At each step of the case process, the people responsible for the next steps are alerted electronically about the information they have to fill in.

- Speakers at an upcoming conference have to provide a biographical statement for inclusion in the conference proceedings, along with their needs for audio-visual equipment. Each speaker is asked to fill out a form to provide all of this information in a structured way.

SharePoint supports efficient processes and the capture of information in structured ways through its business forms and workflow capabilities. The key idea is that although all of these processes could be carried out by people describing what they want in an e-mail message, and sending various requests to the people they thought were the right ones to deal with their request, forms and workflow enable these processes to be standardized, tracked, and controlled.

Finding Information

Organizations have lots of information available to staff, customers, and partners—and all of these people need some way of finding the information they need for the tasks they have to do. For example:

- An employee is pulling together a report for the proposal for a new client. He needs to find the latest editions of past proposals.

- A customer is having a problem with one of your products, and is trying to find out how to resolve the issue. She needs to find information about how other customers have solved similar problems, in addition to your guidance about resolving the issue.

- With so many documents available inside the firm, combined with no relevancy ranking on search results, the only way to find the right document is to ask someone else to point it out.

- An employee needs to find information about a project that was run a couple of years ago. That information is spread across multiple different systems—file shares, databases, Exchange Public Folders—and each one has to be searched independently to get the required information.

- A customer service representative is on the phone with an important client, but is struggling with some of the questions being asked. She needs to find an internal expert to help answer the questions, but is not sure who she should reach out to.

SharePoint offers Enterprise Search capabilities to meet situations like these.

Summary

SharePoint provides an enhanced way for teams to work on projects, and this chapter has investigated why SharePoint is better than using e-mail for project work. In addition, it has discussed the four benefits organizations derive from team work, and has given a brief overview of five other areas in which people can benefit from using SharePoint.

Chapter 2, "Managing the Project and Finding a Team," looks at how to manage a team project by using SharePoint.

CHAPTER 2

Managing the Project and Finding a Team

ROGER LEANED BACK in his chair to think. He knew now that using SharePoint was the right approach for Project Delta, but the question was how to go about running the project and using SharePoint at the same time? He—and the others he was likely to work with—knew how to get things done using e-mail, meetings, and travel, but not SharePoint. It was too new.

Just before waves of despair came crashing down on him, Roger sat upright again at his desk, and pulled out a pen. "How do we run projects around here?" he wrote in the middle of the page, followed by "And how do we make this work in SharePoint?" He looked up from the sheet of paper, thought for a moment, and then wrote again: "SharePoint is just a tool. I need to learn how to wield it effectively."

Managing Projects: The Five Phases Project Life Cycle Model

Every project in an organization is unique, or at least it should be. Many projects will exhibit some similarities to other projects that have already been done, but there has to be something unique about a particular project—the people are different, the industry is different, the operating assumptions are different, or the technology has changed since two years ago. If projects were the same, the recommendations and conclusions from the last time the project happened could be applied again, saving time and effort.

19

Although every project is different in some way, there is a common process at work (pattern or thread) when a project is being carried out. Successful projects work through five phases as the project goes from start to completion (see Figure 2-1):

1. **Creating a Shared Vision.** Understanding what is to be achieved when the project is completed

2. **Understanding the Options.** Exploring the range of alternative ways to complete the project

3. **Analyzing the Options.** Gathering more information on each of the options, seeking to understand the pros and cons of each, and how each sits in comparison to the other options

4. **Making a Decision.** As a team, coming to a decision as to which option will be recommended or implemented

5. **Concluding the Project.** Drawing the project to a close, and disbanding the team

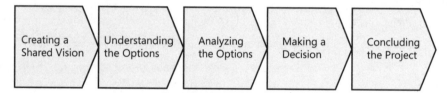

FIGURE 2-1 The Five Phases Project Life Cycle Model

Phase 1. Creating a Shared Vision

Phase 1 is about creating a shared vision for the project, being clear about the boundaries around the project. The team works on the project inside of these boundaries, and everything else exists external to the boundaries. Within the boundaries, the team is working toward a performance outcome, that is, toward making something true that wasn't previously true. Outside of the boundaries are the constraints, the base assumptions that define the boundaries and the people who offer their support to make the work within these boundaries go smoothly. The better the team is able to understand the intended work within the boundaries, as well as the constraints and assumptions outside of the boundaries, the better they are able to target their efforts toward successful achievement of what they're supposed to be doing.

Phase 2. Understanding the Options

Phase 2 requires developing an understanding of the options—thinking up and capturing the ideas that could be possible ways of delivering on the shared vision. The purpose of this stage is to capture as many ideas as possible, to think as broadly as possible, and to consider the crazy ideas as well as the standard way of doing things. If the team is highly creative and innovative, they will come up with more ideas than they have the time and energy to work through in sufficient depth. After the ideas are captured, the team needs to create a short list of candidate ideas for further and deeper exploration—some of the ideas on the shortlist will be rejected, but some will move forward for further assessment in Phase 3.

Phase 3. Analyzing the Options

Phase 3 involves going into greater detail for each of the short-listed alternatives from Phase 2. It is about going deeper and wider into each alternative, and exploring what it would look like to embrace each idea in turn. Each idea is teased apart, is looked at from every angle, and is thought through to determine whether the idea has great merit as a decision candidate or has some clear problems that make it untenable on further analysis. Or maybe there is another idea that is better.

Phase 4. Making a Decision

Phase 4 focuses on making the final decision, or if the team is charged with making a recommendation, preparing that for the powers that be. The analysis from Phase 3 needs to be collated and prepared for presentation to others outside of the core team; the shared understanding that the team has developed over time needs to be captured and shared with others. In some situations, the recommendation can be implemented immediately, but in most cases, and definitely for large and more strategic and important projects, there will be an entire process of socializing the ideas with others for further input and refinement. This is done by writing a document for others, by presenting the ideas in various meetings, and having one-to-one conversations with others.

Phase 5. Concluding the Project

Phase 5 is the project team ramp-down stage, whereby the work of the team is tidied up, people say their goodbyes, and any final corporate work on the project is done. The decision has been made, the work is signed off, but both the social realities and the corporate memory parts of the project need to be attended to. For example, key working documents have to be moved out of the team site and published to the intranet or to the records management system, both of which could be powered by SharePoint.

Recruiting the Project Team by Using SharePoint

Roger has to find the right people to be involved in Project Delta. He has some ideas—after all, he has been at Fourth Coffee for almost two years, and has been very active during that time expanding his network within the firm. But even so, he doesn't know everyone, and more than that, Project Delta requires a strong dose of internationally located people. Thanks to the My Site and People Search capabilities in SharePoint, Roger's job is a lot easier.

> **NOTE** The discussion in this section is predicated on the use of the full Microsoft Office SharePoint Server 2007 product. My Site and People Search are not included in Microsoft Windows SharePoint Services 3.0, which is available as a free download.

WHAT IF YOU DON'T HAVE SHAREPOINT SERVER 2007?

If you have access only to Windows SharePoint Services 3.0, then don't panic. The vast majority of this book is based on the capabilities of Windows SharePoint Services 3.0, and only infrequently refers to the full SharePoint Server 2007 product. In designing SharePoint, Microsoft split most of the collaboration capabilities off into Windows SharePoint Services 3.0, and delivered all of the other SharePoint capabilities in the server product.

So if you don't have access to My Site, chances are that there will be other ways at your organization for doing similar things. Maybe it's a directory of employees with annotations about their expertise. Maybe it's a practice management system that talks about the projects that people at your organization have worked on. Maybe it's good-old word-of-mouth networking, where you know who to ask about finding the right people. Or maybe you just know the right people straight off the bat. Whatever works—go for it.

You may have another reaction. As you read about My Site and some of the enhanced capabilities delivered in the full SharePoint Server 2007 product, you may start to envision some of the possibilities and business advantages that your organization could gain by having more than just Windows SharePoint Services 3.0 in place. If that's the case, then great! Go and seek out your IT people and ask about corporate plans for a full SharePoint deployment. Maybe your support for more of SharePoint will tip the scales and give IT greater insight into the ability of SharePoint to support core business activities.

My Site

My Site provides a "home place" for an individual to live and work within SharePoint. In essence, if you are used to living in your Inbox in Outlook 2007, then My Site becomes the place for you to live within SharePoint. There are two main sides to My Site:

- A public facing profile known as My Profile

- A personal facing home site known as My Home

My Profile

The My Profile part—the public-facing side—of My Site is essentially an online résumé in the organization about your work, with some special features that you can't do with a résumé that's tied up in a document. It provides a set of fields for you to enter details about your work responsibilities, projects you have been involved with, skills, and other interests. There is also a place that lists the e-mail distribution lists and SharePoint sites that you are a member of. Although this membership list is automatically generated by looking up the information in Microsoft Exchange Server and SharePoint, you have the ability to manage the list that is shown to visitors.

My Site is critical to the success of SharePoint as a way to recruit a project team. Here are the key actions that each person in the organization needs to do to make My Site work. To work with your Details page, click Details under My Profile (see Figure 2-2).

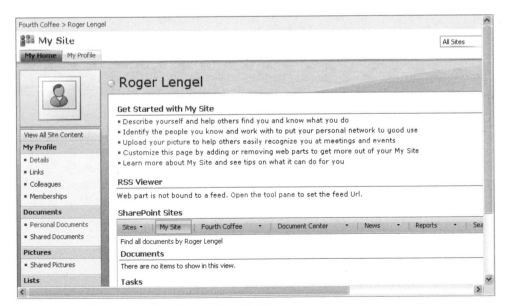

FIGURE 2-2 Navigate to your Details page from My Site.

- **Describe and Show Yourself.** The About Me area is a place to describe yourself, without the constraints of fitting particular information into pre-specified fields (see Figure 2-3). You can write what you want, but remember that SharePoint is used by your business colleagues and the managers in your firm, so be professional. You can also upload a picture of yourself, and you should do this regardless of whether you meet with others in person. It gives your colleagues a personal sense of who you are and who they are dealing with.

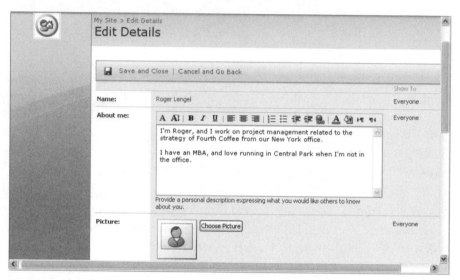

FIGURE 2-3 The About Me area in My Site

- **Work Life.** This is a place to list your work responsibilities, skills, past projects, interests, and schools you've attended. For the Responsibilities and Skills areas, different descriptions of these can be targeted to different groups in the firm. You might want to make a generic statement to everyone, a more formal and complete statement to certain people, and a humor-laced approach with your team. What is displayed on your My Site profile to other people depends on what groups they belong to when they view your profile (see Figure 2-4).

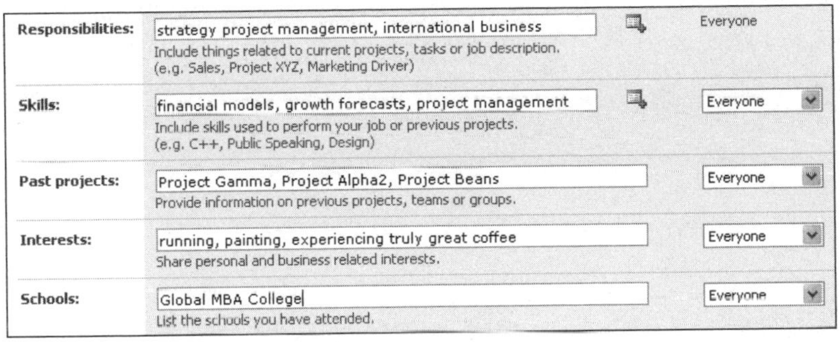

Responsibilities:	strategy project management, international business		Everyone
	Include things related to current projects, tasks or job description. (e.g. Sales, Project XYZ, Marketing Driver)		
Skills:	financial models, growth forecasts, project management		Everyone
	Include skills used to perform your job or previous projects. (e.g. C++, Public Speaking, Design)		
Past projects:	Project Gamma, Project Alpha2, Project Beans		Everyone
	Provide information on previous projects, teams or groups.		
Interests:	running, painting, experiencing truly great coffee		Everyone
	Share personal and business related interests.		
Schools:	Global MBA College		Everyone
	List the schools you have attended.		

FIGURE 2-4 Provide insight on your work life.

- **Contact Details.** This is a place to provide your contact details so that others know how to reach you when they have a great new opportunity for you. As with responsibilities and skills, there are different permissions that can be set for items in the contact details area. If you have an assistant and want everyone to be able to see his or her name, set the permissions to Everyone. However, for your mobile phone, fax, and home phone numbers, you can set permissions to limit the view to just your colleagues. Once again, other people will see different information when they visit your profile, based on their group memberships (see Figure 2-5).

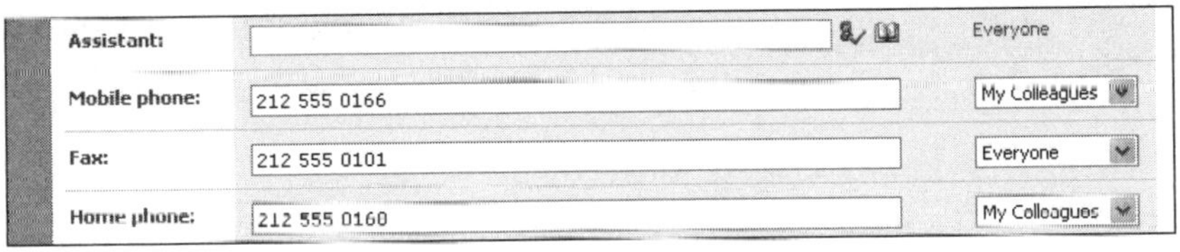

Assistant:			Everyone
Mobile phone:	212 555 0166		My Colleagues
Fax:	212 555 0101		Everyone
Home phone:	212 555 0160		My Colleagues

FIGURE 2-5 Phone and fax details can be shown to certain groups.

- **Colleagues.** This is a place to list the key people who you work with. You can enter the names of people directly, and SharePoint can also suggest people who should be listed based on an analysis of your e-mail patterns and the business department or division you work in. Click Colleagues under My Home, and then click Add Colleagues (see Figure 2-6).

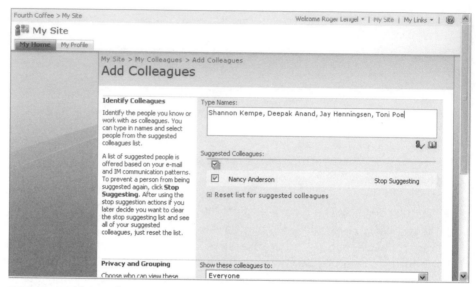

FIGURE 2-6 Add the colleagues who you work with to your My Site page.

Remember, however, that the work you put into the My Profile part of My Site is first and foremost for the benefit of others. If it benefits others by helping them find you and discover skills and interests that they can take advantage of in their work, then it becomes of benefit to you, too.

What Your Profile Looks Like to Others

After you have filled out the information in your profile, when other people visit your My Site page, SharePoint does some standard things and then adds some really cool things.

First, as you would expect, it shows the information that you have entered so that other people can read it. This is shown in a small area so that visitors can scan the information quickly, and assess whether you have value to contribute to a project.

Second, and much more interestingly, SharePoint looks at who is visiting your My Site profile page, and automatically calculates and displays things that they have in common with you. For example, if a visitor and you are both members of the "Weekly Marketing Insights E-Mail Newsletter" distribution list, this will be listed as something that the visitor holds in common with you. Likewise, if both the visitor and you work with Sally, Brent, and John, these names will be listed as colleagues whom you hold in common. Finally, it also looks up the first manager that the visitor and you have in common. All of this information is shown through the "In Common With You" Web Part. The purpose of doing this is to create an awareness of shared and common ground so that initial conversations are not so difficult. Web Parts are components, such as My Calendar and Colleague Tracker, that can be added or removed from SharePoint sites based on preference or need. For more information about Web Parts, see the sidebar "What's a Web Part?" in Chapter 3, "Setting Up SharePoint."

The third thing that your My Profile page shows to visitors is any document that you have written and that is publicly accessible. This works by looking into all of the SharePoint sites that you are a member of, and pulling out a consolidated list of documents that you have authored. Note that these documents are not shifted into your My Site account— each document in the list points back to the Document Library they live in. So if visitors see a document listed that is of interest to them (which is good for you!) and clicks it to read the full version, they will be taken to the original SharePoint site.

10 Tips on Establishing Your Profile

As mentioned in the previous section, the profiling component of My Site is absolutely critical to the effective use of SharePoint for recruiting a project team. Here are 10 tips on establishing your profile for maximum effect:

1. **Make your areas of expertise interesting, not generic.** A rich description of who you are and what you are interested in is much better than using generic terms. So don't write "Marketing" as an area of expertise; write "Marketing strategy for expanding into new international markets." Someone doing a search on the term "marketing" will still find you, but you will have provided much more at-a-glance information than the person just writing "Marketing."

2. **Be exhaustive and list everything.** One of the real powers of your profile is the matching that happens between you and your visitors, to show things that they hold in common with you. If you only list three or four items in each area, the possibilities that matches are found are greatly reduced. Err on the side of more, not less.

3. **View your profile as your online résumé.** We used to keep our résumés locked inside text documents, but those days are gone. Your My Site profile is going to become the most up-to-date and most widely looked at statement of who you are.

4. **Be professional.** Your colleagues and managers in your firm will be reading your profile, so keep it professional. By all means list personal interests, but only if they are socially acceptable within your firm.

5. **Don't be all business.** Although it is important to keep your profile professional, tell others a bit about the non-business you. Do you enjoy running? No harm in saying so. Ditto for enjoying traveling, writing a blog, reading certain genres of books, and other interests.

6. **Actively seek new colleagues.** Who you know, and by implication who knows about you, is really important to the effectiveness of your work in the firm and the opportunities that will come your way. Look for people who share common interests with you, and reach out to them. Learn about their work, their perspectives, and their challenges. Get to know them, and earn the right to call them a colleague.

7. **Ask a trusted colleague—or your manager—to review your profile.** They will notice where you have left out things about yourself that should be there, and will give insightful feedback on how to best describe your accomplishments.

8. **Don't be bland.** Don't settle for doing the minimum with your My Site profile— listing a few words and phrases here and there. Go for the top! Aim to make your profile the best statement of who you are.

9. **Keep your profile up to date.** Make a recurring appointment with yourself to revisit and update your profile every month. If you have projects that change on a weekly basis—as in projects where you are making a good contribution— update it more regularly.

10. **Become a My Site champion!** Encourage other people you meet in the firm to establish their profile in My Site, and to keep it up to date.

My Home

The My Home part—the private and personal side—of My Site is your new online home. It's the place where you should start each day in SharePoint, because it pulls together all of the separate parts of your work in SharePoint into a single view. You can store private documents, keep a list of Web or intranet links that you need to access frequently, and establish workspaces for running your own projects both on your own and in collaboration with others. The big difference with the My Profile part is that where My Profile is firstly for the benefit of others, My Home is directly for your benefit.

My Home offers two key capabilities for enhancing project work: Colleague Tracking and Document Workflow.

Colleague Tracking

After you have established your list of colleagues, you can keep an "electronic eye" on their movements and actions through SharePoint. This means that when something changes in their profile, or in the work they are doing, you will be notified within My Home. You won't have to go looking for changes—SharePoint will bring the changes to you through the Colleague Tracker Web Part, and you can easily modify what changes get tracked for your colleagues so that it works for you (see Figure 2-7).

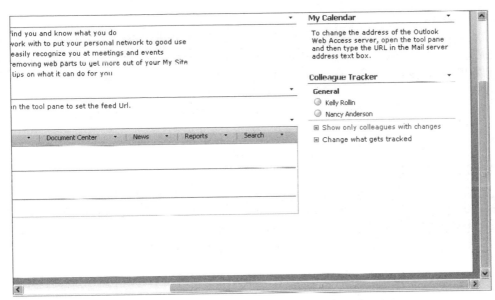

FIGURE 2-7 SharePoint can alert you about changes to your colleagues' information.

Under the Colleague Tracker area, click Change What Gets Tracked. This opens your My Home page in Edit Mode. In this mode, you can select the changes that you want to track for your colleagues (see Figure 2-8).

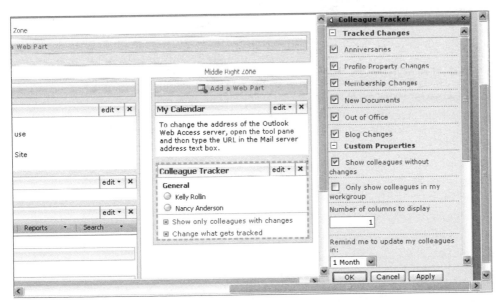

FIGURE 2-8 Customize what you want to know about your colleagues.

Document Workflow

You have a shared document library in My Site, and you can request others to review and comment on any document in the library. This means that they get an e-mail notification requesting a review—and when they click to review the document, it is opened out of your Shared Documents library. The formal projects that you are involved in should be run out of project team sites, but this workflow capability for your own documents provides a way of doing ad hoc collaboration as required.

People Search

After everyone in the firm has established their profile in My Site, the People search capabilities in SharePoint come into their own. People search means that the search target of interest is people, rather than documents and SharePoint sites. People can be found based on looking for them specifically—by first or last name—or by looking for them by their metadata—the things that describe who they are; for example, their department, job title, responsibilities, skills, and memberships.

Open the People search screen under the Search tab on the main SharePoint screen, and then enter your search criteria (see Figure 2-9).

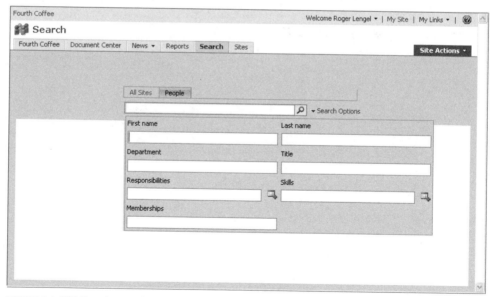

FIGURE 2-9 With People search, you can find others based on multiple criteria.

Here are some approaches for using People search to recruit a project team:

- **Look for someone you know.** After you have been around your firm for a while, you will meet others and get to know who they are and what they do. If you are looking for people to join a new project, and someone comes to mind, type their name into People search and explore what they are currently doing and currently interested in.

- **Look for a representative in a specific department.** If your project needs a representative from a specific department, check out the possibilities by searching for people in that department. After you get back a list of possibilities, click through and read their profile information. If the list of possibilities is too long, refine your search by entering additional search criteria in one of the other fields. For example, if you need someone from the "Corporate Development" department, and that turns up 50 people as possibilities, narrow the scope of your search by specifying that they should have responsibility for "Commercialization" as well.

- **Look for someone based on a job title.** If your project needs significant input from a "Research Director," but you are not sure which department they reside in, search on Title. If the resulting list is small enough to review, go through each and see what you find out. See who looks good. If the list is too long—there is a plethora of Research Directors at your firm—narrow the scope of your search by entering other details, such as responsibilities or skills.

- **Look for someone based on their responsibilities.** The responsibilities that someone has are another way to look for people who could join or contribute to your project. Perhaps the search based on title didn't turn up anyone good enough. Try the search based on responsibilities then, and see if that elicits anyone better.

- **Look for someone based on their skills.** The area of skills is a great example of where formal responsibility can diverge from informal capability. People are put into formal roles based on the skills and capabilities they show, but many other people in the firm can have the same skills but not be in the formal role. With a search based on skills, you can find everyone—regardless of formal position—who says that they have skill in the area you are looking for.

- **Look for someone based on their memberships.** Looking for someone based on memberships in e-mail distribution lists and other SharePoint sites is a way of proving that they have interest and expertise in an area. It is one step for a person to claim interest and expertise in certain areas, but the second step that adds credence to their claim is membership of and active involvement in that community within the firm.

- **Look for someone based on multiple areas.** The great thing with People search is that you can use all of the fields to find just the right person to join your project team. You can start with a broad search to find who is out there, and then use one or more of the other fields to narrow the scope of your search and hone in on a smaller and smaller set of possibilities.

People search is a fantastic way to discover other people in your firm who have the clout, interests, and expertise to join your project team and contribute to the success of your work. But remember that People search only works if the profile part of My Site is established broadly across the organization. You have a role to play in making this work for your firm—create your own profile to the best of your ability, and encourage others to do so, too.

Visiting Someone Else's Profile

When you visit someone else's profile to consider whether they might be suitable to have on your team, form a quick judgment based on what they say about themselves. If they look like a good candidate, spend a bit more time looking around and reading in more depth about their work and life. Make sure that you read their blog, if they have one, and note any recurring themes or common interests that you may be able to reference when you get to speak to them.

After looking at their profile, if you think that they would be a good person for the team, the next step is to talk to them about the project. If you know them, you can send an e-mail message or phone them, but if you don't know them, you will probably need to get clearance to approach them through their manager. Talk to your manager about the right way to do that at your place of work.

If you decide that someone isn't right for the team, there's no harm done in sending an e-mail message to say that you visited his profile and enjoyed learning about his work, or in leaving a comment on one of his blog posts. You never know—he might be looking for a team member in the months ahead and you might be just the person!

What about External People?

People who don't work for your organization are not going to have a My Site in your SharePoint system, so how do you learn about them if you need people from other firms to take part in a project? Cross-organizational teams are very common, after all, so how do you find the best people to work with?

There is no universal answer, but here are some ideas. If your firm regularly works with specific other firms, then there will be an awareness of the particular people who work there. If you need to work with a market research firm, for example, and your firm has a formal agreement with one or more such firms, then try to find people from your firm who have worked with people from those firms. After you have found the people from your firm—by asking colleagues if they know of anyone, or contacting your Corporate Legal Department to ask who set up the contract in the first place—you can enquire about the specific people who they worked with. As your enquiries continue, build a dossier regarding the people you learn about so that you can make an integrated and informed decision when the time comes.

Another place to search for information about specific people that you could work with is through their firm's Web site. They may have a profile page discussing their work and past projects, and such a profile may give you as much as a well-done SharePoint My Site page will give you within your firm. If you can't find something official on their firm's Web site, call the main phone number and enquire about securing access to the profiles of one or two of their staff members for an upcoming work project.

Don't forget to scour the Web. There are so many options for people as private citizens to have a voice on the Internet and to share their thoughts, photos, and videos. Do a search for their name and see what you find—you may just hit their personal Web site and learn a whole lot of interesting (and perhaps even startling!) things that confirm their applicability to be on the team or immediately squash that prospect.

You may even find their blog. With the rise of blogging in the past couple of years, people from all sorts of places have started blogs as a demonstration of their competence and capability. Do a Web search for some of the key words or phrases that you are interested in, and see what comes back. Or subscribe to a key word or phrase (a "tag" in blog-speak) from a service like Technorati (*www.technorati.com*). You'll be amazed at the people you discover, and the ideas that are given away for free. Sometimes the ideas can be picked up and run with directly, and other times they need greater thought. Or they mean that you should actually bring the person inside the team for a short period of time to offer ideas and guidance.

Look who is speaking at conferences in the topics that are related to your work. Experts often do, and for a fairly minor fee, you can go to the conference and check out their ability to inform and inspire. Perhaps they would be an ideal person to have on the team for a short time, or maybe they would be good as an external reviewer when the time comes to seek outside validation. Regardless, start looking for such people now, so that when the time comes, you have a short list of people available to help you with your work.

If your firm doesn't have a particular business relationship in place with established providers and you need to find someone in a certain niche in a specific region, you will have to become a quasi-detective! Think about the type of person who would be ideal, such as their skills, their interests, and the type of projects that they should have worked on to suit what you have in mind. Then go looking, using the Web to search for blogs, using the phone to track down association and professional groups in the region of interest, and using the proceedings from past conferences on the topic to see who spoke at the event.

Finally, if you find that there are other people from other firms who you and your colleagues work with on a regular basis, use SharePoint to build a shared dossier about working experiences. Such a shared dossier could be as simple as a SharePoint site with a wiki page for each person, or it could be an official My Site page within your SharePoint system as a result of other people being given official access to your firm's SharePoint site as a result of their working relationship with your firm. But whatever you do, start to share what you know about others. This will greatly help the other people who come after you and have to go through a similar process.

The Project Delta Team

Roger has found the team for Project Delta, thanks to the My Profile part of My Site. He used name search to find a couple of people he already knew, and then to ensure that they would be good for Delta. And he used the skill and departmental search options in People search to find the others. Doing so netted him four people, besides himself, from Fourth Coffee to work on the project:

- Nancy Anderson (Boston)
- Robert O'Hara (London)
- Shannon Kempe (London)
- Gregory Verny (London)

For the outside market research and marketing strategy firms, Roger approached some of his colleagues in Fourth Coffee to ask who they had previously used, and the key people who they would recommend. For the market research firm, Trey Research and two of its principals came highly recommended, and for the marketing strategy firm, Fabrikam, Inc. was said to be the way to go. After extending an invitation through Kelly Rollin and the Corporate Legal Department, both firms willingly signed up for involvement on the core team. The four other team members were:

- Matthew Carroll, Trey Research (London)
- Yvonne McKay, Trey Research (Australia)
- Laura Giussani, Fabrikam, Inc. (Edinburgh)
- Eric Gilmore, Fabrikam, Inc. (France)

The final person involved in the team is Gareth Chan from the Corporate IT Department. Gareth is based out of California, but that shouldn't be a major issue, because he won't be involved in the day-to-day working of the team, but rather as an IT support person. Because this is the first time that Roger and the team will be using SharePoint, Gareth is the designated contact for all questions related to the effective use of SharePoint.

CHAPTER 3

Setting Up SharePoint

WITH HIS TEAM on board and raring to go, Roger was chugging down his fourth coffee for the day when he realized that it was time to stop using what other people had done in SharePoint and to start creating an effective working place for his team. He recalled seeing some announcement on one of the pages in SharePoint about how to set up a SharePoint site for effective team collaboration, and searching SharePoint, quickly found it again. "Geek speak," he said to himself after reading the announcement, and picked up the phone to call Gareth Chan in California. "It's 4:00 P.M. here in New York, so it's 1:00 P.M. in California," Roger muttered to himself. "I hope he's not at lunch."

"Hey, Roger," said Gareth answering the phone. "It's great to be working with you on Project Delta. How can I help you today?"

"Hi, Gareth," Roger replied. "I have to set up an effective working place in SharePoint for my team, and although I've read the document on the SharePoint intranet, I'm still at a loss to know what to do. Can you give me any guidance, please?"

"Yes, absolutely!" said Gareth. "Sorry the document is hard to understand; I'll take another look at it, but for the moment, we need to start by talking about the three groups of people involved in your project."

"Three groups?" Roger was perplexed. "But it's just me and the team."

"I'm not surprised you're perplexed, Roger," replied Gareth, "but let me explain, and then let's get you an effective working place in SharePoint before you head home today."

The Three Constituencies in Any Project

For any project—Delta included—there are three broad constituencies of people who are interested in what happens:

- **The project team.** The people who are doing the actual work on the project on a day-to-day basis. They are charged with delivering an answer or an outcome to the performance objective of the project, and they have to work with each other to do so.

- **The project sponsors and stakeholders.** The people in the firm who have a stake in the outcome of the project—that is, they will be affected by the outcome in some way—and the people who are sponsoring the project within the firm. Although they also have a stake in the outcome, they have a greater stake in the process because they are the ones supporting it at a political level.

- **Everyone else.** All the other people in the firm who are not in the first two groups.

When SharePoint is set up for the project, all three constituencies need to be supported. However, the needs of each constituency are different, and if we just have one general place where all of the three constituencies work in together, it can lead to misunderstandings.

A SharePoint Site for the Project Team

The team itself needs a secured place where they can do the work they have been asked to do, without constantly having to explain all of the nuances of what they are doing and to justify all of the decisions they are making. They need a place where draft documents can be thrashed out without having to feel worried that a key stakeholder is going to misinterpret the draft document as a final recommendation, and that they will be hauled into a meeting to explain themselves. Thus the team needs a separate place where they can work, without the constant interference of others.

A SharePoint Site for the Sponsors and Stakeholders

The sponsors and stakeholders of the project need to be kept informed about what is going on in the project, and they also need a place where they can talk about the progress the team is making. These conversations should be private to the sponsors and stakeholders—they need to know that they can talk freely and think out loud without members of the project team misinterpreting what they are saying. At the same time, the sponsors and stakeholders don't need access to the place where the project team is actually working—because they lack the shared cognitive awareness that the team members have developed, they may misunderstand the work in progress and jump to invalid conclusions.

The site for the sponsors and stakeholders fills two purposes:

- Providing a place for the project team leader to communicate status and needs to the sponsors and stakeholders. The team leader has a way of managing what the sponsors and stakeholders hear, and can run interference for the work of the team.

- Providing a place for the sponsors and stakeholders to have their own meetings and discussions.

Both groups have a right to have a private place to work and discuss how things are going, without having the other group involved necessarily knowing everything that was said. That's absolutely no different to current organizational practices where the team can have a meeting without the sponsors and stakeholders actually being there, and vice versa. Each may know that the meeting happened, and that certain decisions were made, but the moment-by-moment account of what happened is left to those who were actually there. The same applies with SharePoint.

A SharePoint Site for Everyone Else

The third constituency is everyone else. They aren't on the team, and neither are they a business stakeholder or sponsor of the project, but for some reason, they have an interest in what is being decided and recommended. Here are two examples:

- They have an overlapping interest in part of the project, but the overlap is not sufficient for them to be formally recognized as a stakeholder.

- The project finished two years ago, and a new person to the firm needs more information on what actually led to one of the decisions.

Regardless of their interest, "everyone else" has a right to know in broad terms what was decided or recommended, where to find more information, and in particular, who to go to for more information. Thus when someone visits the home page of the project, which should remain as a perpetual landing spot, they should find the following information:

- A summary statement or abstract of the work, along with an outline of the timeframe of the project and the key decisions that were reached

- Pointers to where more information can be found, such as documents and presentations in a SharePoint Document Library, or a section on the intranet

- A list of all the people who were involved

- The name of the key contact person for the project to whom any questions should be addressed

One more comment about "everyone else." If you don't create a landing page, all SharePoint does is say that a visitor to the site doesn't have access, and gives the name of an IT administrator who may grant access. But apart from the name of the site, and the description of the site, there is nothing else to indicate what the project is actually about. And maybe it's not appropriate for this person to have access to the inner workings of the team. Perhaps they just need to know a bit more about when the project was completed, and where to go for more information.

Creating the Three Sites in SharePoint

When it comes time to creating the three sites in SharePoint, we take the idea of building design and access and apply it to SharePoint. In an office building—and even in a home for that matter—there is an accessible area for "everyone." In an office, it's the foyer. In a home, it's the entrance way at the front door. In order to get past the foyer or the front door, you have to be granted access by someone—a security guard at the office, or one of the people in the home. After you pass the public area, you progressively enter into more secured areas. The most secured areas are generally in the middle of the building, or at the top of the building, thus creating physical distance between the entry place and the secured place.

We take the same approach in SharePoint. When anyone visits the project site, they come to the "foyer" of the project. Foyers in buildings have summary statements about the work that happens in the firm—say a mission statement on the wall, plaques of the awards the firm has won for its work, and copies of the latest annual report or firm newsletter. So when the project foyer is hit by a visitor, they see the same sorts of things.

If the visitor has the right level of access to get past the project foyer, they can go deeper into the site. If they are a member of the Project Sponsors and Stakeholders group, they can enter that area. If they belong to the Project Team, they can enter the area designated for the project team (see Figure 3-1).

SharePoint works on a hierarchical basis, so that sites contain subsites. This means that we create the "Everyone Else" site first, and then the other two sites inside it. Although the Everyone Else site has open access to anyone who can access the firm's SharePoint implementation, the Project Team site and the Project Sponsors and Stakeholders site have controlled access.

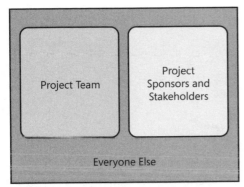

FIGURE 3-1 Every project is of interest to three broad constituencies, and SharePoint needs to support all three.

Create a SharePoint Site for Everyone Else

The Everyone Else site is very simple: it's just an Announcements list and a Links list that show on the first page that anyone hits when they visit the project site. It's possible to make it complex, but the Announcements list makes it nice and easy to express the summary information we want to show. And the Links list provides us with a way of giving people on the team or in the sponsors and stakeholders group with a quick way to get inside the appropriate site.

Step 1. Create a Blank Site

SharePoint ships with numerous templates for sites, but none of those come with just an Announcements list and a Links list. So start by creating a blank site. You will need to first go into the place where business projects are created in your firm's SharePoint system, so that you create the site in the correct place. You will need certain rights in SharePoint to set up these sites, so if it appears that you can't do it, talk to your SharePoint contact in IT about how to proceed. In this book, we will be using the SharePoint system for Fourth Coffee as an example, and projects are created under the Business Projects area.

In the upper-right corner, click Site Actions, and then click Create. On the Create page that opens, click the Sites And Workspaces link under the Web Pages column to start (see Figure 3-2).

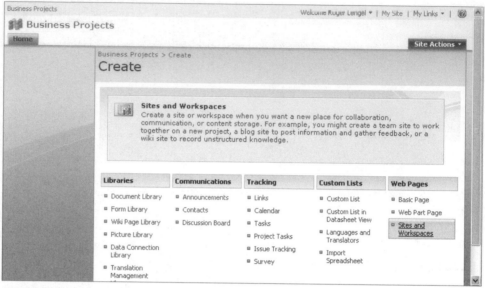

FIGURE 3-2 Open the Create page to start a new blank site.

After clicking Sites And Workspaces, you are asked to fill out the key details about the project site you are creating:

- The title of the project site.

- A description for the project.

- The URL name for the project on the SharePoint system. This is what people will type in to the address bar of their browser when they want to visit the site.

- The template for the site. For this example, click Blank Site on the Collaboration tab (see Figure 3-3).

- The permissions for the site. These need to be unique, and not merely a copy of the parent Business Projects site.

- Various questions about navigation. Leave all these as Yes for this site (see Figure 3-4).

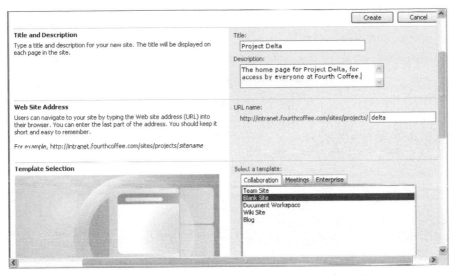

FIGURE 3-3 Give your new site a name and description, and use the Blank Site template.

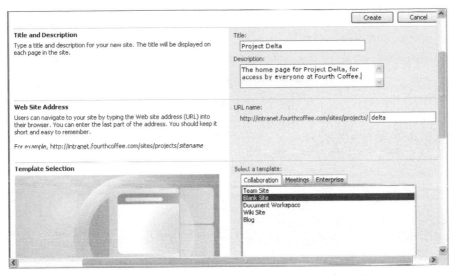

FIGURE 3-4 Set permissions and navigation options for the Everyone Else site.

When you are done, click Create. SharePoint takes a few moments to create the new blank site for you.

Step 2. Set the Permissions for the Everyone Else Site

After the new site is created, SharePoint prompts you to configure the unique permissions for the site. There are three levels of access that can be set for a site (see Figure 3-5):

- Visitors, or people who can read what's happening within the site. Because this is the top-level site for Project Delta, we want everyone in the organization to be able to access the site and read what's happening. There should be an existing group in your SharePoint system for this. For Roger at Fourth Coffee, that's the All Fourth Coffee Employees group.

- Members, or people who can use the lists and libraries that have been made available in the site, but cannot change the design of the site. For this top-level site, this group can be left empty for the moment.

- Owners, or people who have access to both the content and the design of the site. For this top-level site, that's the project leader and the SharePoint contact person from IT.

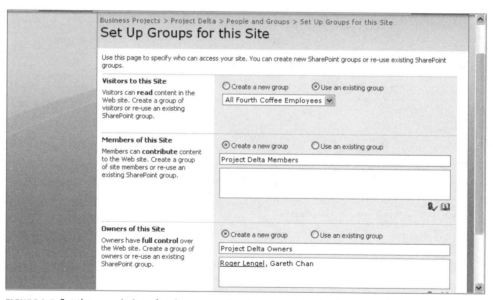

FIGURE 3-5 Set the permissions for the groups that have access to the Everyone Else site.

After you have selected the appropriate "All Employees" group and entered the names of the people who belong in the Owners group, click OK. You are now taken to the main page of the new blank site (see Figure 3-6).

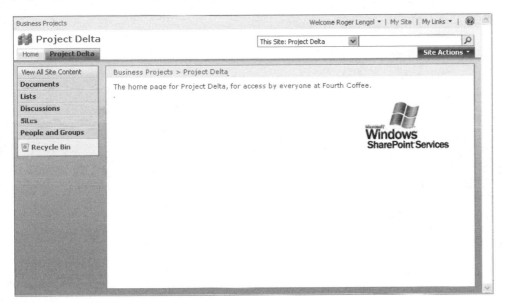

FIGURE 3-6 The blank Everyone Else team site

Step 3. Create the Announcements List

The third step is to create the Announcements list to contain the information that will be made available to everyone. To do this, in the upper-right corner of the screen, click Site Actions, and then click Create. This opens the Create page, from where you can choose the Announcements list from the Communications column. There are lots of other choices, but for the moment, we will just create the Announcements list (see Figure 3-7).

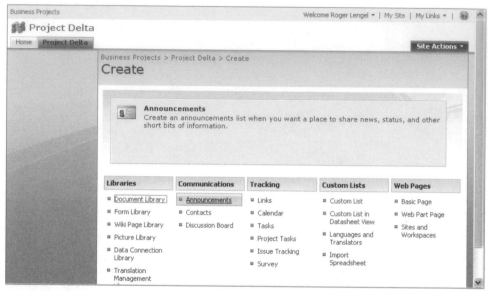

FIGURE 3-7 Add an Announcements list to the Everyone Else site.

As with creating the site itself, there are some fields that you have to complete (see Figure 3-8):

- Name of the Announcements list. This will show in future pages, so choose something that others can relate to at a glance. For this example, enter **Welcome to Project Delta**.

- A description for the Announcements list. This is really helpful if you have multiple Announcements lists in the same site, something we won't be doing in this one. But for the time being, write something interesting (and accurate!) about the role of the Announcements list.

- A navigation choice, about whether you want to show the new list in the Quick Launch area. We will turn off the Quick Launch bar in Step 9, so choose No.

When you have filled out the details, go ahead and click the Create button. You are then taken to the new Announcements list (see Figure 3-9).

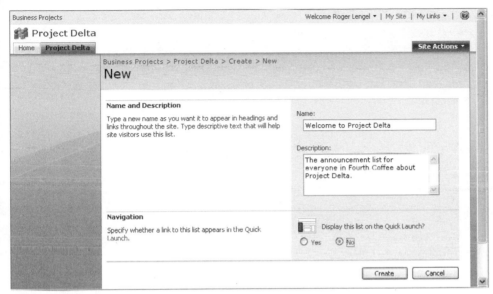

FIGURE 3-8 Give the Announcements list a name and description.

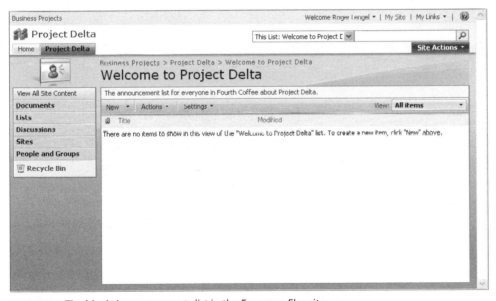

FIGURE 3-9 The blank Announcements list in the Everyone Else site

The other place to take a quick look is the All Site Content page, accessed by clicking the View All Site Content link on the left side of the page. This will show you all of the libraries, lists, discussion boards, sites and workspaces, and more in the current SharePoint site. Because this one only has an Announcements list that we have named *Welcome to Project Delta*, that and the description we entered are the only things that show (see Figure 3-10).

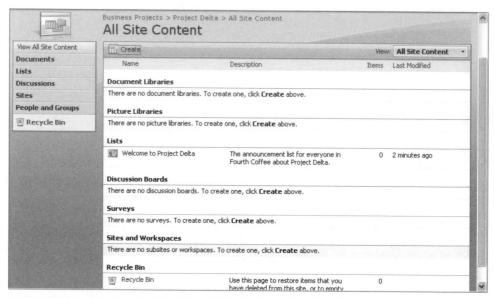

FIGURE 3-10 You can view all of the lists and libraries for a given SharePoint site.

Step 4. Link the Announcements List to the Main Page

Now that we have the Announcements list created, we want to set it so that it's the first thing that people see when they visit the home page for the site. To do this, we click back to the main page of the Everyone Else site, and then choose Site Actions and Edit Page from the upper-right corner. This allows us to modify what the main page looks like. The first thing we want to do is to add a Web Part to the main section of the page.

WHAT'S A WEB PART?

Let's talk about language for a minute. We'll start by talking about a Web page, then a SharePoint site, and finally a Web Part.

A *Web page* shows information, images, links, and other things to people visiting a Web site through a Web browser. It's what you read or view when you are browsing the Web. When you visit a particular Web site, for example *www.microsoft.com*, what you see when first getting there is the home Web page.

A *SharePoint site* is a Web site for collaboration (although given the broad nature of SharePoint, it can be for other things, too). What's important to realize right now is that a given SharePoint site can contain multiple sub-elements—a document library, a shared list, a team calendar. When you visit the document library, for example, you see the library displayed as a Web page.

Web Parts enable you to visit a Web page in SharePoint and see multiple sub-elements of a SharePoint site on a single page. Think of it as the front of a multistory house, where each room behind the frontage is a different sub-element of a SharePoint site, and a Web Part is the window into each room. Each room will be decorated differently—a girl's bedroom is often different colors than a boy's bedroom for example, or at least has different posters on the wall—but by looking in the window, you get to see a little bit of what's inside each room. When you enter the room, on the other hand, you get to see everything in there. The same holds true for a Web Part—it's a mini-window into one of the sub-elements in a SharePoint site, viewable side by side with Web Parts for other sub-elements. They are really powerful because they provide an at-a-glance snapshot of many different parts of what makes up a SharePoint site.

To add a Web Part to the page, click Add A Web Part in the middle of the screen. This opens the Add Web Parts dialog box (see Figure 3-11). This dialog box shows us a list of any lists and libraries in the site, along with the total list of all Web Parts that are available for the current site. In this instance, we want to link the page with the Welcome To Project Delta list. Select Welcome To Project Delta, and then click Add.

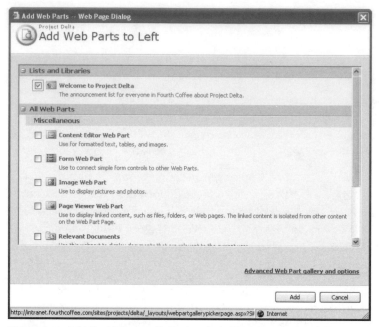

FIGURE 3-11 Add the Welcome To Project Delta Web Part to the page.

After SharePoint creates the Web Part, it displays the updated Web Part page (see Figure 3-12).

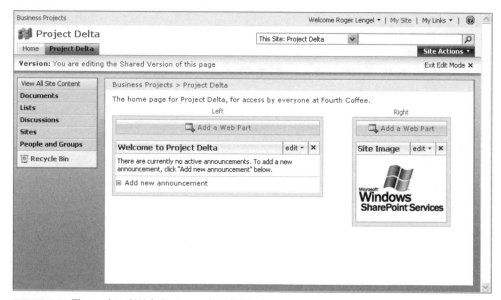

FIGURE 3-12 The updated Web Part page in Edit Mode

Before leaving this page, delete the Windows SharePoint Services logo on the right side. You don't need it for this project, so click the Edit arrow, and then click Delete (see Figure 3-13).

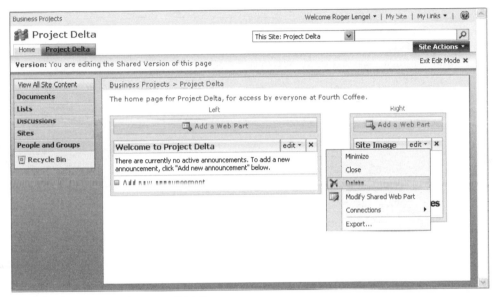

FIGURE 3-13 Delete the Site Image Web Part.

After the screen refreshes, click Exit Edit Mode in the upper-right corner to save your changes.

You are returned to the main page of the new Project Delta site, with your new Announcements list (named *Welcome to Project Delta*) showing there. The new list does not have any announcements in it at the moment, so the page is blank. We'll change that next.

Step 5. Ghost Write the Five Announcements

There are five main areas that we want to outline in this top-level site for everyone who visits:

- A brief summary of the project
- A brief statement about the objectives of the project
- A listing of the people who are involved in the project
- The name of the key contact person
- Advice to people about how they can subscribe to updates on the project

The way that Announcements lists work is that they show the latest announcement at the top, and the oldest announcement at the bottom. Because we want visitors to start with the brief summary, we need to create the announcements in reverse chronological order. Doing it this way means that you don't need to fiddle around with the design of the Announcements list, and can just get straight to work.

To start on the first announcement, click the Add New Announcement link. This opens the New Item window. The last item that we want to show in the list is Subscribe For Updates, so create this first. Leave the body for the moment; we just want to create the order first, and then we will come back in the next step and write the first cut at the content (see Figure 3-14).

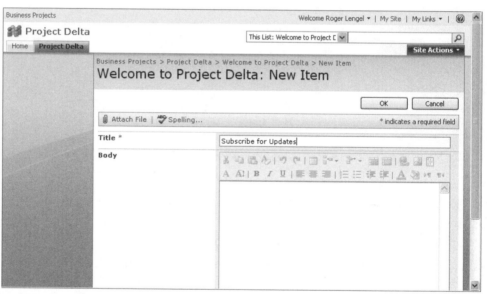

FIGURE 3-14 Write the first announcement.

After you enter the Title, click OK to be taken back to the Welcome To Project Delta Announcements list. The announcement that you just created appears in the list (see Figure 3-15).

Now go through and create these other four announcements, in this order:

- Key Contact Person

- The People of the Project

- The Objectives of the Project

- About the Project

When you finish, the Announcements list has the five announcements in the correct order (see Figure 3-16).

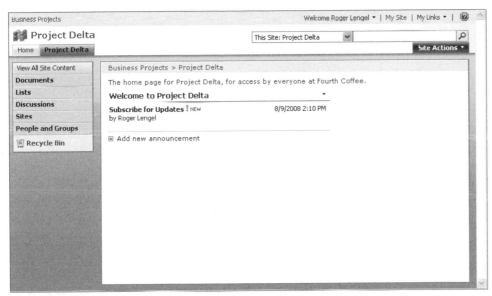

FIGURE 3-15 Your first announcement is displayed in the Announcements list.

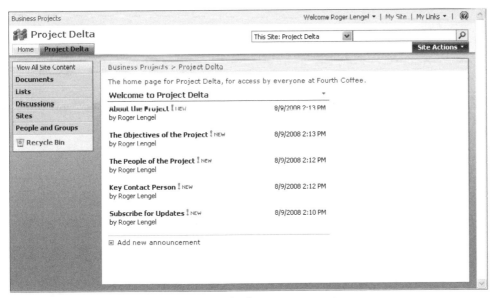

FIGURE 3-16 The Announcements list displays the five announcements.

Step 6. Write the Announcements

You have the structure of what people will see when they come to the Everyone Else site, and now it is time to add the first cut of the content into each announcement.

Let's start with the Subscribe For Updates one. From the list you just created, click Subscribe For Updates. This opens the announcement in its own screen, so you can read everything that it says. What we want to do, however, is to edit the announcement. So click the Edit Item button to change back to the original editable screen that you had when you first wrote the title. Go ahead and write a paragraph—or at least a couple of sentences—about how to subscribe for updates.

For example, Roger would write something like the following for Project Delta (see Figure 3-17):

> *The best way to keep track of what we're doing in Project Delta is to subscribe for e-mail updates or take this Announcements list as an RSS feed. See* http://intranet.fourthcoffee.com/help/sharepoint-alerts.html *for details*

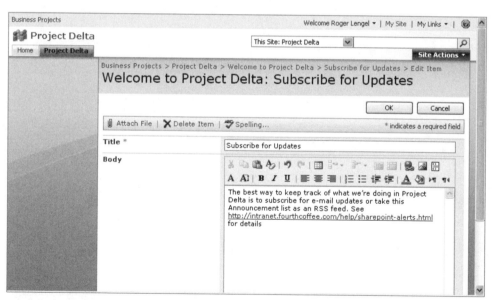

FIGURE 3-17 Write the announcement for Subscribe for Updates.

When you finish, click OK. You are taken back to the main page, and what you have just written appears there. This means that anyone visiting the main page can see at a glance how to subscribe to updates about Project Delta (see Figure 3-18).

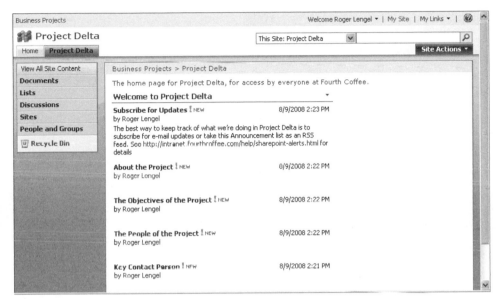

FIGURE 3-18 The Announcements list shows an at-a glance view of each announcement.

Now go ahead and fill out all of the other ones, too—you have to do them in reverse order or SharePoint will change the ordering from what you've set up already.

Here are examples of what Roger could write for each announcement in Project Delta:

- **Key Contact Person.** The key contact person for Project Delta is Roger Lengel, who is working out of the New York offices of Fourth Coffee. E-mail address for Roger is roger@fourthcoffee.com and phone number is 212-555-0167.

- **The People of the Project.** A select group of people have been brought together for Project Delta, with Roger Lengel taking the project lead. From Fourth Coffee there is Nancy Anderson (Boston), Robert O'Hara (London), Shannon Kempe (London), and Gregory Verny (London). We are also working with two external firms—Trey Research is providing key market research information through Matthew Carroll (London) and Yvonne McKay (Australia), and Fabrikam, Inc. is supplying marketing strategy direction through Laura Giussani (Edinburgh) and Eric Gilmore (France).

- **The Objectives of the Project.** The purpose of Project Delta is to explore the ways and means for expanding into select international markets, so as to drive top-line revenue growth and enhance the global brand value of Fourth Coffee.

- **About the Project.** Project Delta is going to look at some of the new ways that Fourth Coffee can expand into international markets. The project team is charged with developing a recommendation to present to the board of directors for approval.

After the five announcements have been created, the main page of the Everyone Else site shows a snapshot for each one (see Figure 3-19).

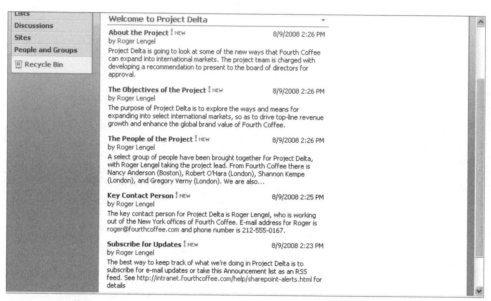

FIGURE 3-19 The completed Announcements list with the five announcements

Step 7. Create the Links List

Because the Everyone Else site is the top-level site for our project, we need to provide a way for linking to the two subsites for the project. Using a Links list is the best way to do this, because it supports security trimming, which means that it will show only specific links to the people who are supposed to see them. When someone comes to the Everyone Else site, SharePoint looks to see whether they are a member of the project team or the sponsors and stakeholders group. If they are, SharePoint displays the link to the appropriate subsite; otherwise the links are not displayed. Right now, we need to set up the Links list.

Follow the same approach as we did in Step 3 when we created the Announcements list, but this time, create a Links list. Click Links from the Tracking column (see Figure 3-20).

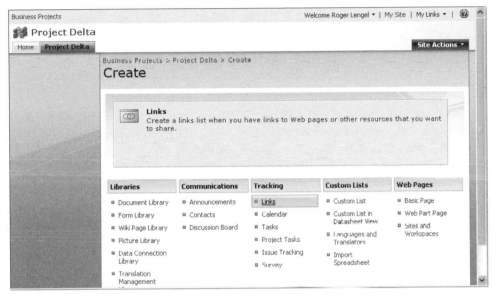

FIGURE 3-20 Add a Links list to the Everyone Else site.

Name the Links list **Project Delta Subsites**, give it a description, do not display it on the Quick Launch bar, and click Create when you are done (see Figure 3-21).

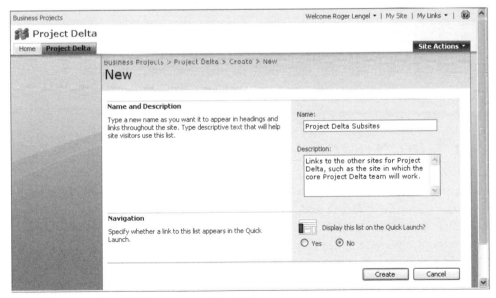

FIGURE 3-21 Give the Links list a name and description.

Step 8. Add the Links List to the Main Page

When someone visits the main page of the project, if they are a member of the project team or the sponsors and stakeholders group, we want them to see a link for getting into one or the other subsites. For this to be displayed on the main page, we need to create a Web Part for the Links list.

To add the Links list to the main page, follow the same approach that we took in Step 4 when adding the Announcements list to the main page. When you add the Links list, however, add it to the Web Part zone to the right of the page (see Figure 3-22).

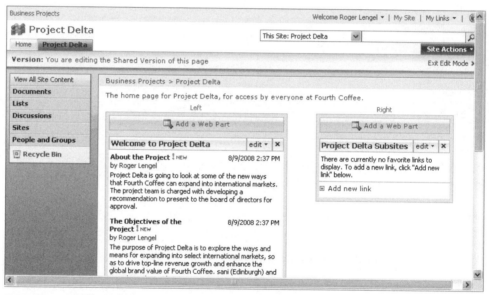

FIGURE 3-22 Add the Links list to the Web Part page.

Step 9. Turn Off the Quick Launch Bar

One of the keys to making SharePoint easy to use is to turn off user interface elements that are not needed for a specific user group. If someone doesn't need to see something on the screen, because it doesn't add any value to their work or experience in a given SharePoint site, then turn it off. One of the default user interface elements that you can turn off in this Everyone Else site is the Quick Launch bar.

Turning off the Quick Launch bar involves going into the Site Settings area, by clicking Site Actions and choosing Site Settings. Under the Look And Feel column, choose Tree View. Clear the Enable Quick Launch check box, and then click OK (see Figure 3-23).

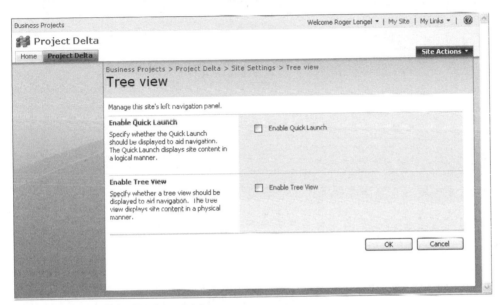

FIGURE 3-23 Turn off the Quick Launch bar.

Step 10. Pretend to Be a Visitor to the New Site

With the overall Everyone Else site set up and populated with the initial Announcements and links lists, and the Quick Launch bar turned off, visit a colleague who only has Read access rights to the Everyone Else site, and ask the colleague to open the main page. The colleague will be able to see what you set up, but will not have the ability to add new announcements or new links. And that's what you want—the colleague can read what you have prepared, but can't change it.

Because Roger's boss, Kelly Rollin, works just down the hall from Roger's office, he pops over and asks her to visit the new site. Roger is delighted to note that he's set it all up correctly, and although Kelly can read what he's written, she does not have the ability to make changes—specifically, the Site Actions menu does not appear for Kelly whereas it did for Roger, and she is unable to add new items to the Announcements or Links lists (see Figure 3-24).

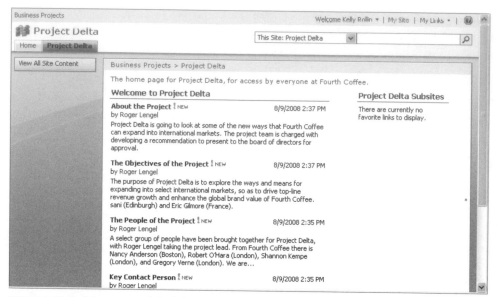

FIGURE 3-24 A visitor can read the information on the Everyone Else site, but cannot make changes.

Create a SharePoint Site for the Project Sponsors and Stakeholders

The second site to create is for the project sponsors and stakeholders. The key is to create it as a subsite within the Everyone Else site, not directly under the Business Projects area. To do this, go to the Everyone Else site that you have just created, click Site Actions, and then click Create to get going.

Step 1. Create a Team Site and Set the Permissions

The sponsors and stakeholders site can be based on one of the existing templates—to start with, it needs a place for announcements, a place for documents, and a calendar for planning upcoming meetings and noting key milestones. The Team Site collaboration template will be fine for this purpose.

Fill out the details to create the new site (see Figure 3-25):

- The title of the new site, noting that it's for the sponsors and stakeholders.

- A description for the new site.

- The URL name for the new site.

- The template on which to base the new site, in this instance Team Site.

- The permissions for the new site. Because this stakeholders site will be used by a specific set of people, click Use Unique Permissions.

- Whether to display the site on the Quick Launch bar of the parent site—this should be a No. We will link the two together through the Links list, not the Quick Launch bar (which we have actually turned off already!).

- Say Yes to using the top link bar from the parent site.

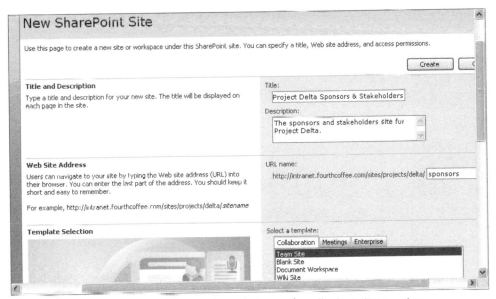

FIGURE 3-25 Give your new site a name and description, and use the Team Site template.

When you are done, click Create. SharePoint then creates the new site under the Everyone Else site. As happened when you created the Everyone Else site, you are asked to create permissions for the new Sponsors and Stakeholders site (see Figure 3-26). Enter these settings:

- **Visitors.** The only people who we want to access the Sponsors and Stakeholders site are the sponsors and stakeholders themselves. So for the moment, give the group a name but don't put anyone in it.

- **Members.** This is the group where all the names of the sponsors and stakeholders will eventually be added. In the case of Project Delta, an immediate person to add is Roger's boss, Kelly Rollin.

- **Owners.** Include the name of the lead business sponsor, and the name of your SharePoint support person from IT. In the case of Project Delta, the latter is Gareth Chan. Also, while the site is being designed, your name will need to be there too.

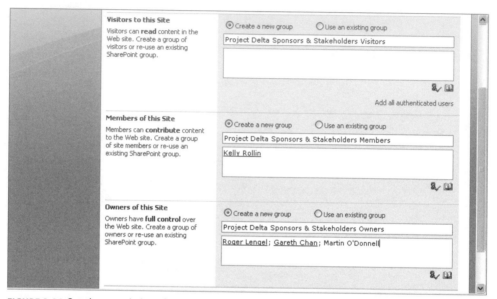

FIGURE 3-26 Set the permissions for the groups that have access to the Sponsors and Stakeholders site.

When you are done, click OK.

Step 2. Add a Link to the New Site in the Everyone Else Site

With this Sponsors and Stakeholders site created, go to the main page of your new site, and copy the URL from your Web browser to the Clipboard. You'll need this in a moment for creating a link between the Everyone Else site and the Sponsors and Stakeholders site. After you have copied the address of the site to the Clipboard, go to the main page of the Everyone Else site and click the Links list.

Click New to open the New Item form, and paste the Web address for the Sponsors and Stakeholders site into the URL field. Type a description—**The SharePoint site for the Sponsors and Stakeholders for Project Delta**—and any notes that you think are pertinent. Then click OK (see Figure 3-27).

This takes you back to the main list of links. For the new link you have just created, point to the item, click the arrow on the right side of the name, and then choose Manage Permissions (see Figure 3-28).

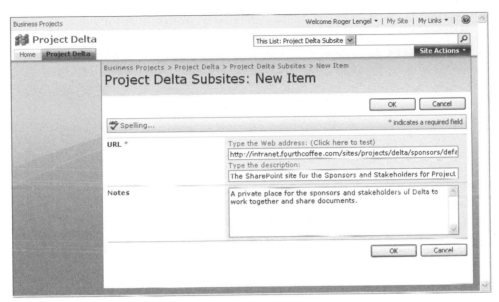

FIGURE 3-27 Create a link to the Sponsors and Stakeholders site.

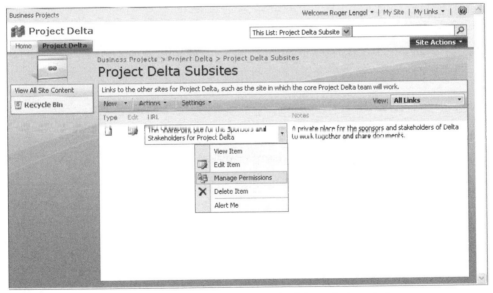

FIGURE 3-28 You need to change the permissions to see the link you just created.

What we're doing is tightly specifying who can see this link in the list, nominating people in the sponsors and stakeholders group, and eliminating anyone else. First, you need to break the tie between the wide-open permissions of the Links list in total and this specific item. Do this by clicking Actions and then Edit Permissions. This copies in the current set of permissions for the list as a whole, and then breaks the connection between the list and this particular item in the list. When you are asked to confirm this, click OK (see Figure 3-29).

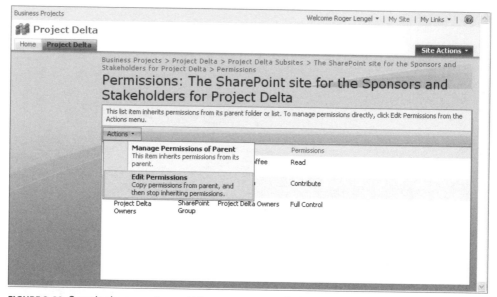

FIGURE 3-29 Copy in the current permissions so you can edit them.

The permissions list now looks a bit different, with the essential difference being that you can select the check boxes of individual items (see Figure 3-30).

What you want to do now is to add the sponsors and stakeholders groups you created in Step 1 to the link item, and delete the others. Click New, and then Add Users. To search for groups to add, click the Browse icon—the one that looks like an open book—at the lower-right of the Users/Group box. On the Select People And Groups form, find the names of the various groups by searching for the name of your project. Roger entered **delta**, and he found the three relevant groups. Select the group names you want to add, and click the Add button. Then click OK (see Figure 3-31).

Set the permissions for this link to Read – Can View Only. Apart from the Owners group (which we'll fix in a moment), they do not need to be able to control, design, or contribute in this case, and they don't need to get an e-mail message advising them of this new link either (see Figure 3-32). After you are done, click OK.

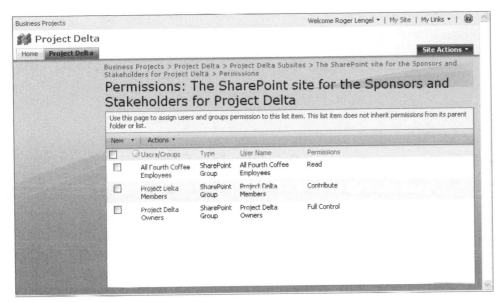

FIGURE 3-30 Change permissions for the groups.

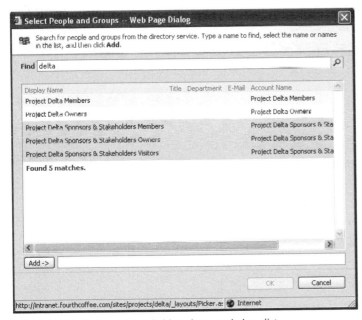

FIGURE 3-31 Select groups to add to the permissions list.

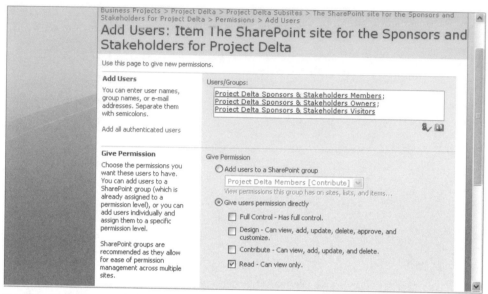

FIGURE 3-32 Set the permissions to Read for the various groups.

There are two more things to do. First, find the relevant Owners group in the new list, and give them higher permissions. Select the group's check box. On the Actions menu, click Edit User Permissions (see Figure 3-33). Then update the group to Full Control – Has Full Control, and click OK (see Figure 3-34).

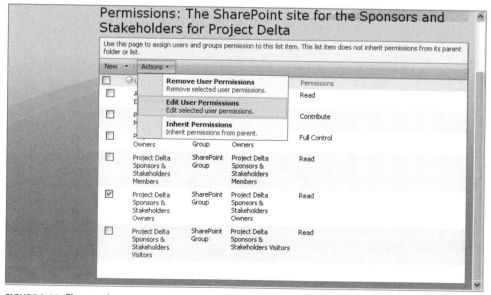

FIGURE 3-33 Change the user permissions for the Owners group.

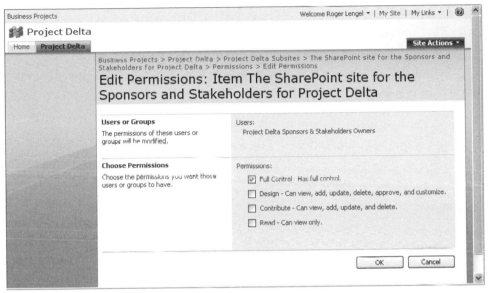

FIGURE 3-34 Give the Owners group Full Control.

The second and final thing to do is to remove the names of people who are not permitted to see the link item. Do this by selecting the check box next to their names, and then clicking Remove User Permissions from the Actions menu. Confirm by clicking OK in the dialog box (see Figure 3-35).

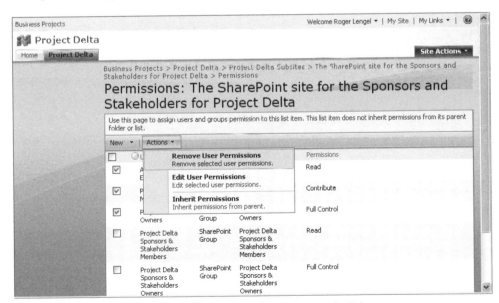

FIGURE 3-35 Delete the permissions for groups that should not see the link.

Step 3. Visit Everyone Else as a Member of the Stakeholders Group

To ensure that the rights have been created properly, log in to SharePoint as someone who is a member of the sponsors and stakeholders group you just set up, and go to the top-level Everyone Else site. On the Project Delta Subsites links list, you should see *The SharePoint site for the Sponsors and Stakeholders for Project Delta* link. If you can, that's a good sign! Click the link to open the new site. Roger has asked Kelly to take a look (given she's a member of the group), and yes, it's there (see Figure 3-36)!

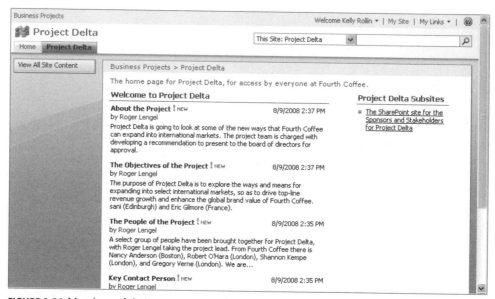

FIGURE 3-36 Members of the sponsors and stakeholders group see the link.

Step 4. Visit Everyone Else as a Non-Member

Now log out from SharePoint, and log back in as someone who is not a member of the stakeholders group, and again visit the Everyone Else site. This time, you should not see the The SharePoint Site For The Sponsors And Stakeholders For Project Delta site listed in the Project Delta Subsites Links Web Part. If you don't, it has been set up correctly! If you do, go have another look at Step 2.

Roger asked Nancy Anderson to test it, and because she is not a member of the sponsors and stakeholders group, she can't see the link (see Figure 3-37).

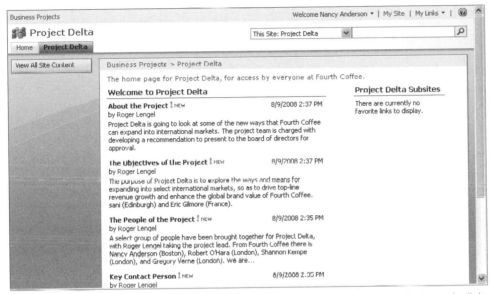

FIGURE 3-37 People who are not members of the sponsors and stakeholders group don't see the link.

Create a SharePoint Site for the Project Team

The final site to create is the actual working place for the project team. Like the stake-holders site, the project team site will allow limited access to the people who are actually directly on the team—the purpose is to give them a secure place to work. Like the stake-holders site, the project team site should be created directly under the Everyone Else site, and a link created within the Everyone Else site to the project team site.

What Does the Team Site Actually Look Like?

At the beginning of all things, the team site needs seven areas:

- An announcements list

- A team calendar

- A team task list

- A team document library

- A team wiki

- A team discussion list

- A team blog

Step 1. Create the Team Site, Groups, and Link

As with the stakeholder site, start with the basic Team Site template in SharePoint and set up the project team site. The Team Site template does not include the wiki, so we will add that in step 2. Look back at the five steps under the sponsors and stakeholder site section detailed earlier:

1. Create a Team Site.

2. Set Up the Groups for the Inner Team Site.

3. Add a link to the Inner Team site from the Everyone Else Links list and set the permissions for the Inner Team groups. The Visitors group should have Read access, the Members group Contribute access, and the Owners group Full Control. Remove all the other groups that will not have access to the Inner Team site.

4. Visit the Everyone Else site as a member of the Inner Team group.

5. Visit the Everyone Else site as a non-member of the Inner Team group.

After you have completed the five steps above, your new team site will be displayed (see Figure 3-38):

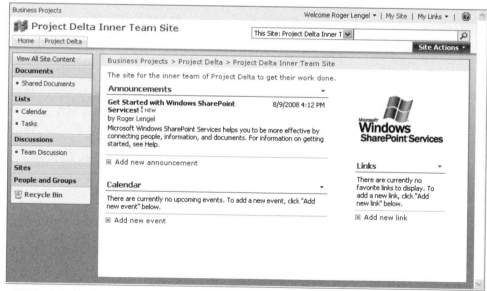

FIGURE 3-38 Your new team site for the Inner Team on Project Delta

By default, the Announcements list is not linked to the Quick Launch bar, but we want it to be linked. To create the link, open the Announcements list by clicking its name in the Web Part page, and from the Settings menu, click List Settings (see Figure 3-39).

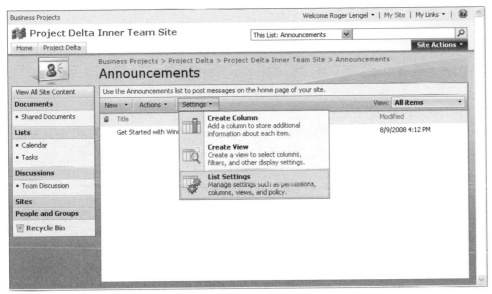

FIGURE 3-39 Change the List Settings to display the Announcements list on the Quick Launch bar.

Under the General Settings column, choose Title, Description And Navigation. On the List General Settings: Announcements page, click Yes to displaying this list on the Quick Launch bar, and then click Save (see Figure 3-40).

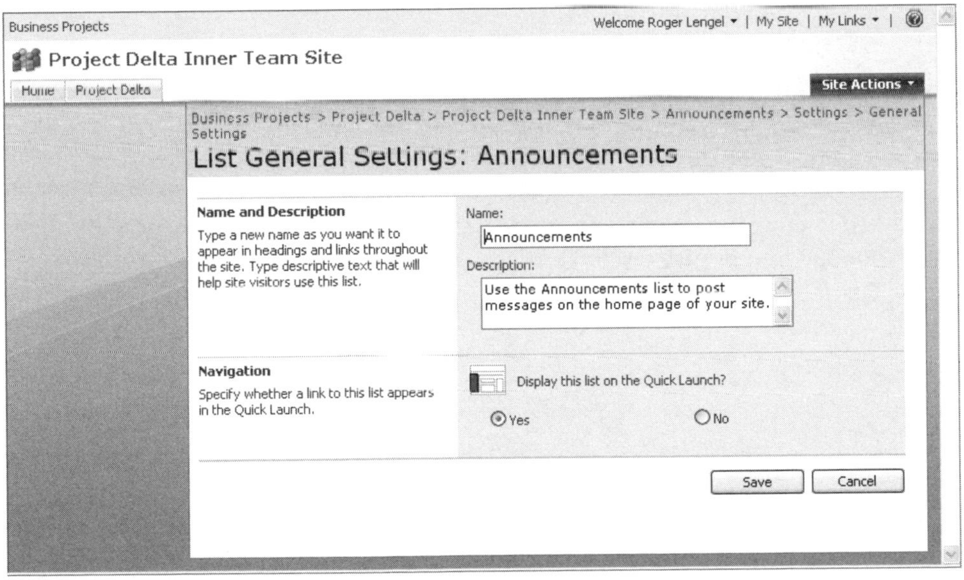

FIGURE 3-40 Click Yes to display the Announcements list on the Quick Launch bar.

Step 2. Add a Wiki Page Library

The team is going to need a wiki for its work. The SharePoint Team Site template does not include one by default, so we need to add one. In SharePoint, there are two options when creating a wiki capability: as a subsite or as a wiki page library. We'll explore the difference in a moment.

Ensure that you are within your Inner Team site. Click Site Actions in the upper-right corner of the screen, and then click Create from the menu. After the Create page opens, choose Wiki Page Library under the Libraries column (see Figure 3-41).

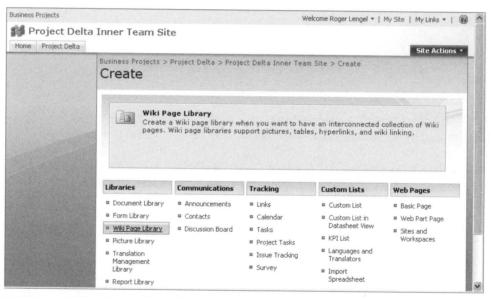

FIGURE 3-41 Add a wiki page library from the Libraries column.

You are asked to enter a name and description for your new wiki page library, and whether you want it to display on the Quick Launch bar. Enter the first two, and say Yes to the Quick Launch option. Click Create when you are done (see Figure 3-42).

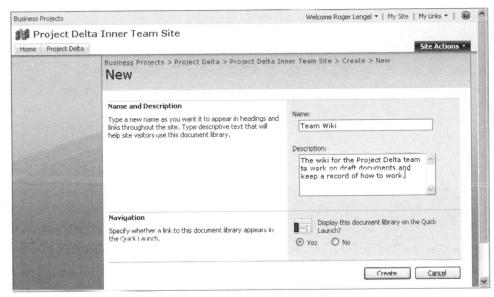

FIGURE 3-42 Give the wiki page library a name and description.

After SharePoint has created the Team Wiki, it will be displayed under Documents in the Quick Launch bar (see Figure 3-43).

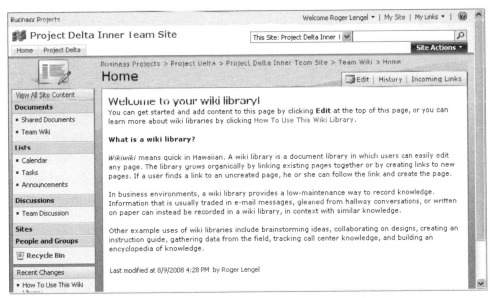

FIGURE 3-43 Wiki page libraries display under the Documents title on the Quick Launch bar.

SharePoint offers two ways to set up a wiki—either as a SharePoint site or as a page library. What's the difference? With respect to what the team can do with the wiki, whether it is created as a site or a page library has little impact. Either will be fine. Here is what a wiki site looks like when it has been created. Notice that the whole focus of the site is the wiki.

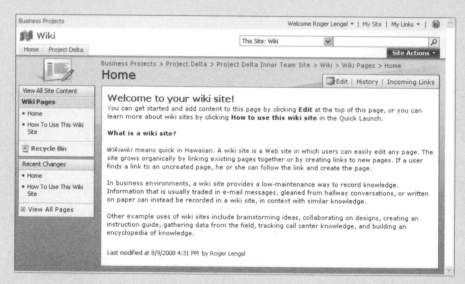

After you have created a wiki site, you can add other libraries and lists, just like you can with other sites.

A wiki page library has subtle differences:

- The wiki page library shows under the Documents heading on the Quick Launch bar, and a wiki site shows under the Sites heading on the Quick Launch bar.

- A wiki page library can be used within the context of the current team site, and you can see the other parts of the team site—the document library, the calendar, and so on—when you are working in the wiki page library. The wiki site is a bit different— you go down into the site and get a different Quick Launch side panel. It feels like a different place.

For teams that will orient their work together primarily based on a wiki, start with the wiki site. Or for intranet applications where what you need is a wiki to capture intelligence and let people write down what they know, go for the wiki site. For the purposes of this book, a wiki is one of the capabilities needed by the team, rather than the focus of it, and so a wiki page library is the way to go.

Step 3. Add the Wiki Page Library to the Main Page

When people first visit the Inner Team site, they will see the Team Wiki link under Documents. We want to go a step beyond that, however, and give a snapshot overview of the contents of the wiki page library itself. To do this, we add a Web Part for the wiki page library.

Once again, click Edit Page from the Site Actions menu. This switches the main page of the Project Delta Inner Team site into a design layout mode as we did with the Everyone Else site, so that you can add and remove Web Parts—snapshots into libraries and lists—to and from the page. After the page has switched into Edit Mode, click Add a Web Part in the Left Web Part zone. This will open a menu for choosing the desired Web Part. Select the Team Wiki check box at the bottom of the Lists And Libraries section, and then click Add (see Figure 3-44).

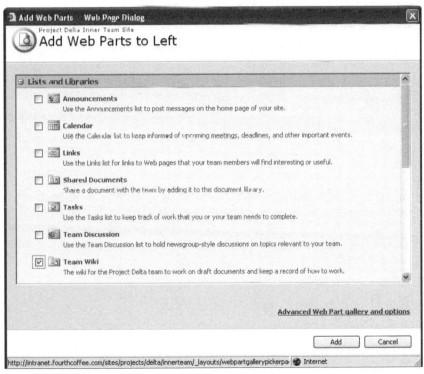

FIGURE 3-44 Add the wiki page library to the main Web Part page.

SharePoint creates the Web Part in the Left zone, and then shows you the screen still in Edit Mode. By default, the new Web Part is displayed at the top of the list, but we really want it lower in the list. To move the Web Part, drag it to where you want it to go in the list. Point to the title bar of the Web Part—Team Wiki—and then click and hold the left mouse button. Still holding the button down, drag the Web Part to the bottom of the list, and let go. A red line will move underneath the Web Part to show you where it is going to end up when you release the mouse button. If you don't drag it far enough the first time, drag it until it is at the bottom of the Web Part zone (see Figure 3-45).

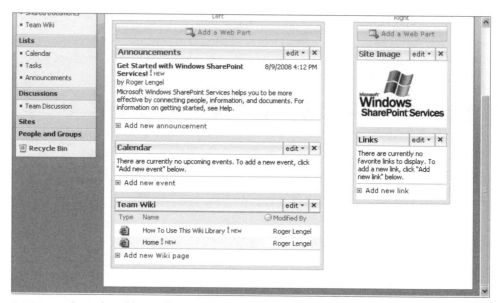

FIGURE 3-45 Drag the wiki page library to the bottom of the Web Part page.

Now scroll back to the top of the screen and click Exit Edit Mode directly under Site Actions. This puts the Inner Team Site back to work mode.

Step 4. Revise the Home Page of the Wiki

When a wiki page library is created—or a wiki site for that matter—a default home page is created with a few paragraphs of explanatory text about what a wiki is and what to use it for. Now that we have the wiki page library created, we need to get rid of that default text, and put in something that makes a bit of sense for the team.

To do this, click into the Team Wiki library (using the Quick Launch bar or the Web Part on the main page), and click Edit to revise the default text. Highlight all of the default text, and delete it.

Now type the name of three new wiki pages:

- One for the name of the project
- One for comments about the process aspects of running the project
- The final one for a page about the team members on the project

To create a clickable page name in the wiki, you have to use the SharePoint wiki markup of double square brackets before and after the page name (see Figure 3-46).

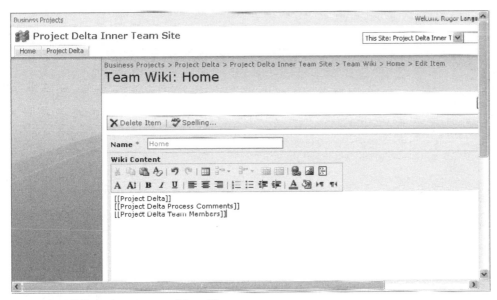

FIGURE 3-46 Edit the home page of the wiki.

When you are done, click OK.

Step 5. Add a Web Part for the Discussion List

When we created the Inner Team SharePoint site based on the Team Site template, a team discussion area was included. We need to add a Web Part to the main page so that team members can get a snapshot view of current discussions. Go through the same process as above, but this time add Team Discussion, and drag it in between the Calendar and Team Wiki Web Parts. And while you are at it, drag the Calendar Web Part over to the top of the Right Web Part zone, and delete the Site Image Web Part. When you are finished, your team site should look like this (see Figure 3-47):

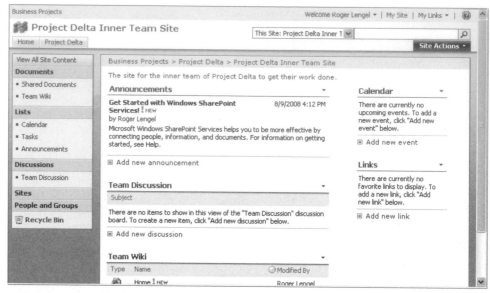

FIGURE 3-47 Your revised Inner Team site in SharePoint

Step 6. Add the Site Users Web Part

Working with people who you can't be with in person means that everyone on the team needs some way of sharing information about who they are, how to contact them for questions, and for interaction on the shared project. With a bit of creative thought, we can use the standard SharePoint User Information Form and the associated Site Users Web Part. Creative thought is necessary because the User Information Form has no pre-defined areas for some of the information that we want to track for each user—such as their blog address, country, or even organization name. So we have to re-interpret out-of-the-box definitions to fit what we want to happen. For example, where you see the term *Department* on the User Information form, tell everyone on the team to think "Organization and Country." Where you see *About Me*, think "free form entry of interesting things about me that others can use" (see Figure 3-48). Please note the following:

- The Department field is automatically populated from Active Directory, so you will need to ask your SharePoint contact in the IT department to make that change.

- Some of the information on this page is populated from the user's My Site—About Me, responsibilities—and other pieces of information come directly from Active Directory—e-mail addresses, phone numbers, and other information.

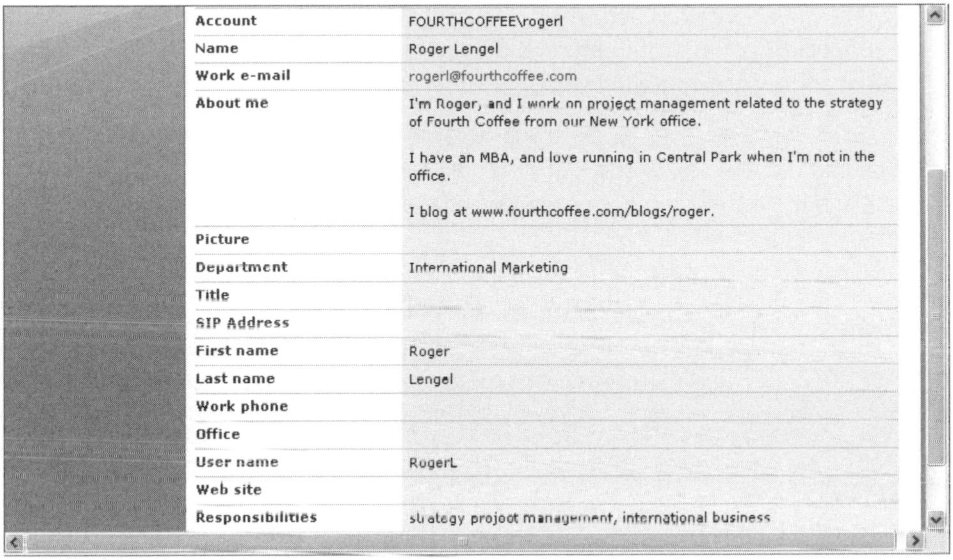

Account	FOURTHCOFFEE\rogerl
Name	Roger Lengel
Work e-mail	rogerl@fourthcoffee.com
About me	I'm Roger, and I work on project management related to the strategy of Fourth Coffee from our New York office. I have an MBA, and love running in Central Park when I'm not in the office. I blog at www.fourthcoffee.com/blogs/roger.
Picture	
Department	International Marketing
Title	
SIP Address	
First name	Roger
Last name	Lengel
Work phone	
Office	
User name	RogerL
Web site	
Responsibilities	strategy project management, international business

FIGURE 3-48 The About Me area should tell other people interesting things about you.

This involves a bit of a leap of faith (or at least a shared agreement!), and you have to tell people to do something different than what the screen actually says, but there are three key benefits to doing it this way:

1. User information isn't stored in just one SharePoint site, but is rather shared across a collection of sites. So when the user updates their information in one place, it is updated everywhere. That helps minimize the amount of work people have to do when they are involved in many projects, and ensures that the information is kept consistent across all of SharePoint.

2. The Site Users Web Part displays the list of people who have access to the site along with their online presence from either Microsoft Office Communications Server 2007 or Microsoft Windows Live Messenger. This means that every time you visit the SharePoint site for your project, you can see who else is currently online, regardless of where "online" happens to be physically. They could be in their standard office, they could be in an airline lounge, they could be lying on the beach connected via their laptop and fast data connection ... but for all intents and purposes, where they are physically is irrelevant because they are accessible virtually.

3. The third major benefit is that when Microsoft next releases an update to SharePoint (in 2010 or 2011), this configuration should transfer across to the upgraded edition without any specific migration work.

To add the Site Users Web Part, follow the process we undertook in the previous Step 3 section, and add it to the top of the Right Web Part zone (see Figure 3-49). (Note that the Site Users Web Part is listed under the Miscellaneous area in the Add Web Parts dialog box.)

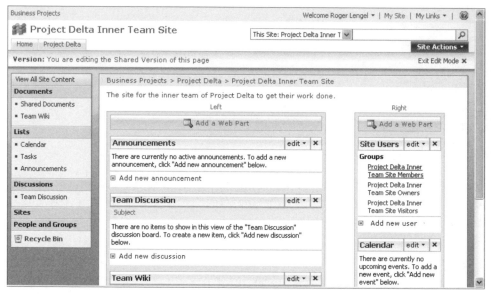

FIGURE 3-49 Add the Site Users Web Part to the Inner Team site.

Note that what is shown is the names of the groups that can access the Inner Team site. What we want to see is the names of the individual people. To make the change, click Edit on the Site Users Web Part while still in Edit Mode, then Modify Shared Web Part. This opens the option pane for the new Web Part. Change the setting under Display Type to Show People In This Site's Member Group, and click OK (see Figure 3-50).

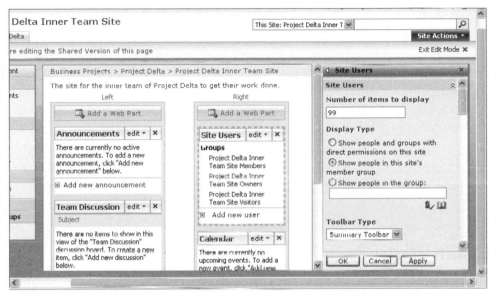

FIGURE 3-50 Change the settings for the Site Users Web Part.

Turn off Edit Mode to see a list of the users of the site (see Figure 3-51).

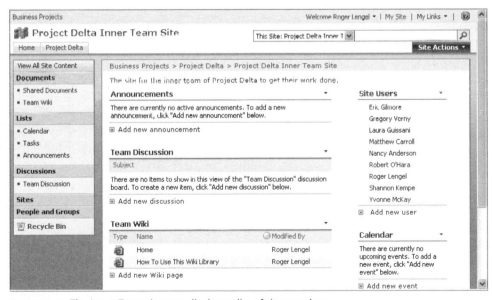

FIGURE 3-51 The Inner Team site now displays a list of site members.

Step 7. Add a Team Blog

The final capability you need to add to the team site for the core project team is a blog. In SharePoint terms, a blog is a site, not a list or a library. Create a new site within the Delta Inner Team site, and choose Blog on the Sites and Workspaces page. Give the blog a name—something like Team Blog—type a description for the new blog, use the same permissions, link from the Quick Launch bar, and use the same top bar as the parent site (see Figure 3-52).

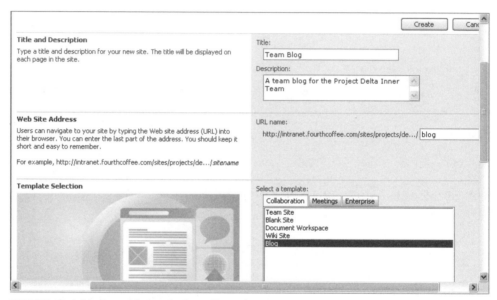

FIGURE 3-52 Add a team blog to the Inner Team site.

Click Create when you are done.

SharePoint creates your blog and you are taken to the default home page, much like you are with a SharePoint wiki page library or wiki site (see Figure 3-53).

Before leaving, create a little bit of structure in the blog in advance of other team members coming by. First, get rid of the three default categories—Category 1, Category 2, and Category 3—by clicking the Categories heading. Delete each of the three default items in turn by right-clicking the item's name and then clicking Delete Item (see Figure 3-54).

FIGURE 3-53 The default home page of a new blog

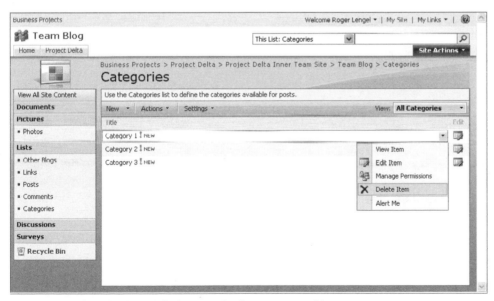

FIGURE 3-54 Delete the three default categories from your team blog.

Now add three categories that are better suited to the team blog for the purpose it will be used for: Upcoming Work Plans, Project Happenings, and People Happenings. Just click the New button to enter a new category name on the New Item page (see Figure 3-55).

FIGURE 3-55 Add a new category to the team blog.

After you enter all three category names, you have a new list of categories for the blog (see Figure 3-56).

FIGURE 3-56 The three new categories for the team blog

Click Team Blog in the breadcrumb trail at the top of the screen to get back to the blog home page. The breadcrumb trail is the sequential listing of pages that you have clicked through to get to this point in the site, and it provides quick access to clicking to an earlier place in the site.

The second change to make to the blog is to edit the default blog post. Open the default blog post by clicking its name—Welcome To Your Blog!—and then click the Edit button on the far right of the screen (see Figure 3-57).

As with editing a wiki page, you will be able to select the current text, delete it, and then write a more appropriate first blog post for the other team members to read when they first visit the team blog. Write something that welcomes the team members to the blog for the project, and explain that you will be talking to them more about using the blog soon.

Don't forget to edit the title, too, and add the post to the Project Happenings category. When you finish, click Publish (see Figure 3-58).

FIGURE 3-57 Edit the default blog post.

FIGURE 3-58 Write an initial blog post to welcome the team to the new team blog.

And You're Done!

Congratulations! With the completion of these steps, the SharePoint site for the core team of Project Delta is ready to be used.

Do You Have to Do This for Every Project?

Do you have to go through this process—creating three nested sites, with different security groups and rearranging the Web Parts—for every project? Yes, you should. Any business project where you have a terms of reference document, a group of sponsors, and a nominated team should be done this way. But it's not onerous to set up, and indeed, after you are in the swing of managing projects in this way, whenever you work without this approach, you will feel lost. The normal things that you expect (the various constructs of SharePoint and the way of working with SharePoint) will not be there, and the way of working with others that you have become familiar with will be gone. Indeed, the entire setup can be done via a SharePoint template and very easily provisioned by IT for a new project.

There's another benefit to doing things in the same way for every project. You will get into a habitual way of working with SharePoint, and the technology will become an invisible part of your working style. Thus it won't get in the way and will just become "the way we do things around here." All of the different pieces will be where you expect them to be, and you won't have to go looking for where the team calendar is, or for where you should put a certain document, or where you should put a certain task. What is for one project is for all projects, and what is for one person is for everyone.

CHAPTER 4

Team, Meet SharePoint

ROGER WAS PLEASED with himself after he finished setting up the three SharePoint sites. The structure that he had created would give each of the main groups of people involved in the project a place to work and a place to see what was going on. For the moment, the main part of his work was completed, and it was time to get the team members involved in their new work place.

Roger pulled out his trusted piece of paper again, and found his favorite pen. "Now before we get started on Project Delta," he mused to himself, "there are some things that I, for one, want to know." And then putting pen to paper, he quickly wrote down:

- Who are these people?

- How are we going to work together?

- How will we each know when other people want us to do something?

His writing was interrupted by the phone ringing, and when Gareth Chan's name flashed on the little screen, he quickly reached over and picked up the phone. With a great big smile in his voice he said, "Just the man I need to speak with!"

Welcome to Your New Team Home

The *Seamless Teamwork* approach is to embrace the capabilities of SharePoint to support both the doing of the team's work and the cultivation of the health and well-being of the team. The doing of the team's work is expressed through several SharePoint tools: a wiki page library, a document library, a discussion list, a calendar, a task list, and an announcements list. The health and well-being of the team is also cultivated through SharePoint tools, with the two key ones being the wiki page library and the team blog.

At the top-level, there are three parts that describe how the *Seamless Teamwork* approach works (see Figure 4-1):

- **Doing the Work.** The work of the team is done by using shared artifacts (in the wiki page library and the document library), with the team calendar used for coordinating in-person meetings.

- **Coordinating the Work.** The work of the team is coordinated by using the process part of the Team Wiki for describing a common working approach, the announcements list for team-level coordination, and the task list for individual-level coordination.

- **Sharing the Context.** The context of the team and its members is shared by using the team blog.

FIGURE 4-1 *Seamless Teamwork* embraces SharePoint for doing the work, coordinating the work, and sharing the context of the work.

Knowing What's Going On

One of the challenges to teamwork with a SharePoint site is the simple matter of forgetting to check for new information and new action items on a regular basis. People on the team will write a draft document and post it into SharePoint, create a new meeting event, or update one of the existing wiki pages, but they should not have to tell everyone else what they have done. They should be able to trust that everyone else will either make it a regular habit of checking for new information in SharePoint, or that they have some way of being alerted to the changes that have been made.

The best approach is to have some way of being pulled back into the SharePoint team site when a relevant change is made, without having to go there and manually check for changes. For the first couple of days, team members may be diligent in checking the site, but there should be an automated way for SharePoint to alert team members that something has changed in their world.

Thankfully, there is.

Getting Pulled Back into SharePoint

SharePoint offers a couple of key ways for alerting users about changes that have been made by other people within the SharePoint sites they belong to:

- E-mail notification, whereby an e-mail message is sent when something is added or changes

- RSS notification, whereby the same type of update is distributed by a file called an RSS feed, rather than by an e-mail notification

> **SEE ALSO**   For an explanation about RSS, see the sidebar "What Is RSS?" later in this chapter.

Either alert type will work fine, but it is vital that each team member chooses one or the other or both.

Setting Up E-Mail Alerts in SharePoint

E-mail alerts are set up for each list or library in SharePoint. Rather than having a global e-mail alert option, users are able to choose which lists or libraries they want to be notified about. The key list of interest for Roger and the team is the announcements list, because that will be the central place for coordinating the things that are happening in the project. To create an e-mail alert for the announcements list, Roger first opens the announcements list, either by clicking Announcements in the Lists area on the Quick Launch bar, or by clicking Announcements on the home page of the Project Delta Inner Team site.

After the Announcements list opens, click Actions, and then click Alert Me to set up an e-mail notification (see Figure 4-2).

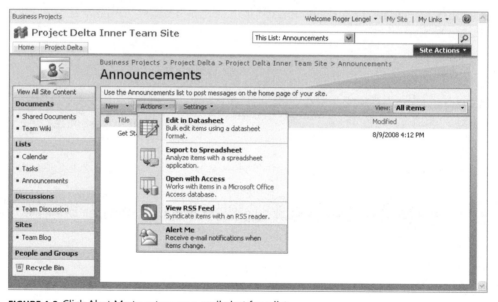

FIGURE 4-2 Click Alert Me to set up an e-mail alert for a list.

Roger can create e-mail notifications for himself and for other people on the team from the New Alert page. He first gives the alert a descriptive name, and then enters or selects the list of people on the team in the Send Alerts To box (see Figure 4-3).

The lower half of the New Alert page provides options about the alert itself. For announcements, this is things like the type of change that should trigger an alert, specific criteria for the alert, and the timing of the alert. Because the key objective is to let everyone on the team know as soon as anything changes on the Announcements list, Roger goes for All Changes, Anything Changes, and Send E-Mail Immediately (see Figure 4-4).

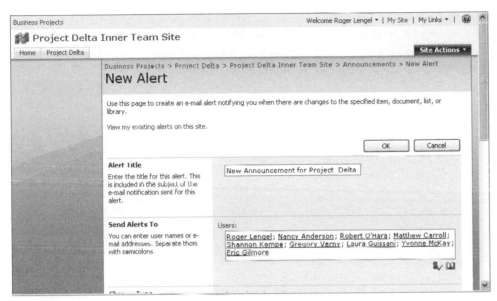

FIGURE 4-3 Give the alert a name, and enter the people to receive the alert.

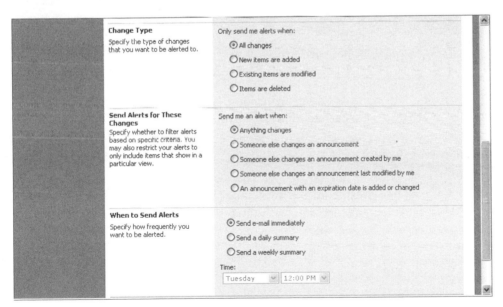

FIGURE 4-4 Set the options for the alert.

When done, he presses OK at the bottom of the page, and the alert is created.

Roger's next action is to create the first announcement in the list, welcoming everyone to the project and letting them know that SharePoint is ready for them to use. To create the first announcement, he clicks Add New Announcement from the main page of the Project Delta Inner Team site (see Figure 4-5).

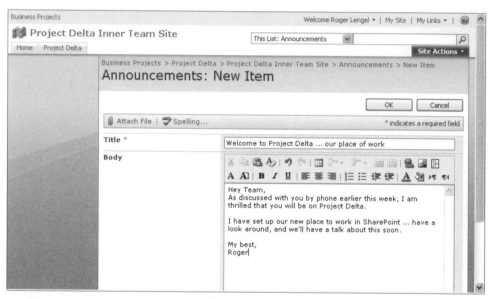

FIGURE 4-5 Add the first announcement welcoming the team to the Inner Team site.

After Roger clicks OK on the Announcements form, it is saved to the Announcements list and an e-mail alert is sent to each of the team members.

Receiving an E-Mail Alert

When the alert that Roger has just configured is triggered by activity in the Announcements list, a message will be created and sent out to Roger (and anyone else with the same alert). The subject line of the message says that it is an alert from a specific SharePoint site, and the message provides a link for pulling the user back into SharePoint to view the change (see Figure 4-6).

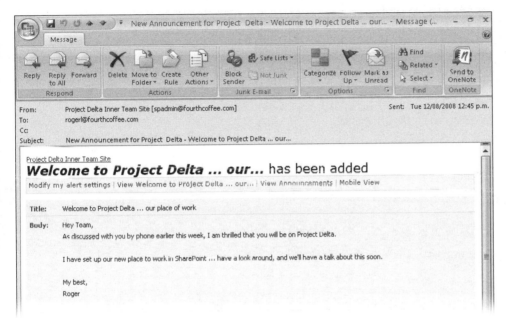

FIGURE 4-6 SharePoint distributes alerts in e-mail messages so that people are advised quickly of relevant changes.

Deleting or Modifying an E-Mail Alert

Although Roger has created the alert for everyone on the team, the team members individually can delete or modify the alert if they don't want to recieve it every time something changes. They can see their own personal list of alerts by first clicking My Settings, which they can access from anywhere in a given SharePoint site by clicking on their name in the upper-right corner of the page (see Figure 4-7).

Then click My Alerts on the User Information page to review your active alerts for that specific SharePoint site (see Figure 4-8).

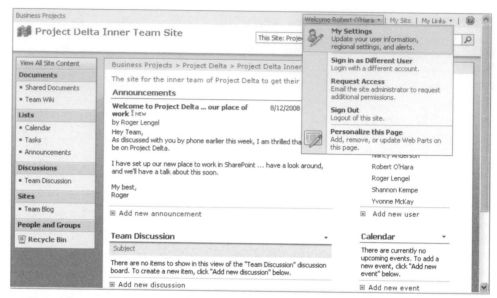

FIGURE 4-7 Open My Settings to review your alerts for a SharePoint site.

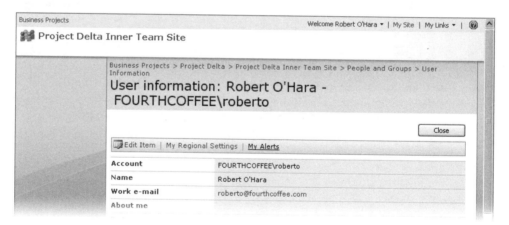

FIGURE 4-8 Access the Alerts page through your My Settings page.

The My Alerts On This Site page lists all of your alerts for the current site, organized by frequency of notification—immediate, daily, and weekly. Because only one notification has been set up for Robert O'Hara, he sees only the New Announcement For Project Delta alert. He can select it and delete it, or he can open it to make changes (see Figure 4-9).

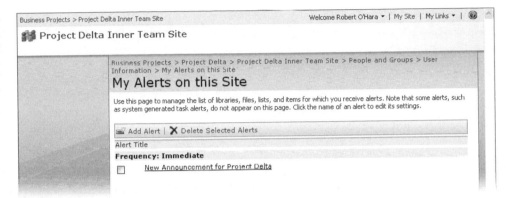

FIGURE 4-9 Individuals can review their alerts for a SharePoint site.

Robert opens the alert, and decides that for his requirements, an alert only when New Items Are Added is the way to go, so he selects that and then clicks OK (see Figure 4-10).

Alert Title	New Announcement for Project Delta
Enter the title for this alert. This is included in the subject of the e-mail notification sent for this alert.	
Send Alerts To	E-mail address:
This alert will be sent to the e-mail address indicated	roberto@fourthcoffee.com
Change Type	Only send me alerts when:
Specify the type of changes that you want to be alerted to.	○ All changes
	● New items are added
	○ Existing items are modified
	○ Items are deleted
Send Alerts for These Changes	Send me an alert when:
Specify whether to filter alerts based on specific criteria. You may also restrict your alerts to only include items that show in a particular view.	● Anything changes
	○ Someone else changes an announcement
	○ Someone else changes an announcement created by me
	○ Someone else changes an announcement last modified by me

Delete | OK | Cancel

FIGURE 4-10 Users can change or delete alerts.

MANAGING E-MAIL ALERTS IN SHAREPOINT

Let's have a deeper discussion about setting up e-mail alerts in a SharePoint team site. It is important to strike a balance between creating more discordant e-mail noise for yourself with too many alerts of the wrong kind, and being swiftly informed of new happenings by e-mail that make your life and work easier. SharePoint offers an e-mail alerting capability, but how you use it will determine whether it has positive or negative effects for you.

The first rule in creating e-mail alerts is selectivity. Don't do it for everything. When you are waiting for a certain document to be added to SharePoint, set up an alert (New Items Are Added, then Send E-mail Immediately). After the document has been added, delete the alert. When you have asked a team member to review a document for you, set up an alert (When Existing Items Are Modified Then Send E-mail Immediately). After your team member has reviewed the document for you, get rid of the alert. Even if the alert is only current for three hours in the system, you haven't had to worry about or think about it during that three-hour period, but were able to get on with your other work knowing that you would be told as soon as something happened.

The second rule is to create alerts that align with your current areas of focus. If working on a project like Project Delta is a major part of your time and energy investment at the moment, create a set of alerts so that you know what's going on without having to look. These alerts act as a personal butler, announcing changes that you may want to know about, and thus allowing you to at least have been told. It is totally within your power to do nothing about the alerts, but you have had that choice with an investment of three to five seconds to scan an alert, rather than a couple of minutes to head off to SharePoint and check to see if anything has changed.

The third rule is to take an "easy-come, easy-go" approach. It is very easy to create a new alert request in a SharePoint site, and you should create one whenever it makes sense within your work. Hey, create one just for the fun of it ... and then see if the alert is working for you and is proving to be helpful in your work. If you find yourself checking a folder for new things, or just to see what's changed, you need to create an alert for yourself, most likely of the Send A Daily Summary variety. That's the easy-come half. The easy-go part is that when you find an alert is no longer helpful, get rid of it. Delete it. And do so without any regret or concern. If you made a mistake in deleting it, and find yourself missing out on key things because you don't have the alert any more, add it back. But don't keep alerts hanging around that have outlived their usefulness and are proving to be annoying.

The fourth rule is to automatically shift your alerts from SharePoint into a special "SharePoint Alerts" folder in Outlook. Create an e-mail rule in Outlook to automatically move all of your alerts out of your Inbox into a separate folder of SharePoint project alerts. This means that the alerts are not mixed in with all of your other messages, causing even further e-mail overwhelm. This way, you can see quickly and easily know what's changed in the various projects you are involved with. Extending this idea for even greater benefit is to create a Search Folder in Outlook 2007 to highlight the particularly urgent and immediate-attention-required alerts from SharePoint.

The fifth trick is to choose an e-mail Alert Title that really helps you in your work. When you look at your list of alerts in a specific SharePoint site, they are categorized by frequency (immediate, daily, and weekly), and then only the Alert Title shows. Hence, if you have 10 to 20 alerts set up, the only piece of information you are given to help differentiate between alerts is the title. So make it a good title. For example, why do I have an alert named *Tasks* (immediate) and one named *Daily Summary of Michael's Tasks* (daily)? What's the difference between the two? What warrants me having two? Unless I click the title and review the alert information, I have no way of knowing from the title what it does and where it works within the site. So I need to make the title more descriptive.

Having clicked into both of these, there is a good reason there are two. The Tasks alert is to tell me whenever I get a new task assigned to me; I want to see what people are telling me to do ASAP! So the better title for it is *A New Task Is Assigned To Michael*. But what happens if an existing task that was originally assigned to someone else is suddenly re-assigned to me? The way that I have created my alert means that I won't see it. So I really need to request an alert for All Changes" when A Task Is Assigned To Me. Then I will get both the new ones and the changed ones. And as a consequence, the title of the alert should be written as *A Task Is Assigned to Michael*.

Setting Up RSS Alerts in SharePoint

The alternative way of being pulled back into the SharePoint team site is for users to create an RSS alert for themselves. This means that e-mail alerts are not being sent, but rather they are told about changes through a relatively new technology called *RSS*.

WHAT IS RSS?

RSS stands for "Really Simple Syndication" (and a couple of other variants), but the essential idea is that every time a Web site such as a SharePoint team site changes, a list of changes is automatically created and maintained as a special page on the Web server. When an RSS reader on the user's computer—such as Microsoft Office Outlook 2007—requests the latest copy of the RSS page, all of those changes appear within an Outlook RSS Feeds folder. Outlook 2007 displays the RSS page as a list of messages, one for each change on the master Web site.

To create an RSS alert for a list or library, for example the Announcements list, open the list (as you did when creating the e-mail alert), click Actions, and then click View RSS Feed (see Figure 4-11).

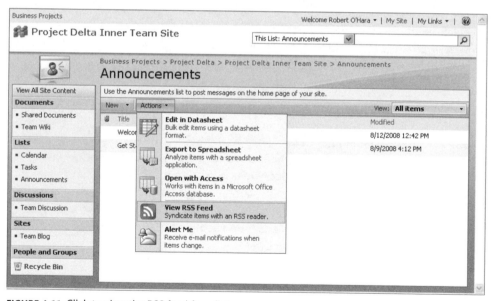

FIGURE 4-11 Click to view the RSS feed for a list.

This opens a page for the RSS feed, and asks you to confirm that you want the RSS feed for the Announcements list. Click the Subscribe To This RSS Feed link (see Figure 4-12),

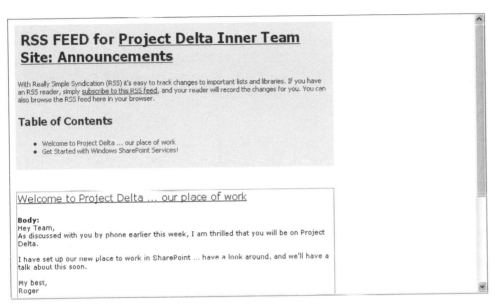

FIGURE 4-12 The RSS feed is shown in Internet Explorer.

If Outlook 2007 is set up as your RSS reader, you will be prompted to add the feed to Outlook. Click Yes in the dialog box (see Figure 4-13).

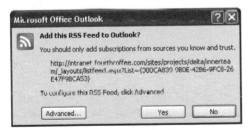

FIGURE 4-13 Outlook asks you to confirm your subscription to the RSS feed.

Because you may end up having lots of RSS feeds for different SharePoint sites, and even multiple feeds for your Inner Team site, create a project-specific folder to store your Inner Team feeds, and then move the feed you just added into that folder (see Figure 4-14).

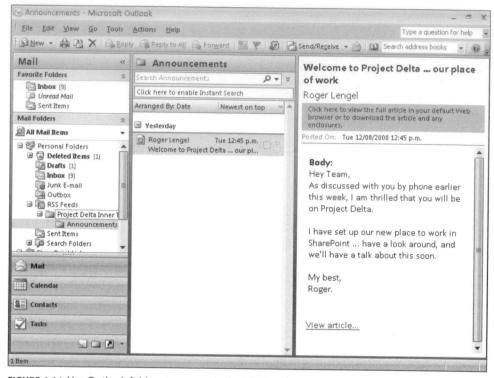

FIGURE 4-14 Use Outlook folders to group similar RSS feeds.

This means that you can group all of your feeds related to specific projects together, for an at-a-glance view of what's going on.

Finally, note that other people cannot create RSS alerts for you. Only you can do it, giving you total control over what you receive RSS alerts for. And when you have had enough of being alerted by RSS, you just delete the RSS alert from Outlook 2007 and it will no longer pull it in for you. So you have total control, and only get what RSS alerts you want to get.

RSS IN WINDOWS VISTA

In Windows Vista, RSS feeds are handled by the operating system, and then shared among RSS readers. That's a major difference from earlier versions of Windows, where RSS is handled as an application issue—for example, RSS is handled by Outlook 2007 in Windows XP, but in Windows Vista, RSS is handled by the operating system, and one of the places where the feed can be displayed is in Outlook 2007.

Entering Your Details in SharePoint

When you work with new people on a team, you generally know so little about them at the beginning of the project. You are told some things, but you have to find out everything else for yourself. It would be really helpful if you had an approach to learn more about the other people who you are working with as early as possible in the project, so that you can more fully make use of their skills, expertise, and interests. Saying with a groan halfway through a project, "I didn't know that you were interested in that!" signals a great loss of opportunity.

Learning about other people on a team is easier when you work with them in person. When you can see them working at their desk, when you can notice the books on their shelves and the magazines they subscribe to, you pick up a lot of this insight in an implicit way. When the others who you work with do not work in the same place as you, your job is more difficult.

But there is hope.

In this section we are going to look into using SharePoint to capture contextual and contact details about each team member.

What Do We Want to Know?

Roger's project—and yours, too—involves working with other people whom have particular areas of expertise and interest. Teamwork is more effective when people know more than just the task information required to get the joint work completed. It's helpful to know who the other people really are, what they are interested in, where their passions in life lie ... so that the interaction can be richer and extend beyond a pure work focus, and more than that, so that the work can be structured to call on people's unique contributions and insights.

There are at least five key areas where it is helpful to have insight into the other people you work with:

- **Contact Details.** When you need to contact someone else on the team, what are the range of options that are open and available to you? E-mail address, instant messaging address on the different services, phone number, mobile number ... all of these are different ways of getting in contact with the other people on your team. In addition, if you are working on a team with people from other organizations, knowing that information is helpful to give context to conversations and the positions that people take in discussions.

- **Home Location.** Where are they based, as in the geographical location they call "home"? When you are working with team members located around the world, the opportunity for joint, real-time work becomes less and less as more and more time zones are crossed. When some team members really do live on the other side of the world, the overlap in working hours is nil, and so someone has to take an out-of-work meeting appointment when you have to work together.

- **Current Location.** With the travel that is often a part of regular business life, people aren't always at their usual place of work. So where are they now, and where do they expect to be in the coming days?

- **Skills and Expertise.** What specific areas of skills and expertise does each person on the team have? What do they bring to the team for the benefit of all? It's good to be clear about what people see as their areas of strength, so maximum use can be made of these.

- **Passions in Life.** What are people really interested in and passionate about? What do they fill their out-of-work time with? Many people have started writing and sharing about such things on their personal blog.

Filling Out Your My Settings Page

If you want to know this information about other people, then the place to start is with yourself. You need to share as much as you feel comfortable sharing, so that others can learn about you. From within the Project Delta Inner Team SharePoint site—or actually anywhere within SharePoint—click your name at the top of the page, and then click My Settings from the list. As we have already seen, this opens your User Information form in SharePoint. There are two types of information on this form:

- **Information that is intended for use by the system.** This is the data that SharePoint needs to know about you for granting access to SharePoint sites. Your IT department will manage this, and you won't be ble to change it. This is primarily the Account field at the top.

- **Information that is designed for other people to see, understand, and use.** This is everything else on the form, including your name, e-mail address, the About Me field, and the rest of the fields. This information is displayed on the User Information form, but is maintained in two other places—your My Site and in Active Directory.

To update and revise what is noted about you, click over to your My Site and edit the details stored in the My Profile part of My Site. We talked about this in Chapter 2, "Managing the Project and Finding a Team," for the project leader, and now that same information should be shared with everyone on the team.

Be sure to upload a picture! When you work with people in person, you don't wear a black mask so they can't see what you look like. Find a picture you like, and upload it. It really helps—for some reason that is hard to explain—to have some visualization of what the other people you are dealing with actually look like.

A couple of other best practices and ideas to consider embracing:

- The picture of you will be resized to a fairly small scale. If there are other good photos of you that you are willing to share, include a link to them in the About Me field.

- If you write a blog outside of work, include the link. If it covers some sensitive areas that you are not sure your colleagues will appreciate, either leave it out or include a warning. Tell people what to expect, so if they do go there, they won't die of shock.

- The information that you enter here is available everywhere across SharePoint— all of the sites that you are involved in use this information and will display it. If there are project-specific things that you want to say, don't put it here. Use the wiki—which we'll talk about soon.

- If you have a Web calendar that shows where you are going to be for work in the coming weeks and months, include the link in the About Me section.

- Your My Site page includes a lot of information about you and your work. Include a link to that.

What About Project-Specific Information?

Because the user information that you enter about yourself is shown everywhere in SharePoint, you will need to exercise some judgment over what specifically you want everyone to see. And remember too that your My Site page includes a lot of good information about you and your work. If there are specific disclosures that you want to make specifically to everyone else in the team, do this in the SharePoint wiki in the Project Delta Inner Team site.

Head over to the Team Wiki, and click the Project Delta: Team Members link that Roger set up in Chapter 3, "Setting Up SharePoint" (see Figure 4-15).

FIGURE 4-15 Open the Project Delta: Team Members page from the Team Wiki home page.

If that page has not been created yet, a blank page will open (actually a dashed line under any page name signifies that the page has not been created), otherwise the current version of the page will open for editing.

- If your name is on the list, click it and add some more details about yourself.

- If your name isn't on the list, edit the Team Members page. Create a new page for yourself using the SharePoint wiki markup of double square brackets before and after a word or phrase to signify a new page, save the page, and then click your new link and make notes.

For Project Delta members, Roger has already created the structure of the page, and has even noted the organizations that each team member works for (see Figure 4-16).

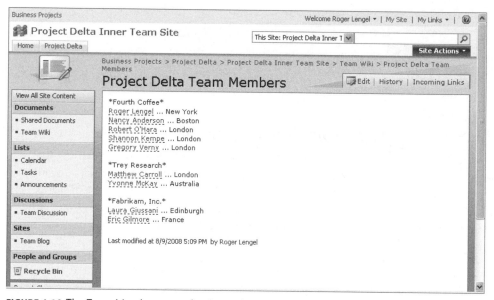

FIGURE 4-16 The Team Members page for the project

To add details about themselves, team members only have to click into their own wiki page, add any project-specific information they want to add, and then click Create (see Figure 4-17).

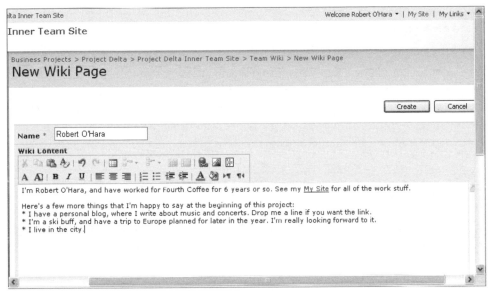

FIGURE 4-17 Write project-specific information about yourself on your wiki page.

Discovering Common Working Hours by Using the Team Wiki

When you work with people across multiple time zones, it is a challenge to remember the right time in all of the different places. You may be able to remember two or three different places and get it right most of the time, but as the number of time zones increase along with the number of team members, it gets more and more likely that mistakes will be made. You can use SharePoint to help with time zone coordination, but more than that, you can use SharePoint to make it clear what overlap exists between standard working hours in the various places that people work from.

One of Roger's first requests to everyone on the team is to go into the Project Delta wiki, open the page named Common Working Hours that he has just created, and fill out the column of working hours during which each person will generally be available. The trick to make this work, however, is for everyone to enter the times against a common time standard, or in other words, a time list that is time zone friendly. When Roger on the East Coast looks at the page, he will be able to see which other members of the team are available for real-time interaction at 4 P.M. his time. The purpose of doing this is to make it evident to everyone on the team when others are generally available for work; of course, emergencies are one thing, but regular working hours are another, and as much as possible, team members need to show respect to each other by keeping requests for real time meetings by phone or IM within the bounds of the identified common working hours page.

It is better to create this as a wiki page rather than as a Microsoft Office Excel 2007 worksheet, for two reasons. First, it is faster to edit the wiki page than to open and edit an Excel worksheet. Second, by doing it on the wiki, people can create a browser link to the actual page and the information on the page, rather than having to download and open the latest edition of an actual document. So it's faster and easier to use the wiki.

Creating the Common Working Hours Page

Roger goes into the Project Delta wiki, clicks into the Project Delta Process Comments page, and creates a heading named *Team Information*. (Using the rich text editing control, Roger can type the text **Team Information**, select it, and click the Bold button). Directly under that, he types **[[Common Working Hours]]**, which tells SharePoint that he wants to create a new page named *Common Working Hours*. Within SharePoint, the "[[" and "]]" around a word or phrase are code tags that tell SharePoint to create a linked page (see Figure 4-18).

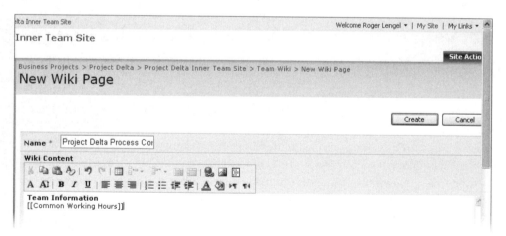

FIGURE 4-18 Create a linked page in the SharePoint wiki.

When Roger saves the page, a link is created with the words *Common Working Hours* high-lighted. This means that he has entered the information correctly, and can now click that link to create the page. Roger does so, and gets another blank page in the SharePoint wiki.

He looks at the list of nine names on the team, and notes the place that each comes from and works from. He creates a table in the SharePoint wiki page, with nine columns and 26 rows. He clicks the Insert New Table button to create the new table (see Figure 4-19).

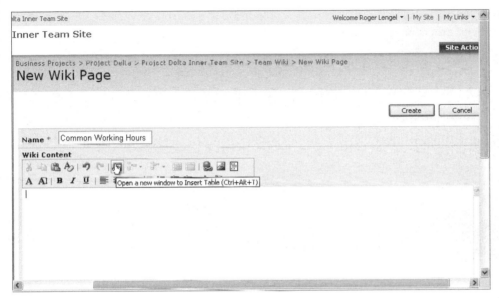

FIGURE 4-19 Add a table to the wiki page.

SharePoint opens a dialog box to ask Roger to specify the number of columns and rows in the table (see Figure 4-20).

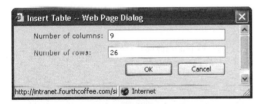

FIGURE 4-20 Specify the number of columns and rows in the table.

Across the first row, Roger enters **London** in columns 1-4, **Edinburgh** in column 5, **France** in column 6, **Boston** in column 7, **New York** in column 8, and finally **Australia** in column 9. He has laid it out this way to show the general flow of a working day for the team ... who starts first, and who works latest.

In the second row, he enters the names for the nine team members, based on where they live and work. From left to right, that's **Robert**, **Shannon**, **Matthew**, **Gregory**, **Laura**, **Eric**, **Nancy**, **Roger**, and finally **Yvonne** (see Figure 4-21).

He then enters the working hours that he can generally do. It is important to note that these times are a general statement of Roger's working reality, and don't take into consideration other meetings, scheduled travel, or other things. It's just what his normal working day looks like, and what he is willing to do at a pinch to ensure he can actually talk with others on the team (see Figure 4-22).

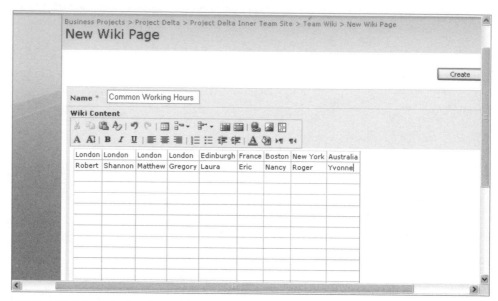

FIGURE 4-21 Set out the locations of the team members.

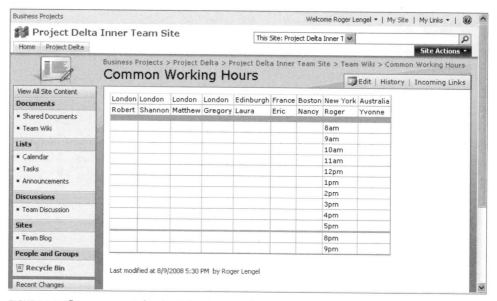

FIGURE 4-22 Roger sets out the times that he is available to work on Project Delta.

Thus, when looking at Roger's working hours, we see that he works 8–6 P.M. each day, and is also available between 8 and 10 P.M.

After Roger has filled out his general day, he creates a new announcement in the Announcements list, telling the team about what he has done, and requesting that they do the same (see Figure 4-23).

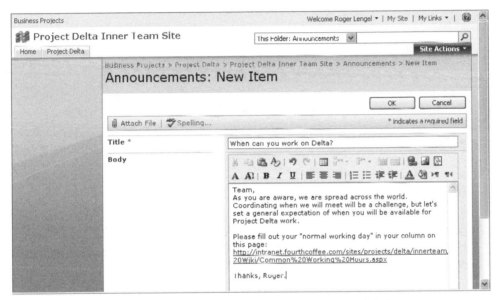

FIGURE 4-23 Create an announcement to request team members to fill in their times.

Because all the team members have either an e-mail alert or an RSS subscription to the Announcements list, Roger knows that they will see his announcement and the request within a few hours. Once everyone has filled in their columns, he will be able to see about setting up the meeting times when he can view the overlapping working hours; and if there are no times that are self-evident, then he can consult with a couple of team members to see if he can make it work.

Taking this approach to figuring out when people will generally be available to work means that people can work on this project at times that are best for them. If someone wants to sleep all day and work all night, then it doesn't really matter ... but what does matter is that such a decision is made clear so that others can see when they can rely on that team member to be available for conversation and interaction.

Once again, it doesn't really matter when people are available, just that everyone knows when others are generally available so they get a sense of when things will be done.

Roger is delighted to note the next day that the page is all filled out (see Figure 4-24).

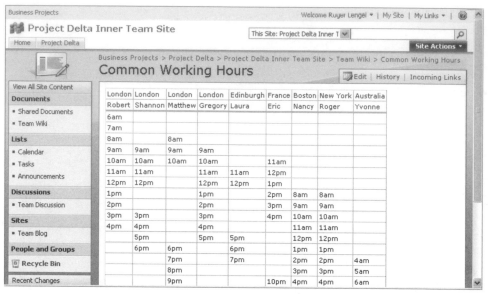

FIGURE 4-24 Everyone has contributed to the Common Working Hours page.

It is, however, immediately clear that there are no overlapping times for everyone on the team, so meetings that require the attendance of everyone will need to be carefully planned.

Establishing a Teamworking Protocol

At the beginning of working with other people on a shared project, team members need to agree on the general approach to how they will work together, particularly when technology such as SharePoint is involved. Because everyone not in the same room is invisible, a shared mental picture is needed by everyone to know what has been planned to happen. "How does what I am working on by myself here relate to what Yvonne is doing in Australia and what Robert is working on in London?"

At this stage of the team's work, a few broad principles and agreements are in order. For example, it is very helpful to have shared and common expectations about the following:

- How often people will respond to announcements posted in the SharePoint announcements list. Is a response within a week sufficient, or is something faster expected?

- How people will react if they do not understand something that another person says. Do they push ahead on their understanding, or do they go back to the other person?

- How people will share the contextual information about what is going on for them.

- That it is expected—and absolutely beneficial—that people have disagreements and differences of opinions about key matters in the project. If everyone thinks the same, a team will not be necessary. However, the key is that we will not allow disagreements to derail the progress of the project, because we agree to listen carefully and resolve our disagreements through candid dialogue and debate. When we can't do this by ourselves, we agree that after making our case to the wider team, we will abide by the decision of the wider team.

Making the point of agreeing with these principles upfront is very helpful to ensuring that the difficulties of working remotely do not overshadow the work of the team, and ruin it for everyone.

The best way to start the agreement toward a shared way of working is for the team leader to make an initial statement of approach, using the SharePoint Team Wiki. This should be on a page linked from the Project Delta Process Comments page, and should be named **Agreement on Working Approach** (see Figure 4-25).

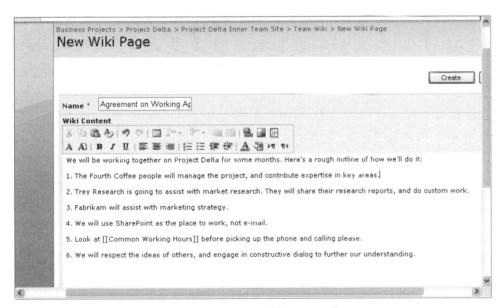

FIGURE 4-25 Use the wiki to describe the common working approach.

After the initial statement has been made, the team leader should create an announcement linking back to the page, asking the other members on the team to read it over and make any suggestions or recommendations that make sense. These can be made directly on the page in the wiki.

Giving Others Insight into What's Happening

When you work with other people in person, you get to see what is going on in their work and life. And that means everything that is going on, not just the project work that you are jointly involved with. For example:

- The meetings they attend and the issues that they get particularly fired up about, in good and bad ways!

- The people who come by to speak with them, both about current and future work. And sometimes you even get to hear the totality of the conversation, because while you are working away at your desk, they are standing just over there and having a good-old talk.

- The magazines and books they're reading—you can see them on their desk, or they discuss them at morning break.

- The trips that they have planned, for business and pleasure, because you hear them talking about upcoming travel and see the dates marked on their calendar.

When you share a work life with others, you get all of this extra information as a natural consequence. It is an implicit thing that happens, rather than something that you need to search out. But it often helps you understand better the people who you are working with, and the range of skills that they have to offer.

When you work with people who are not in the same place as you, the sharing of this contextual information is much more of a challenge. It is actually one of the hardest things to get done. It's not hard because it is difficult, but rather is hard because your contextual information is so self-evident to you because you are in the midst of it. It's almost invisible to you, and you can't imagine that others could be interested in it. Resolving the sharing of contextual information is completely within the control of team members, and SharePoint provides a great way to do it: the team blog.

Writing on the Team Blog

The key to making the team blog work is that everyone on the team should regularly post an update on their work. Everyone should post at least once a week, and many people on the team should post every day or every other day. Here are some topics that team members should write about on a frequent basis.

The first topic is what's happening with the project at your location. For example, the scraps of information about who came to the office to discuss the project today may seem like "scraps" to you, but can be very interesting to others. Ditto the project meetings that you were a part of, and how the various pieces of the work that you are responsible for are going. Each day, or after each meeting that has relevance to the project, post a short summation of who attended and what was discussed, and what decisions and next actions were determined.

A second topic is a summary of any in-person meetings you had with others on the core project team. Talking about in-person meetings that you were able to arrange gives others on the team something of a sense that they were there too and that they therefore didn't miss out. Writing out in short terms or in long detail about the sorts of topics that you discussed during the meeting helps other people form a sense of how the project is going for you, and what you are currently doing.

A third topic is your work plans for the coming day or week. It's really helpful to others to have a sense of the current work activities that you are undertaking, because it helps them to know what to expect from you in relation to their work and the overall progress of the project. If your list of work activities changes daily, then make a three-line or four-line blog post updating everyone on the team about what you will be working on today. If a week is a better planning horizon for you, make a blog post once a week about your plans for the next week. If it's the same as last week, make another post anyway, noting what you did achieve and what specifically you will be doing this week.

A fourth topic is any upcoming vacation time that you have planned, as well as any upcoming public holidays that happen in your country. With respect to the vacation time, knowing that others on the team will be away "next week" or "in a fortnight" helps everyone else set expectations about what to expect from you. It also sends the signal that if they have things they want to discuss with you, that they should talk to you sooner rather than later.

After you get to know the other people on the team a bit better, you may even write about the movies you watched out of work time, because you know that others on the team like the same movies that you do. Or they like the same sports team. Or whatever— the point is that it celebrates the commonalities that do exist and goes some way toward covering over the huge number of differences that team members who are not together have to overcome.

Letting Everyone Post Without Approval

When a new blog site is added to a team site in SharePoint, the default setting is that the person who created the blog is able to publish new blog posts directly, and everyone else has to have their blog posts approved first. We don't want that in the Inner Team site—everyone needs to be able to post directly. It's really easy to make the change.

Open the team blog, and click Manage Posts on the right side of the page, under Admin Links (see Figure 4-26).

FIGURE 4-26 Click the Manage Posts link to set posting permissions.

This opens the team blog in a list view, much like we have seen already with other types of SharePoint lists. Click Settings, and then click List Settings to open the Posts page (see Figure 4-27).

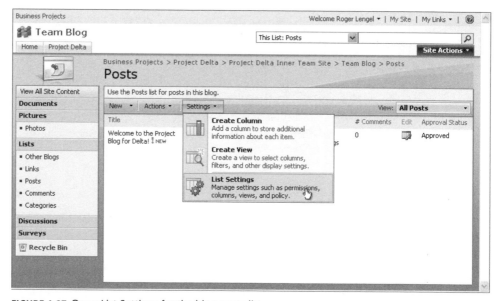

FIGURE 4-27 Open List Settings for the blog posts list.

Click Versioning Settings under the General Settings heading, and change the Content Approval option at the top from Yes to No (see Figure 4-28). Then click OK to exit the settings page.

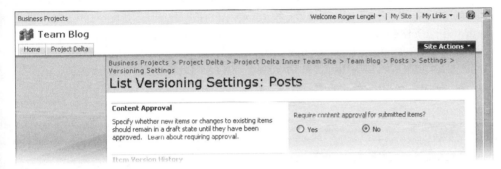

FIGURE 4-28 Turn off content approval for blog posts.

With this change, any team member will be able to post directly on the team blog, without having to wait for their blog posts to be approved by the blog owner.

Creating a Blog Post

Creating a blog post in the team blog is super-easy. Click into the Team Blog on the Quick Launch bar, and then click Create A Post on the right side of the page (see Figure 4-29).

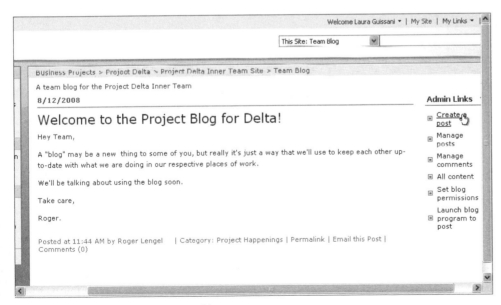

FIGURE 4-29 Team members can create blog posts.

When the new blog post page opens, enter a title, type what you are going to say, and assign your blog post to one of the categories. For example, you are going to interview a number of prospective channel partners for your project in the coming week, and that will take you out of the office. Although you will have your mobile phone with you, you will have Internet access at the hotel each night. Because it is really helpful for the others on the team to know what's happening with you in the coming week, make a blog post saying what's going on. And because the post relates to upcoming travel, include your name in the title, so others can see at a glance who the post is about (see Figure 4-30).

FIGURE 4-30 Write a blog post about what's happening in your life and work.

Now when others on the team visit the Team Blog, they'll be able to see what's up with Laura, and why she is so quiet this week!

Winning Trust Through Blogging

Being diligent about keeping others on the team appraised of your work through the team blog greatly assists with the building of trust. When we develop trust in another person when working with them face to face, we formulate our trust quotient in them over time through repeated observation on work and react in the hurly-burly of moment-by-moment work. When we work with others who are at a distance, we form our trust based on the things that are shared between us, and on whether they do the things that they say they will do and therefore that we expect from them. If they do what they say when they say, that signals to us that they are worthy of our trust—we can trust them: they are trustworthy. When they don't do what they say or what we expect of them (based either on job description or mutually agreed task or project division), we say that they are not worthy of our trust.

Tracking the Team Blog Through RSS

Your fellow team members can read what you write, directly within SharePoint or by subscribing to the RSS feed for the team blog and reading it within a news reader. If you say something that they are particularly interested in, hopefully they'll leave a comment, either thanking you for what you shared, or asking you for more information. And the same applies to you; others have taken the effort to write and share what's going on in their work world, so make the effort to thank them for doing so, or to ask a question.

To subscribe to the RSS feed for the blog, click the RSS Feed link at the bottom of the Quick Launch bar for the team blog. As with the RSS feed to the announcements list that we looked at earlier, doing so will give you the option of reviewing the RSS feed that you are about to subscribe to. Click Subscribe To This RSS Feed to confirm your subscription, and be sure to put the RSS feed for the team blog into the same folder as the other RSS feeds for your project—thus keeping them all together.

Finally, if you would prefer to receive e-mail alerts about new blog posts, you can set that up too, by clicking Alert Me from the Actions menu on the team blog. Follow the same approach that you did when you set up the e-mail alert for the announcements list.

Overcoming Silence Through Blogging

Regular blogging about your work is an antidote to another major challenge of working on a virtual team: how to interpret silence. Your team members are already invisible to your eyes, and if they are not talking to you, they also become inaudible to your ears. What do we make of this?

Silence can mean many things. It can mean that people are schedule-slammed, and have so much on their task list that they just cannot get a few spare minutes to respond to your question. Or it can mean that they are ignoring you, that they don't want to engage with you on the work that you are jointly involved with. Or it can mean that they are working away diligently on the next thing that they are supposed to be working on, and don't think it worthwhile saying that that's what they're doing, because that's what they are supposed to be doing. Or it can mean that they are angry with you, and they never want to speak to you again. Although the fact of silence is just one message (they are silent or they are not), it has many different interpretations! It's no wonder that unexplained silence can be such a challenge to the efficacy of team relationships.

When each team member writes a regular update on the team blog in SharePoint, the interpretation of silence is a lot easier. If people are schedule-slammed, a post at the beginning of the week to say that they have a super-busy week coming up, and that they'll be pretty much out of the loop goes a long way to allay fears and make it clear what's actually going on. If they are busily working away on the next deliverable that they are accountable for, they can say that. Thus the team blog can adequately deal with two of the good reasons for silence, and a well-timed comment from others on the team can remind a person that it's time to write more, or that they should keep on with what they're doing. By setting out in advance what is coming up, and what is likely to happen over the next week, the team members provide a strong basis of trust for what's coming up.

But how do you use a project blog if you're struggling with one of the other reasons? You have a grievance against one of the other team members, and it's festering away. Or you're really, really angry with what someone said to you on the last conference call, and you just want to avoid that person as much as possible. Is the project blog the place to air this?

No. It's not blog content.

You need to approach the person privately, and request a meeting. If they are in another location, as is likely to be the case, it will have to be a phone call. When you talk to the person, outline your view of what's happened, and ask how he or she sees things. Hopefully, you can come to a place of agreement or resolution. If you can't and you feel that the other person hasn't listened, you need to request the presence of another person in a second conversation, perhaps the team leader (Roger, in the case of Project Delta). If the team leader isn't the right person and you want someone external to the team, approach the right person and request his or her help. If a second conversation with someone else present (on the phone or in person) still doesn't resolve it, take it to the wider team for an all-hands-on-deck discussion. Others may be able to force a resolution that you cannot do on your own, or may drive the removal of the troublesome team member with someone better suited to the task at hand.

A powerful strategy to overcome the possibility of silence being attributable to avoidance behaviors or anger with another is for the team to have a frank conversation at the beginning of the project and agree to keep a short account with each other. For example, during one of the initial teleconferences—and definitely in the team's written working protocol—a senior member of the team should say that it is very likely that disagreements will arise during the course of this work, and that these items aren't personal but are reflective of different interpretations of what is right according to a certain frame of reference, and that when this happens the people involved agree to resolve the issues quickly. This sets the ground rules so that when each person signs up to the team, they equally give their word of honor to be honest with their colleagues, to speak quickly about what is going on and what they are finding difficult, and to agree that they will resolve disagreements to a point that everyone can accept. Such an agreement will need to be kept alive by practice and goodwill during the course of the work, but having it in place from the beginning is a powerful counteracting strategy to something that is bound to happen.

Remember, when we work in virtual teams, all of our interaction is much more difficult than when we are together in person. In person, it somehow seems a lot easier to hash the problem out, to draw things on the board to explain our position, or to speak frankly about the problems we are experiencing than when we have to do these things remotely. But the reality is that much of our interaction with others is at a distance, and we need to get better at dealing with silence and coming to mutually agreeable resolutions when silence signals a breakdown in interpersonal relationship capability.

Does Offline Mean Out of Touch?

We don't live in the office, and as more of our work is facilitated through SharePoint, we need to work with our team members, the documents we are sharing, and the conversations we are having when we are offline. As a browser-based tool, SharePoint does not natively offer offline capabilities. What are people to do—like Laura, who will be interviewing channel partners for a week—when they need access to SharePoint but will not be connected to the network?

There are three approaches: two from Microsoft, and one from Colligo Networks.

Microsoft Office Outlook 2007

The first Microsoft alternative is Microsoft Office Outlook 2007. Some of your information in SharePoint can be linked to Outlook and accessed when you are away from the office. Information like team calendars, team to-do lists, lists of contacts, and libraries of documents, among some others, can be connected to Outlook for access when offline and out of the office. For example, a SharePoint team calendar can be displayed in the Calendar part of Outlook 2007. To do this, open the calendar in SharePoint, and click Connect To Outlook on the Actions menu (see Figure 4-31).

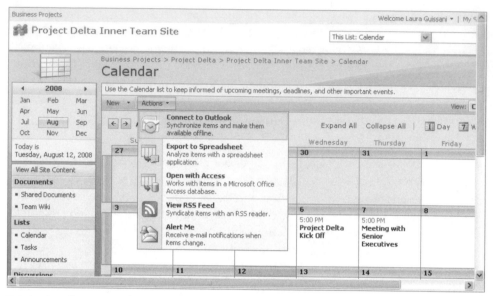

FIGURE 4-31 Connect a calendar list in SharePoint to Outlook.

You will be prompted to confirm the connection; say Yes. You can connect multiple SharePoint calendars to Outlook 2007, and you can see a threaded view of all your calendars. This means that you can see your personal calendar in light of all of your SharePoint meetings and milestones (see Figure 4-32).

Outlook 2007 is a great choice under two conditions. First, when your need is focused on reading or viewing the information in your SharePoint project site when you are away, connecting the information from SharePoint to Outlook 2007 is the way to go. Second, if you will want to add new items into standard lists on the SharePoint project site when you are away from the office, Outlook 2007 is a suitable tool. It doesn't let you add new documents to document libraries or view and modify custom lists, however. If you would like to save documents (such as e-mail messages) in SharePoint document libraries or folders, or need to change existing information in libraries and custom lists within Outlook 2007 when you are not connected to the network, the Colligo Contributor Add-In for Outlook, explained later in this chapter, is a better alternative.

> **SEE ALSO**   For more information about Outlook 2007, visit *office.microsoft.com/en-us/outlook/default.aspx*, or read *Microsoft Office Outlook 2007 Step by Step*, by Joan Preppernau and Joyce Cox (Microsoft Press, January 2007). Visit *www.microsoft.com/mspress/books/9602.aspx* for information about this book.

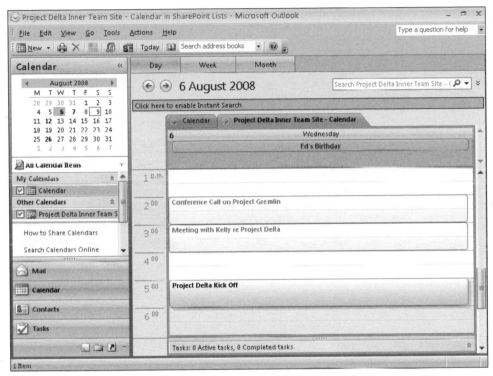

FIGURE 4-32 SharePoint calendars can be threaded with your Outlook Calendar.

Microsoft Office Groove 2007

The second Microsoft alternative is Microsoft Office Groove 2007, a collaboration tool for teams that offers many of the same team collaboration functions that SharePoint does. Microsoft acquired the maker of Groove—Groove Networks—in April 2005. One of the capabilities offered by Groove 2007 is the ability to connect a document library from a SharePoint site with a Groove site. This means that an individual who travels frequently can take a SharePoint document library with them via Groove, and read and edit those documents while they are away from the office. When they next connect to the corporate network, Groove sends any changes made in those documents back to SharePoint, and brings down any updates since the last time the user was connected. But remember, it is only for documents—not for everything else in the SharePoint site (see Figure 4-33). We talk more about Groove 2007 for document sharing in Chapter 7, "Analyzing the Options."

SEE ALSO   For more information about Groove 2007, visit *office.microsoft.com/ en-us/groove/default.aspx*, or read *Microsoft Office Groove 2007 Step by Step*, by Rick Jewell, John Pierce, and Barry Preppernau (Microsoft Press, January 2008). Visit *www.microsoft.com/mspress/books/11848.aspx* for information about this book.

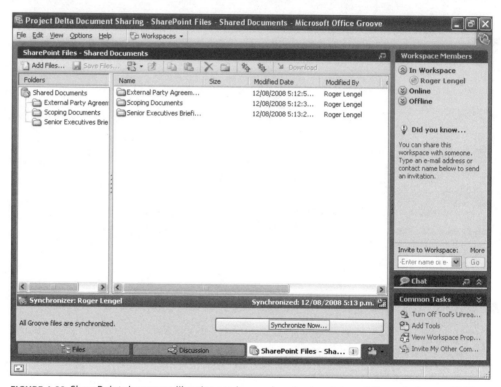

FIGURE 4-33 SharePoint document libraries can be synchronized and shared through Groove 2007.

Colligo Contributor

Colligo Networks is a Microsoft business partner that sells desktop applications for Microsoft SharePoint. Using Colligo Contributor, a user can connect a complete SharePoint site—or a selected subset of the site—to their desktop for access when they are offline. There are three editions of Contributor:

- A standalone client for offline access to SharePoint

- A Microsoft Outlook add-in for SharePoint document and e-mail management

- A professional edition that includes both of these interfaces

Colligo Contributor Client enables users to work with a SharePoint site through a client interface rather than a browser. The layout of the Contributor Client looks pretty much the same as it does within SharePoint. Colligo Contributor Add-In connects SharePoint document libraries, folders, and lists to a mailbox in Outlook. Users can drag documents into SharePoint and access documents and list items online or offline, directly within the Outlook interface.

With either the Contributor Client or Add-In, individuals can read items such as documents and tasks, they can make changes to the information that is in there, and they can add new items to any of the lists or libraries. When individuals are connected to the network again, any changes will be uploaded back to SharePoint, and any updates in the SharePoint site will be downloaded into Contributor. If someone else has changed the same document, task, calendar event, or other item that you changed, Contributor will tell you about the conflict and ask how you want to resolve it (see Figure 4-34).

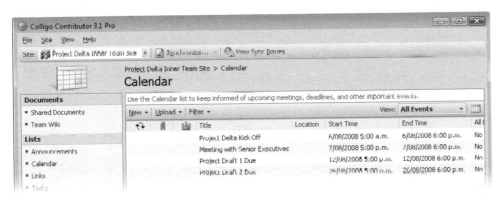

FIGURE 4-34 Colligo Contributor Pro offers full synchronization with SharePoint sites for offline access.

Contributor is a great choice for individuals when they are required to travel frequently as part of their work, but also need to stay in the loop on what's happening with various projects. It enables them to have their team data with them at all times, and be able to follow what's happening within the wider team, and to contribute regardless of where they happen to be. Do be aware, however, that the current edition of Colligo Contributor does not support working with wiki page libraries or wiki sites when you are offline.

SEE ALSO For more information about Colligo Contributor, visit *www.colligo.com*.

CHAPTER 5

Creating a Shared Vision

WITH HIS HAND-PICKED team ready-to-go, a SharePoint site set up for effective use, and the team having a clear grasp of how it will use the various capabilities of SharePoint for the project, Roger turned his thoughts to the next couple of days. It was time to get motoring on the actual work of the project—not that what he'd done to date wasn't important to the health and vitality of the team and the project over the next couple of months, but it was time to kick into gear on the substantive content work of the project.

"I know what the senior executives want," Roger mused to himself, "but I'm less clear about what all of the other stakeholders want out of this. I just do not have a good grasp of their requirements and conditions." He paused to think for a moment. "And I know what I want out of doing this project—evidence that I'm ready for the next step at Fourth Coffee—but what about everyone else? What do they want? How do I help each of them maximize the outcomes that they're in this project to achieve?"

Roger sat quietly for 15 minutes, thinking about everything he knew about achieving project goals, and about how important it is to know upfront what you are working toward. And then it came to him in a blinding flash of the obvious: the first major piece of work that everyone needed to get onboard with was the definition of the shared vision for Project Delta.

■ "Being a Team" Isn't Enough

> *"The essential feature of a common thought is not that it is held in common, but that it has been produced in common."*
>
> —MARY PARKER FOLLET (1868–1933)

Teams do really badly when all they want is the ability to claim that they are a "team." When there is nothing that drives them together, and to which they mutually aspire and work toward, "team" is merely a label and not a reality.

What we really need is for a group of people to jointly recognize a compelling outcome or purpose that they each want to see happen—launch a great new product on the market, beat a competitor in obtaining a customer account, double the firm's market share in a particular market over the next 12 months, and other achievements. Such compelling ideas drive cooperative and collaborative work, and transform a random collection of people into a cohesive and high-performance team. Playing for power or position with the team gives way to mutually focusing on what needs to happen in order to reach the compelling outcome—the shared vision that everyone has bought into.

■ The Three Sides of Shared Vision

When a team is assigned to a specific project, they have to jointly work together until the project is completed. Note that "completion" is attained when the activity or the outcome that brought them together in the first place is realized. It is critically important, therefore, to be very clear as a team about what completion looks like. This is done in the form of a written statement at the beginning of the work that describes in sufficient detail what the outcome is supposed to look like. In other words, in a couple of weeks or months when the team has expended a whole lot of effort, done a whole of lot of things, and produced something that they think signals completion, how can they be sure? What does that look like?

Getting to the point of being able to describe what the outcome looks like involves a process of creating a shared vision. A shared vision has three main sides to it—the delegated vision, the contextual vision, and the personal vision (see Figure 5-1).

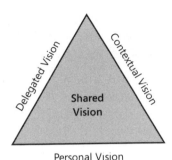

FIGURE 5-1 The three sides to shared vision

The Delegated Vision

Most business projects have an imposed or delegated outcome from someone higher up the chain of command or from somewhere else in the organizational structure. Perhaps it's your boss, or your boss's boss, who wants something different than what you have today, and so has formulated a project to make the change a reality.

Projects can also have imposed or delegated outcomes from clients. They are the ones paying the bill, after all, and so they will want to have a say in calling the shots. It is unlikely that they'll want to micro-manage the work—if they wanted to do that, they should do it themselves—but they will have a sense of what they want different in their organization or in their world.

For Roger Lengel and Project Delta, there is a very clear statement of delegated outcome from the senior executives: drive growth of Fourth Coffee in select international markets. What's true for Roger and his team, however, is true for you and your projects too: don't take the delegated outcome at face value. You will need to invest some personal thinking and team discussion time into teasing apart the delegated outcome and thoroughly understanding it. For example:

- What level of growth are the senior executives seeking? The team knows the high-level statement, but needs to get more specific.

- What international markets are the senior executives excluding on the front end from consideration? Are there some places where Fourth Coffee will never consider doing business, due to legal policy, economic conditions, or human rights abuses?

- What's the timeframe for growth that the senior executives are seeking? Do they want a short-term boost to profits, and therefore the share price in anticipation of a higher buying price, or are they looking for longer term, consistent growth?

All of these aspects may not be immediately obvious to a team, because they have not been disclosed, but obviously a choice on any one item signals major differences in how the work is approached by the team. How the sponsors specifically define what they want—the full delegated vision—can drastically change the nature of the project.

The Contextual Vision

There is a second side to shared vision, and that's the contextual one. It represents the outcomes and requirements of the key stakeholders from the work. These people, departments, regulatory boards, government agencies, and other organizations have some level of investment or impact from the decisions that are made as part of the project work. Whatever is decided through the process of the project work has an impact on them, in some shape or form, and in greater or lesser amounts, depending on what precisely is decided.

Because these other parties are impacted by the decisions of the project, and because the degree of their embrace of the decision often ensures either its success or failure, knowing early on the other things that the project has to live up to is essential to long-run success. Unlike the delegated vision, the contextual one will not fall so easily into the lap of the project team, and will involve some careful thought as to who will be impacted and how to understand the team's requirements. But like the delegated vision, what is learned from stakeholders should not be taken at face value, but should be teased apart so as to understand what they are saying and to clarify that understanding with the stakeholders. For example, for Project Delta, part of the contextual vision could include the following:

- With international expansion comes the need to ensure that the supply chain doesn't fall over. The supply chain manager is not one of the sponsors, but is a stakeholder because what is decided by the team will impact her group. She may specify that all coffee beans should be sourced locally in new markets, for example, or that all existing supply lines must be able to extend into the new markets. That makes a difference to the team's work.

- Corporate Legal will have certain requirements and stipulations about expanding into international markets. For example, they will want input on building acquisitions or lease agreements for new premises, and some of their requirements will shape the work of the team. It's good to know about these upfront. Likewise, with international expansion comes the question about the appropriate legal structures for operating businesses in other markets. Having a sense of the differences may be helpful to the team.

- Human Resources will have strategies and approaches that have been honed within the home market, but with international expansion, there will be a need to consider a wider range of strategies. For example, the regulations on hiring and firing, and the requirements for vacation time differ by country.

- Corporate IT will need to extend the IT infrastructure to the appropriate international markets, either through putting new people on the ground, or by extending current outsourcing agreements with third parties.

The Personal Vision

The final side to shared vision is personal vision, or what the successful realization of the project means for the individuals on the project team. Although delivering a successful project for the business has some meaning and reward in and of itself, many people are motivated by what happens next. As a result of being successful with the project, what does that make true or mean for each person?

If Project Delta is successfully delivered, then what will it mean for Roger? We know that he's on the fast track within the firm, and so perhaps Roger's next promotion within Fourth Coffee is based on Roger being successful in leading this project.

What about for Nancy Anderson? She's wants to travel to England and have a three-week vacation in London. Nancy's personal vision for the project is to have Fourth Coffee send her to London as part of the project so she can work with Shannon, and then she can tack on her vacation at the end of that week.

What about for the others involved in Project Delta or in your team? It's absolutely fine for a person to have less ambitious reward ideas for a project—perhaps a new article of expensive clothing or a new top-of-the-line laptop bag—but it's good to be detailed and clear even with personal goals.

Using SharePoint to Shape Shared Vision

Your team can use SharePoint to help you shape the three sides to the shared vision of the project. Let's look at how to do this.

Shaping the Delegated Vision

When shaping the delegated vision, the essential input is the outcome statements from the project sponsor. The project sponsors—the people who have commissioned the work of the team in the first place—surely have some picture or idea of what they want to be true at the end of the project. Go and ask them! Schedule a meeting—by phone, in person, or by video conference—and delve into their view of the outcomes, the drivers of the work, the deadlines, the assumptions, and the constraints that the team will be operating within. If you can't talk to them in real time, ask them for a written synopsis, sometimes called a *terms of reference*.

Plan How to Get the Delegated Vision

The information that you learn from the project sponsor should be documented in the Team Wiki, so in order to get ready for this, edit the home page of the wiki and add a link to a new page named *Shared Vision* (see Figure 5-2).

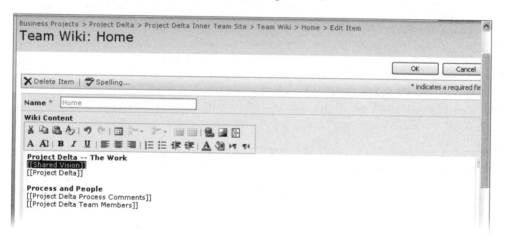

FIGURE 5-2 Create a new Shared Vision page in the Team Wiki.

Save the home page, then click into the new Shared Vision page.

Going to speak with the project sponsors is a great time to involve other people on the team, so they can hear firsthand what is said and can be involved in the conversation. On your new Shared Vision page, write that you are going to speak with the project sponsors shortly, and ask the other people on the team if they want to attend (see Figure 5-3).

Because we are using the announcements list to bring such opportunities to the attention of everyone on the team, create an announcement linking back to the wiki page, and giving people a timeframe for signing up. This opportunity is for a limited time only, so set an expiration date beyond which it's too late (see Figure 5-4).

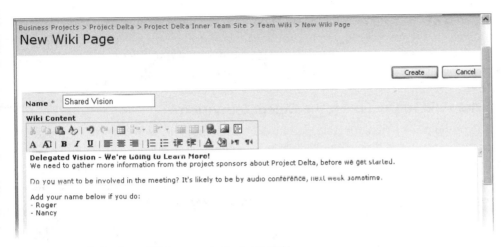

Business Projects > Project Delta > Project Delta Inner Team Site > Team Wiki > New Wiki Page
New Wiki Page

Create   Cancel

Name *   Shared Vision

Wiki Content

Delegated Vision - We're Going to Learn More!
We need to gather more information from the project sponsors about Project Delta, before we get started.

Do you want to be involved in the meeting? It's likely to be by audio conference, next week sometime.

Add your name below if you do:
- Roger
- Nancy

FIGURE 5-3 Draft the Shared Vision page in the Team Wiki.

Business Projects > Project Delta > Project Delta Inner Team Site > Announcements > New Item
Announcements: New Item

OK   Cancel

Attach File | Spelling...   * indicates a required field

Title *   Meeting with the Project Sponsors ... Want to Come?

Body

We will be interviewing the project sponsors about the delegated vision sometime next week ... after the 20th.

Add your name to this page in the wiki if you want to come:
Shared Vision

Thanks,
Roger.

Expires   8/20/2008

FIGURE 5-4 Set an expiration date on the announcement.

Everyone will get an immediate e-mail notification of the new announcement, or an RSS update in the next few hours.

When it comes to setting the meeting time, open the Common Working Hours page in the Team Wiki and find a time slot that works for all of the people who want to participate in the meeting with the project sponsors. Approach the project sponsors with a range of meeting time options that will work best for your team, and see what will work for the sponsors. If you can't find a common meeting time for the team members who want to attend, inform the members of the best option, and give them the choice of attending or not. Some may have wanted to attend only out of interest and so will drop out; others will see it as critical and attend at an otherwise inconvenient time for them.

Use the Wiki to Document the Delegated Vision

When you hold the actual meeting, use the same wiki page to write out your notes of the main points of the discussion. There's no problem deleting what you already have on the wiki page—others can get the history through the history link, and the current text inviting people to the meeting is going to be irrelevant after the meeting has been held, so there's no great value in keeping it there (see Figure 5-5).

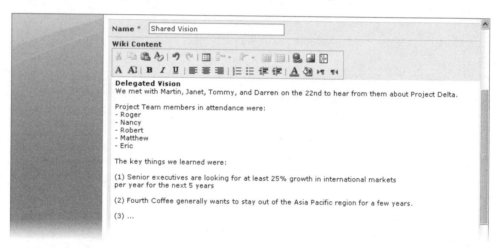

FIGURE 5-5 The revised Shared Vision page in the Team Wiki

When you have edited the Shared Vision page to document what you learned about the delegated vision, you should have a full description of the outcome required by the project sponsor, available for anyone on the team to read both now and in the weeks ahead.

Discuss the Delegated Vision by Discussion List or Teleconference

The final piece of work to do on the delegated vision is for the team to have an opportunity to discuss and agree on their interpretation of the delegated vision. You have two main ways to do this:

- Set up a team teleconference and present what you have learned about the delegated vision. In essence, give a presentation outlining what you have learned about the delegated vision through your explorations, and ask for questions. If people have issues that are unclear, get them resolved.

- Set up a discussion thread in the team discussion area, pointing back to the wiki page and asking people if they have any questions about the delegated vision. Given the importance of ensuring that everyone understands what is expected of them, a teleconference is the best way to go if possible.

WHY A WIKI PAGE AND AN ANNOUNCEMENT?

Because the SharePoint wiki can have e-mail notifications and RSS feeds, just like the announcements list, what's the reason for asking someone to do two things—create the wiki page, and then create a linked announcement? Why not just get the team to pull the new page from the wiki through the RSS feed and take that as the cue for getting on with the work at hand? Before giving my reasoning, let's acknowledge that it's a valid question and a valid approach to the task at hand, and that it is actually the easier approach for the person doing the work—Roger in this case. Then why?

My reason for recommending the wiki page plus announcement approach is this: absolutely clear signaling to team members about what is expected of them. Over time, the wiki page library is going to gain loads of pages, some of which will be for reference, and others of which will be for action. And of course, the status of those pages will change regularly during the course of the project work. Expecting team members to constantly sort through both types and discern which is which is expecting too much, in my opinion, at least at the beginning of the project and while the team is getting used to using SharePoint.

Shaping the Contextual Vision

The contextual vision is the confluence of a set of similar statements from stakeholders—people and groups that will be impacted by the work of the team. In an organization, it could be a different business unit that will be required to use the output of the project in their work. They need to be included in the upfront discussions. Or it could be the marketing and sales people, who will need to develop both go-to-market strategies and sales competencies to deliver the new product or service to market. If people from those groups are not included directly on the team, then at minimum, do them the courtesy of talking about what's coming up that might have an impact on them.

Create a Draft List of Stakeholders

SharePoint can provide the place for the team to brainstorm about the list of people, departments, and organizations they need to consult. On the Shared Vision page, under a new Contextual Vision heading, the list can take shape with the input of everyone on the team adding their insights. The team leader needs to create the heading in the wiki, and an announcement in the announcements list asking people to go there in the next couple of days and add their input (see Figure 5-6).

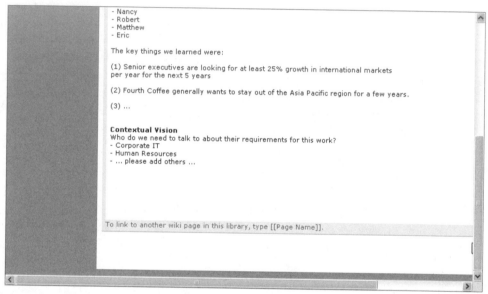

FIGURE 5-6 Add a draft list of stakeholders.

If your team members are watching and acting on the announcement e-mail notifications or RSS alerts, hopefully over the next day or two a good list of candidate people, departments, and organizations will be added to the wiki page. In editing the list, quickly eliminate the duplicates, if any exist.

Who Is Going to Interview Each Stakeholder?

With the list of stakeholders completed, the real work is about to begin. All of the people on the list need to be contacted and the project outcomes discussed with them, and their feedback and input captured for others to read and review. You have a couple of ways of asking the people on the team to contribute to this work.

One option is to take a hands-off approach and ask people on the team who they would like to interview in an ideal situation. Use the Announcements list to do this—create a new announcement and note in it that the list is completed, and now it's time for people to say who they would like to interview. Ask them to add their name next to the names of the people or groups they want to talk to. If you have enough time in the project timeline, take this approach, because it will make the team members feel that they have more of a say in the work. And team members who show a particular interest in certain people and departments are likely to have friends or ex-colleagues there, and so they will be good at getting the information.

A second option is the more directive approach, where the team leader instructs people on the team to interview certain people and groups. Use the task list to do this, creating one task for each team member for each person or group they are to interview.

ROGER TAKES THE HANDS-OFF APPROACH

Roger takes the hands-off approach with the Project Delta team, asking them to nominate who they would like to speak with. He checks the wiki a few hours later and sees that the page has been revamped. Rather than there just being the original flat list of people and groups, he sees that Shannon has created a major section for each of the people on the team, and has moved some of the stakeholder names under her name. Following that, Nancy has moved some of the linked pages under her name, and has also written her name next to a couple of the entries under Shannon's list, indicating that she too would like to be involved in some of the conversations that Shannon is going to set up. Nancy could have moved the linked pages off Shannon's list, but felt that would be rude, and so just appended her name. At this point, she has not created a duplicate entry under her name, but realizes that she can do that after the lists are finalized and the information starts coming back in.

Prepare a Brief Presentation for the Stakeholders

There is common information a team needs from each of the stakeholders that they will be talking to, and so it follows that there needs to be a common way for asking for the information. In conjunction with the "we need this from you" set of questions, there is the "here's what we are going to disclose to you" set of statements. Both of these should be commonly presented and requested, so that every stakeholder gets told the same message.

Take a two-stage approach to developing the common statements and common questions. First, create a page in the wiki linked from the Shared Vision page where draft ideas about the statements and questions can be posted. Whoever creates this page should make some rough first-cut notes about both areas, and then create an announcement asking for input (see Figure 5-7).

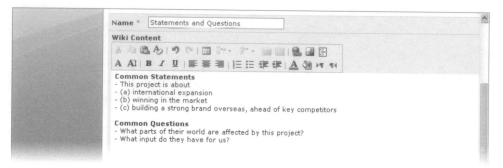

FIGURE 5-7 Use a wiki page to create a shared approach.

NANCY DRAFTS THE STATEMENTS AND QUESTIONS

Roger asks Nancy to create a page in the wiki for brainstorming on questions and approach. Nancy does this, linking from the top of the interview listing page. She notes some ideas, and then posts an announcements item with a link back to the page offering other team members the opportunity to comment and make suggestions. Within a day, three others on the team have taken her up on the offer, and have suggested a fairly good set of interview guidelines and some content ideas for how to pitch what they are working on and what they want from the various people and groups.

When the list of common statements and questions has been fleshed out, turn it into a Microsoft Office PowerPoint 2007 slide deck, and place the deck into the team's document library so that all of the team members can access it (see Figure 5-8). We talk more about using the document library in Chapter 7, "Analyzing the Options."

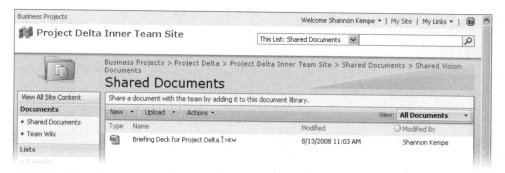

FIGURE 5-8 Save the presentation into the document library.

Engage with the Stakeholders

The team members who have volunteered to interview the various stakeholders should now get on with setting up the meetings. Where two or more team members want to be involved in a given briefing session, they coordinate among themselves and determine times that will work for all involved, using for example the Common Working Hours page in the wiki, so as to keep the time zones and different working times straight!

SHANNON CREATES THE POWERPOINT 2007 DECK

Shannon volunteers to take the material that has been submitted and refined and turn it into a briefing deck in PowerPoint 2007, and she goes ahead and does that. She saves the slide deck to the document library, and creates a link at the top of the wiki page to the slide deck so that all of the team members can quickly get there. She also offers that anyone who wants to make improvements to the deck itself should go ahead, telling them to check out the slide deck before making changes to it. As part of the team protocol, every time a change is made, the person who makes the change makes it directly inside the deck, and also posts a fairly high-level summary of what they did in the comments section of the item in the document library.

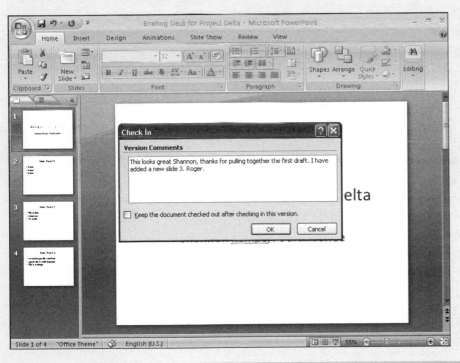

After you have confirmed the time with the stakeholders, log in to Microsoft Office Live Meeting and set up a meeting (see Figure 5-9). You will need to speak with the Live Meeting Administrator at your organization about getting access to the Live Meeting service.

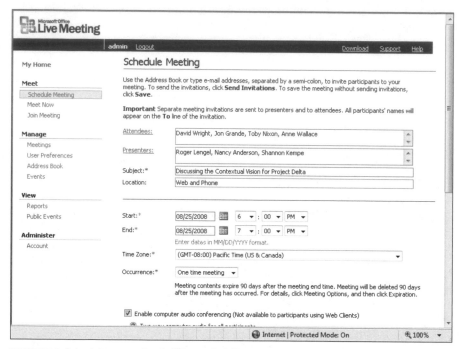

FIGURE 5-9 Schedule a meeting in Microsoft Office Live Meeting.

WHAT IS LIVE MEETING?

Live Meeting—or more fully Microsoft Office Live Meeting—is a Web conferencing service offered by Microsoft. It enables one person to show what's on his or her computer screen to people located in other places. So it provides screen sharing capabilities, saving travel time and expense. Live Meeting supports many capabilities for enabling interaction during a Web conference—polling and voting, switching of presenters, text-based conversation with attendees, and much more.

SEE ALSO   For more information about Live Meeting, see *office.microsoft.com/ en-us/livemeeting/default.aspx*.

This reserves a meeting time in Live Meeting. After you have entered the names of the people who will be attending the meeting, Live Meeting sends them the Web and call-in details. Then after the meeting time actually comes, everyone will have the correct meeting details on their Outlook 2007 calendar and be ready to go.

When the actual meeting time arrives, open the PowerPoint 2007 slide deck from the team's document library by clicking its name. You will be prompted whether you want to read or edit the presentation—click Read Only, and then click OK. This should be opened on the computer of the person who is taking the lead role to give the presentation and solicit the feedback from the stakeholders (see Figure 5-10).

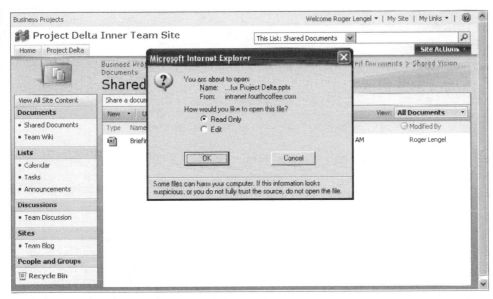

FIGURE 5-10 Open the presentation in Read Only mode.

Open the Live Meeting account on the lead presenter's computer and start the meeting so that everyone else can join and see what is being presented.

After the slides have been shown, a conversation takes place and the team member running the session opens the SharePoint wiki page for the person or department that the member is talking to, and enters notes directly into the page while the meeting is in progress. This note-taking is also displayed on screen, so that the other people can see what is being written down, and can confirm that what they are saying is being heard and captured correctly (see Figure 5-11).

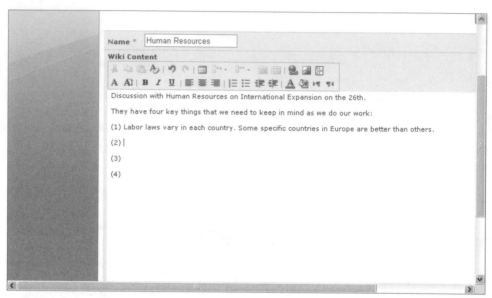

FIGURE 5-11 Use the SharePoint wiki to take notes during the meeting.

At the end of the session, the lead team member thanks the other people, and sets the expectation with everyone on the call as to when and how communication will be maintained. There should be two key parts to this:

- The publication of a new announcement in the Sponsors and Stakeholders site on a monthly basis. The stakeholders on the call should have an e-mail alert for new announcements, or an RSS subscription to the Announcements list.

- The mechanism by which the collated requirements will be distributed to the sponsors and stakeholders. Ideally, this document should be published into the Shared Documents library in the Sponsors and Stakeholders site, with a new announcement telling everyone that it is there.

Collate the Feedback

After all of the feedback from the various stakeholders has been gathered, it needs to be collated. In practice, this means that someone needs to go through all of the written notes in the Team Wiki from the various interviews, and consolidate them into a single page of information. This consolidated page of information should also have links back to the original interview pages, so that other people reading the material in the future can quickly jump to the source information.

There are two key points to look for during the process of collation:

- What are the common points raised by all of the different stakeholder groups? In other words, where are the main themes of agreement?

- On what points do the various stakeholder groups have wild variances in requirements? In other words, where are the main themes of conflict or difference of opinion?

For example, Roger's team finds that there are five key common themes that emerge from a consolidation of the interview process. There are also three areas of significant disagreement and misalignment between the different groups. The five common themes are easily dealt with, and can be written on an overview page in the Team Wiki, with an associated announcement to advise the team when the work is finished and ready for their review.

Resolve the Points of Disagreement

The three areas of disagreement between the desired outcomes of the various stakeholder groups require a bit more thought and work. Such thought and discussion should start within the team, with the different team members looking at the points of difference and trying to work out how to get a resolution that everyone would be happy with. To ensure that everyone is looking at the same material, these discussions can be held person-to-person using Microsoft SharedView.

WHAT IS MICROSOFT SHAREDVIEW?

Microsoft SharedView is a screen sharing tool for teams and groups of up to 15 people. That means that one person can sit at his computer and have what's on his computer screen appear on the computer screens of other people. These other people can be in the same office, or halfway around the world. It doesn't matter where the other people are—they can see what you are looking at, and even more than that, they can be given control so they can click around your screen from where you are.

SharedView is a free tool from Microsoft for screen sharing. It is a great tool to use within a team environment, because the sharing of screens can be whenever it's needed; no "meeting" has to be set up in advance.

SEE ALSO   For a more detailed discussion about SharedView, see Chapter 7, "Analyzing the Options."

After the group has finished their review of the key differences, they need to work them through to a resolution or compromise. There are various strategies available for doing this:

- **Requesting more information from team members.** The team members who did the initial interviews with the stakeholders may recall additional nuance that they did not write down on the wiki page. Because their names show on the original interview page, they can be asked for any more information that will help resolve the breakpoint.

- **Requesting more information from the stakeholders.** Someone on the team should approach the stakeholders for more information, and seek a clarification of their views and requirements. The points of commonality should be highlighted during the call, and the points of disagreement should be noted. With the relevant stakeholders on the call, the points of disagreement can be talked through and greater understanding gained. As a result of having such a frank and forthright conversation with the stakeholders, they may rescind one or more of their requirements, or be willing to live with a lesser outcome than they originally mandated.

- **Seeking direction from the project sponsors.** If it is not possible to work through to an agreed outcome with the different stakeholder groups, then the project sponsors should be asked for input. They are, after all, chartering the work and funding its progress, so they should have a good amount of say in what happens when things are not clear. Perhaps the issue with the other stakeholders is something that can be resolved amicably through higher-level discussions. Or perhaps the issue is related to other firm-wide initiatives that are beyond the scope of the current project, and so the stakeholder requirements can be removed from this project and dealt with in another project.

Roger's view is that one of the issues can be dealt with by adding another requirement to the statement of work, but the other two areas are seriously left-field of where the project was going. Because Roger did not talk with the two groups involved in these areas, he lacks the background on why they have asked for what they have. He requests control of Nancy's screen (she accepts), and he heads over to the wiki to see who did the original interview and what was discussed. Shannon spoke to one of the groups, and Gregory to the other, and given the time, neither of them are in the office—Shannon has left for the day, and Gregory hasn't arrived to work yet. So he and Nancy decide that the best thing, in the first instance, is to ask both Shannon and Gregory to review the notes they made in the wiki about the two interviews, and add any details that make sense in light of the disconnect.

Because the request to Shannon and Gregory are things that only they can do—in other words, it's a task for one person to complete and then mark as done—the work request is created as a task for each of them, one for Shannon and one for Gregory. Both have a task alert set for them, and so when they check their e-mail next, they see a task alert from the Project Delta Inner Team site.

By the next day, both Shannon and Gregory have done what Roger asked them to do, so Roger takes another look. He sees that Shannon and Gregory have filled out some additional details that were not on the wiki page already, and have also added their analysis of why they think the two groups hold the positions they do. Both have also listed the names and contact details of the people involved, so that Roger can reach out to them for a conversation.

Roger decides that this is the best thing to do, and asks Nancy to prepare two slide decks, both with the five points of agreement and one each with the major point of disagreement from the two groups. He then schedules a conversation with both groups, so that the issues can be talked through and so he can gather more insight into why they want such varying things.

The meetings happen within a few days, and by the end of each session—after Roger has run through the slide deck to show the major points of agreement and to highlight the two major points of variance, and after everyone on the call has fully explained their respective positions and why they want the things they want, Roger writes a summary of each meeting and posts his notes to the respective wiki pages. This means that all of the information and content related to these information gathering sessions are displayed together. This allows for easy tracking in the future about why certain things were decided, and why other things were left alone.

Roger felt torn about how to handle the two groups, because he realized that both groups were raising really valid points on the project, even though their points of view were quite different from what was already being pushed ahead with. So he decided that it was time to brief Kelly on the progress and see what could be done about moving the project ahead.

He scheduled a discussion with Kelly (and because they both work in the East Coast office, this meeting would be a "real" in-person one), and brought along both the PowerPoint slide deck that showed the main points of agreement, as well as an analysis of where and how the two other groups had differing perspectives. Kelly listened and asked a pepper spray of questions at certain points, and concluded the meeting by saying "leave it with me."

Shaping the Personal Vision

The personal vision for the project is a succinct statement of what each person on the team hopes to get out of being involved in the project. It's what they want to achieve for themselves beyond the paycheck—it's what they want to be true after the project is finished that isn't true now. Another way of casting the personal vision is to think about it as the meaningful outcome for each person, and it's pretty well guaranteed that each person on the team is going to have a different meaningful outcome.

After every person has set their own personal vision for the project, they need to write it down in SharePoint, so that every time they visit the team site in SharePoint, they are reminded of what is driving their involvement—what's motivating continued contribution and excellence in delivery on their part. The trick is to set up a new list in SharePoint and change the settings so that each person only sees the items that they have contributed to the list. This means that everyone writes out their personal vision directly within the SharePoint site, but only they can see the Personal Vision statement that they wrote. They can't see anyone else's statements, and in all fairness, they don't need to.

Create the Personal Vision List

Add a new announcements list to your inner team site, and name it **My Personal Vision**. Follow the same process that we have followed in earlier chapters to set up a new announcement list (see Figure 5-12).

FIGURE 5-12 Add another announcements list to the site for tracking personal vision.

Change the List Settings

After the new announcements list has been created, open it. Click the Settings button, and then click List Settings from the menu. Under the General Settings heading, click Advanced Settings (see Figure 5-13).

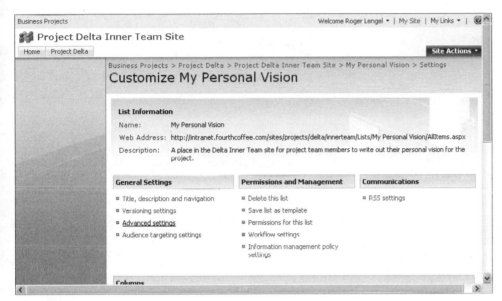

FIGURE 5-13 Change the Advanced Settings of the new list.

On the List Advanced Settings page, change the two entries in the Item-Level Permissions settings area so that each person can read and edit Only Their Own items (see Figure 5-14). When you have done this, scroll to the bottom of the screen, and click OK.

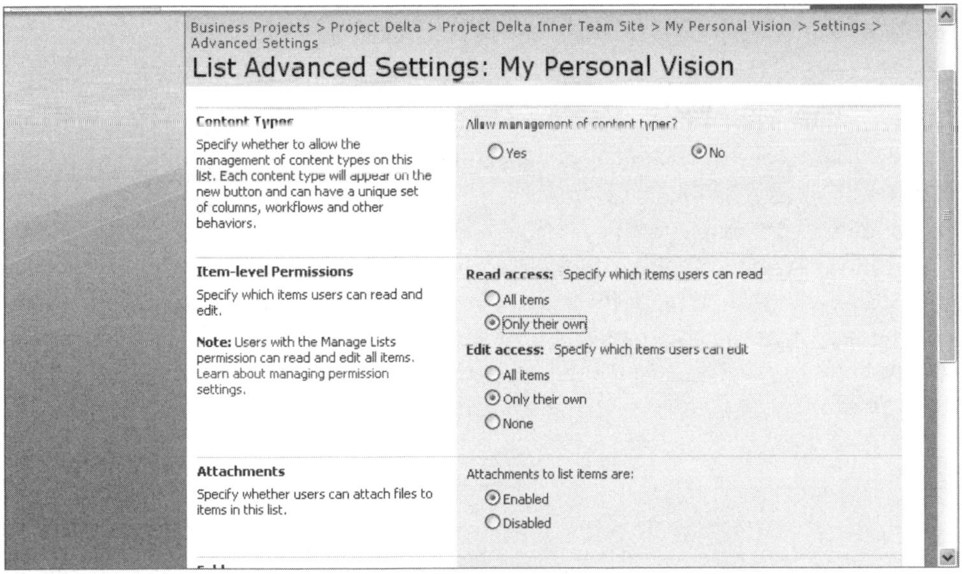

FIGURE 5-14 Change the setting for Item-Level Permissions.

Add the Personal Vision List to the Home Page

The final step is to add the new My Personal Vision list to the home page of the Project Delta Inner Team site, creating a Web Part for it on the right side of the screen. From the Site Actions menu, click Edit Page, and add the list to the right Web Part zone (see Figure 5-15).

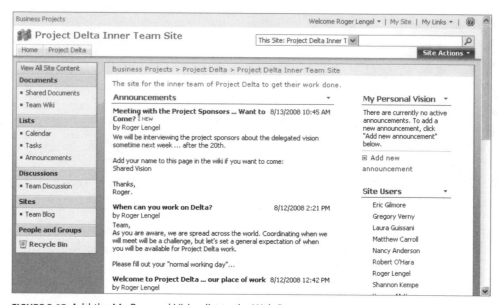

FIGURE 5-15 Add the My Personal Vision list to the Web Part page.

Ask Each Team Member to Write a Personal Vision

Now that the list has been created, create an announcement in the main announcements list, directing the team members to write a short summary of what success in the project will mean for each of them, in the new My Personal Vision list. It should be an inspirational and motivational statement to remind them each time they visit the team site of what a good outcome will or could mean for them. Remind them, too, that whatever they write will only be seen by them, and that what they are wanting will not be displayed for everyone on the team to see. This is a personal and private statement within the context of the shared Web site.

What do you do if you want lots of different things? Choose one or two things, and write those as your personal vision statement for this project. And note other things on the various other projects that you are involved with too, so that each project has a great outcome for you after it is successfully finished.

NANCY WANTS TO GO TO LONDON!

Nancy sees the announcement in the announcements list, and heads over to create her personal vision statement for Project Delta. She's really keen to meet up with Shannon in London as part of this project, and then have a three-week vacation traveling around and seeing some of the sights that she last saw when she was a university undergrad, some 15 years ago.

Nancy creates her personal vision statement in the new My Personal Vision announcements list, writing a short title for her vision, and putting the details into the body of the announcement. This means that when she visits the home page of the Project Delta Inner Team site, she will see and remember why she's in the project.

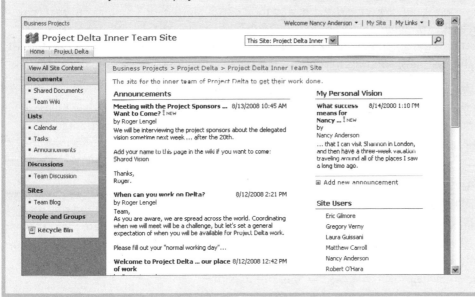

What Takes Team Projects Off Course?

With the three sides of the shared vision clearly stated and documented for everyone to read, it's time to move on to the second stage of the project—Understanding the Options. However, before we do so, let's talk for a few minutes about three factors that can knock team projects off course. Being forewarned about these means that the right preparation can be made to mitigate against these happening, or against them wreaking havoc to the project when or if they do.

Shifting Goal Posts

The first main factor that can knock team projects off course is that the goal posts can be shifted by the project sponsor. In other words, after the project is underway, the project sponsor decides to expand or revise the delegated vision.

Such changes will have flow-on effects throughout the remaining project phases. Sometimes the shifting of the goal posts is a result of the team starting off on what they thought the project was about, and then getting into it, only to find out that they hadn't quite understood. Being rigorous in the initial take on the delegated vision, and in getting sign-off and feedback from the project sponsor is a way of minimizing the risk that this happens, and thus wasting a lot of project time, team member enthusiasm, and energy for the project, not to mention the budget assigned to complete the project.

At least to some degree, the team has control over shifting goal posts if they follow a due diligence process in understanding exactly what the project sponsors are looking for, rather than being quick off the mark on what they thought was being sought.

Changing Market Conditions

A second factor that can throw a team project off course is changes in the market conditions that have an effect on the likelihood of success of the candidate idea. These changes may happen because the project is going to take a long time to complete, and while the project is being executed, a competitor releases a product or service into the targeted niche, which changes the rules of the game.

Another change in market conditions is the result of new government or industry regulation that introduces new conditions and limitations on the product or service being developed. The team doesn't have so much control over these things; but they will have to react to them and make corresponding changes within the work of the team.

Although the team cannot directly control some marketplace changes, there should be an ongoing tracking of the major changes in the market, the tracking of competitor actions that impact internal key projects, and scenario development to ensure that worst-case outcomes can be mitigated effectively. All of these can be done within the Team Wiki, linking off from the Shared Vision page (see Figure 5-16).

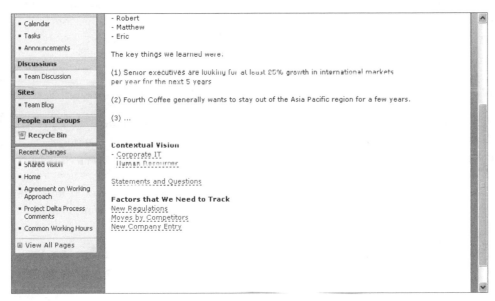

FIGURE 5-16 Track marketplace changes in the Team Wiki.

Changes in Team Composition

A final factor that can throw a team project off course is changes in the composition of the team. The team starts off on good footing, and is into the groove of working together. All of the upfront explicit agreements and discussions that took a lot of time have been internalized by the team, and there's a real hum in the way the team is progressing. And then out of left field, someone announces her resignation from the firm or says that she has too much on her freelancing plate and that she won't be able to contribute any further. Now the team has to scramble to find a replacement team member, and get the new member up to speed on what the team is doing and how they can directly contribute and help. That process takes time, and depending on the criticality of the contributions of the departing individual or the nearness of the final deadline, it can wreak major havoc.

Regardless of when it happens, the impact of changes to the team can be mitigated by using a shared tool like SharePoint as the organizing place of what's going on in the life of the project. No more does a new team member have to struggle to get access to the key data of the departing individual, because merely giving them access into the SharePoint team site provides them with the complete history of where the project has come from, a snapshot of where the project is currently at, and a statement of upcoming work for the departing individual. If this record keeping has been accurately kept in SharePoint, it makes the job of bringing new people on board all the easier.

Being Notified of SharePoint Task Items

At the beginning of Chapter 4, "Team, Meet SharePoint," we talked about using three different tools within SharePoint to assist with keeping team members working in a coordinated fashion. Tasks are one of the three tools that are used for this purpose, and are specifically used for directing one person to undertake a specific action. You will remember that the Announcements list is used to direct the activities of the whole team, and that the team blog is used to share all of the contextual information about what people are doing on the project.

The question, then, is what's the best way to be notified that there is a new task that has been assigned to you? Microsoft built into SharePoint a number of options for keeping team members informed of their task assignments. One of the operating principles of team work in our virtual world is that people are working on multiple projects at once, usually in different spaces and sometimes in different tools. They need some way of being pulled back to each of the projects they are working on, and being told what they are supposed to be doing, and what the other people on the team expect of them.

SharePoint offers three alternatives—an e-mail alert, a link between the SharePoint task list and an Outlook 2007 task list, and an RSS feed of tasks. Which is best?

Notification by E-Mail

If you choose to be notified by e-mail, you can set it up to get a new e-mail every time you have a new task assigned to you, or once a day in summary form, or once a week in summary form. The problem is that you then have another e-mail message to deal with, and most people say that they've had enough of dealing with e-mail. Secondly, if you choose a daily summary of your tasks and you are so highly productive that you get one of the tasks completed on the day it was created, then you will still get a notification in your daily summary of that task. It will say that you have completed it, but it will still say it ... and it's extraneous noise that you don't need to see. This is partially due to how the notification e-mail is created by the end user; you can choose only one alert statement when creating the rule, not a combination thereof. So you can't say "send me a notification whenever I have a task assigned as long as it's not completed." It's one or the other, but not both.

As with setting up an e-mail alert on the Announcements list, to create one in the tasks list, open the task list, and choose Actions from the menu bar, and then click Alert Me. On the upper half of the screen, give the alert a name, specify who should receive the alert, and what should trigger the alert (see Figure 5-17).

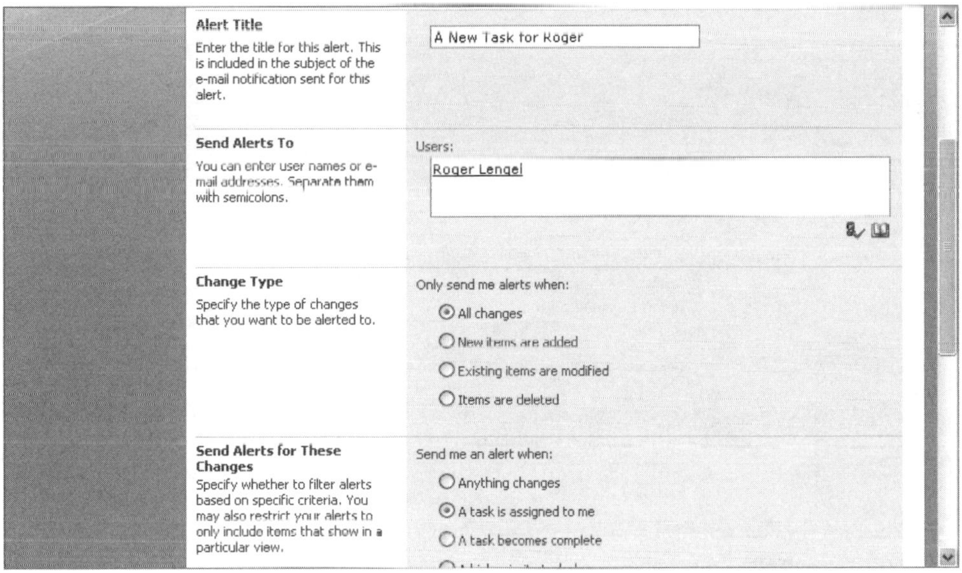

FIGURE 5-17 Create an e-mail alert for SharePoint tasks.

On the lower part of screen, choose the timeframe for being alerted—immediately, daily, or weekly—and then click **OK**.

Notification within Outlook 2007

The second option is to receive notifications through the task capabilities of Outlook 2007. With the Connect To Outlook option, the complete list of tasks from the task part of the SharePoint team site will be synchronized between SharePoint and an Outlook task list. Note that you get every task item on the SharePoint task list, not just the task items that have been assigned to you. This makes it a good option for team leaders wanting to see what everyone is working on.

To set up a connection between SharePoint and Outlook 2007, open the task list in SharePoint. Click Actions, and then click Connect To Outlook (see Figure 5-18).

> **NOTE**   If this in the first time you have tried to connect a SharePoint list to Outlook, you may get a security prompt asking you if you are sure that you want to do this. Click Yes.

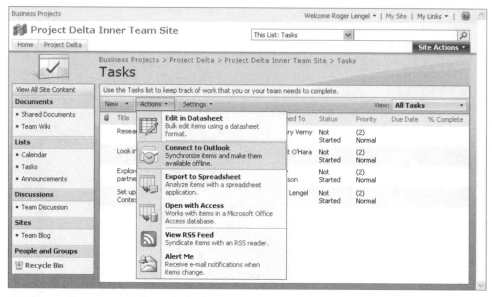

FIGURE 5-18 Connect a task list to Outlook 2007.

Outlook 2007 will be given focus on your desktop, or if it isn't running, Outlook will open. Then it will ask you to confirm the creation of a link between SharePoint and Outlook. Once again, click Yes, and the task list will be created in Outlook 2007 for you. Now whatever shows in the SharePoint task list will also be shown in the new synchronized list in Outlook 2007 (see Figure 5-19).

Any changes that you make in either Outlook or SharePoint will be updated in the other place whenever Outlook 2007 performs a Send/Receive operation.

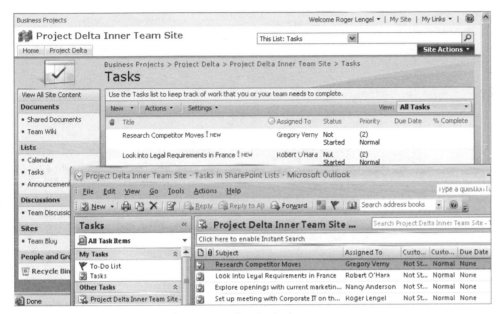

FIGURE 5-19 SharePoint tasks can be connected to Outlook.

Notification by RSS

The third option is to receive alerts of new tasks by RSS. From within the task list part of the Project Delta Inner Team site, click Actions, and then click View RSS Feed, and proceed to add the RSS feed for your tasks to the Project Delta folder (see Figure 5-20).

RSS also solves the distributed teaming issue of everyone not using Outlook and a Windows computer. Even the Mac people on the team will be able to receive a pull-back into the space if RSS is being used!

The other really nice thing about using RSS is that most RSS readers permit you to set up folders for grouping your RSS feeds by topic or interest. Because you have an RSS feed for tasks from the SharePoint project site, and also an RSS feed from the announcements list from the SharePoint project site, you can put both together in an RSS feed folder named Project Delta (the name of the project, in this situation). Then you can quickly see the current state of the project directly from your RSS reader (see Figure 5-21). And this works for everyone—when they are on a Windows Vista computer using Outlook 2007, or when they are using a dedicated RSS feed reader on another computer, for example FeedDemon from NewsGator (see *www.newsgator.com*).

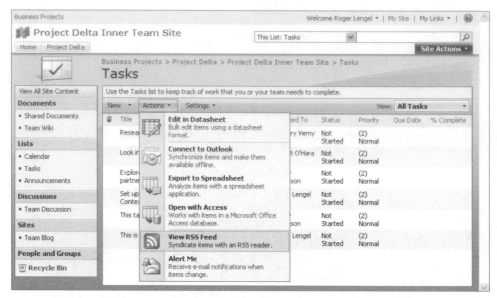

FIGURE 5-20 SharePoint tasks can be distributed by RSS.

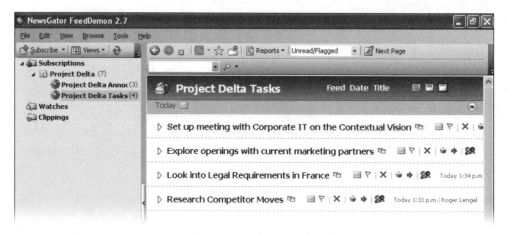

FIGURE 5-21 SharePoint tasks can be displayed within an RSS reader.

Recommendation

So the answer to the question about notification of new task items is that all of the options have their place, and it really depends on what you want to do. Here are some guidelines:

- If you just want to know what has been assigned to you, choose the e-mail alert option.

- If you want to track what's happening with the entire team, go for the Outlook or RSS approach.

- If you don't use Outlook 2007 and want to track what's happening across the team, go for an RSS reader.

What If Some Team Members Are Using a Mac?

Many organizations have people whom use Apple Mac computers as the mainstay of their day-to-day computing work. Mac users are a minority in most organizations, with a vast majority of people using Windows-based computers. Given that SharePoint is from Microsoft, does this mean that Mac users are left out in the cold?

No, it doesn't. A Mac user can be a fully contributing member of the team, just like a Windows user can be. A Mac user can sign into a secured SharePoint site with their SharePoint user name and password, and can work with most of the SharePoint capabilities in the same way as a Windows user with Windows Internet Explorer 7 can do (see Figure 5-22).

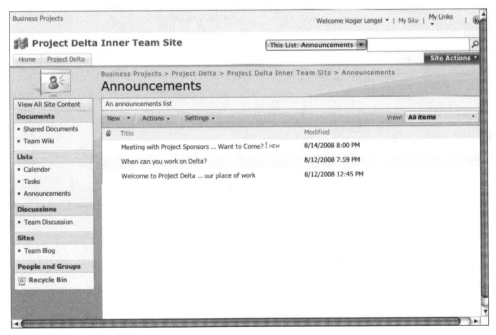

FIGURE 5-22 Mac users can access SharePoint sites from the Safari browser.

Nonetheless, there are some things to watch out for. First, Apple's Safari browser renders some things within SharePoint a bit oddly. For example, if you open a Team Wiki page in Safari to edit it, you'll see extra characters that you don't see in Internet Explorer (see Figure 5-23). If you are going to use a Mac and do wiki work, use Firefox instead of Safari.

Second, documents that are created in the Microsoft Office 2007 programs and saved in their native Office 2007 formats, can only be read by Mac users with Microsoft Office for Mac 2008. The 2004 edition will not cut it. If you have lots of Mac users with Office for Mac 2004, get them to upgrade, or if that's impossible, save the Office 2007 documents in the Office 2003 format. That is a bit of a pain, however.

Third, some of the menu options in SharePoint will not display to Mac users, because they don't have the right software installed. For example, you can't connect a SharePoint team calendar to Outlook 2007 on the Mac, because you can't install Outlook 2007 directly on the Mac. And unfortunately, Office 2008 for the Mac lacks any meaningful integration with SharePoint, so Mac users do miss out on the tight integration that their Windows counterparts enjoy.

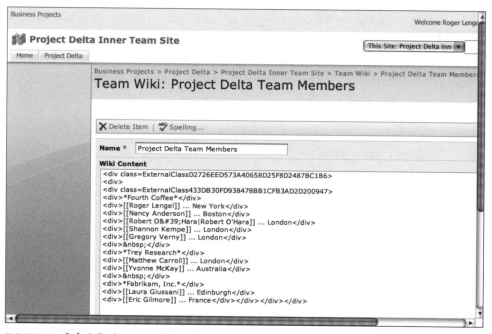

FIGURE 5-23 Safari displays some things from SharePoint a bit oddly.

One way of bringing Mac users fully into the fold, however, is to get them to run Windows by using one of the virtualization approaches—of course there are additional OS license costs to consider. Because the Intel-based Macs can run both the Windows and Mac operating systems at the same time, Mac users can use Internet Explorer (as per everyone else), Outlook 2007 (as per everyone else), and even Groove 2007 (as per everyone else) on their Macs. Talk it over with the Mac people, and see what will work for them and you. It really is a non-issue given the advances that Apple has made with its operating system in the past couple of years.

CHAPTER 6

Understanding the Options

IN THIS CHAPTER, YOU WILL

- Learn about creating ideas through brainstorming.

- Explore how to embrace brain-storming in virtual teams.

- Find out how to use a SharePoint wiki for brainstorming.

- Decide whether to use OneNote 2007 for brainstorming.

- Look into using a conference call for brainstorming.

EVERYWHERE ROGER WENT, people noticed that he seemed to have a lift in his step. Even the train conductor had mentioned it that morning, and that old curmudgeon hardly spoke to anyone. Roger pondered what everyone was noticing, and came quickly to the conclusion that he did have some new energy at the moment. Project Delta had started off well, the team was acclimatizing to SharePoint, and after the recent interviews with the stakeholder groups, everyone on the team had a shared and common vision for what they were working toward. The power of clear thought and focus was having an immediate and positive effect on Roger.

"Well, we know where we need to get to," Roger said, breaking his reverie. "The next question is how? Or more precisely, what is the universe of options that are available to us for getting from here to there?"

He thought some more, and clicked his fingers. "I've got it!" he exclaimed. "It's time to use SharePoint to lay out all of the options that we have available to us—all of the different ways that we could travel from where we are today to a completed project. I bet the team has got some brilliant ideas!"

What "Could" We Do?

The second phase of the Five Phases Project Life Cycle Model is "Understanding the Options." After the team has a sound idea of what they are trying to accomplish, this next step is to understand the options that are available. Achieving the shared vision of a project can usually be met in a variety of different ways, and prematurely settling on one option as the best way of doing things without exploring many options is a recipe for making an okay decision, but not a great one. Thus, the first order of business is to develop a sense of the different possible avenues of meeting the team's challenge, and working through the pros and cons of each. SharePoint can help a team do this.

The Big Idea Behind Brainstorming

The discipline of brainstorming is a well-established process for creating ideas. Brainstorming can be used by people acting alone, or in a team setting. For teams, it gives people a time and a space to have many ideas without having to immediately judge the validity of the idea themselves nor to have other people judge them. The core concept of brainstorming—the big idea that makes it work—is the separation of idea generation from idea evaluation, having ideas versus judging the value of the ideas. Doing so means that people can speak out and propose a range of ideas, some of which will be rejected later as being too crazy, in the hope that at the end of the day, some great ideas will emerge, helped along by some of the crazy ideas.

SharePoint can become the focal point to help a team understand the options, and that includes the idea generation or brainstorming part of understanding the options, as well as the idea evaluation and judging parts.

The Rules of Brainstorming

Brainstorming rules are the guidelines that help a team get as many ideas spoken out and written up as possible, without thought to the validity or rightness of the ideas as they are spoken out. The guidelines for brainstorming are especially directive in terms of separating the creative and idea generation stage from the analytical and judging stage where ideas are evaluated for merit. If the two stages are put together—so that as soon as one person has mentioned an idea, another person immediately judges its merit for all to hear ("That's a really dumb idea")—then the creative idea generation part of people shuts down. Potentially good ideas are sometimes never mentioned out loud, because people fear the immediate judging of others. And even bad ideas are left unsaid, even though a "bad" idea phrased in a particular way (or in a particular context) may trigger a thought in another person's mind that results in a breakthrough and brilliant idea.

Brainstorming in a Face-to-Face Meeting

When a team meets in a room to have a brainstorming session, the meeting leader welcomes everyone and clearly states the rules of engagement that are going to apply for the meeting. If it was a normal meeting, then normal meeting rules apply. But because it is a meeting specifically for brainstorming—or when the brainstorming part of the meeting actually comes—the meeting leader tells everyone the brainstorming rules. This is done with everyone present so that every person in the meeting has a common understanding of what is going to happen. Usually, the meeting leader will then ask if everyone agrees to follow the rules of brainstorming, and will look around from person to person to get a visual agreement of assent to what the meeting leader has said. Brainstorming works only if all agree to follow the rules of brainstorming, and because this involves suspending the normal rules of meeting etiquette, everyone needs to agree.

During a face-to-face brainstorming meeting or session, everyone has to be very careful to suppress the judging and idea evaluation parts of themselves when brainstorming rules apply, in order to not ruin the creative idea-generation spark that is kindled within other people. A snigger, a raised eyebrow, a smirk aimed at one of the participants—all of these can result in the creative juices being shut down and the brainstorming session rendered useless. And worse than that, it can establish bad experiences in other team members, reducing their willingness to more fully engage in brainstorming in the future, thereby reducing the capability of the team to meet its performance outcome.

Brainstorming in Virtual Teams

When we work on virtual teams that can't be together for face-to-face brainstorming sessions, we can use tools like SharePoint to support brainstorming. However, we need to embrace the same core ideas of in-person brainstorming to make brainstorming-by-SharePoint work for us. We need to make it very clear that brainstorming rules apply in the SharePoint tool we are using to support brainstorming at a particular point in time. We do this through a visual marker on the pages being used for brainstorming, so that everyone on the team has the same expectations and will follow the same rules of conduct. When brainstorming rules apply, it means that

1. The team is trying to list as many ideas as possible.

2. The team agrees not to pass judgment on any ideas that are listed at this time.

3. The team is cognizant that idea generation is followed by idea evaluation, and that the team will come back as a collective group later to sort, organize, and judge the ideas.

Brainstorming Through the SharePoint Wiki

Teams using SharePoint to support brainstorming need a blank canvas—something without a lot of structure—to support idea generation. They need something that supports the process of quickly writing out their ideas and quickly reviewing the ideas that other people have noted down. It shouldn't take a lot of time to open and work with. The ideal tool in SharePoint to support brainstorming is the SharePoint wiki.

Create a Page to List the Rules of Brainstorming

To start using the Team Wiki for brainstorming, click to open the Team Wiki. On the main page of the wiki, click into the page named Project Delta Process Comments, put the page into Edit Mode, and create a new page named **[[Brainstorming Rules]]**. Save the page, and then click into the new Brainstorming Rules page. This opens a blank page where you can enter a list of the rules of brainstorming for everyone on the team (see Figure 6-1).

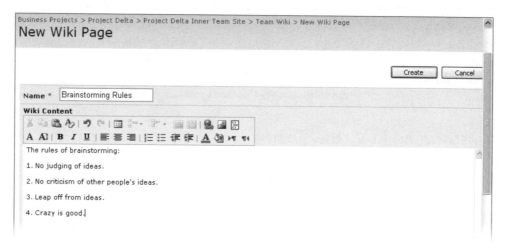

FIGURE 6-1 Create a new wiki page to list the rules of brainstorming.

Create the Pages for Brainstorming

With the page for the rules of brainstorming created in the process side of the Team Wiki, the next step is to create a master page for holding the brainstorming session. Because this is related to the actual content work of the team, the master brainstorming page is created in the content side of the Team Wiki. Navigate back to the home page of the Team Wiki, and click into the Project Delta page.

On the Project Delta page, create a new page named **[[Understanding the Options]]**, remembering to put double square brackets around the page name to signal to SharePoint that you want to create a new page. Save the changes to the Project Delta page, and then click into the newly created Understanding The Options page.

At the top of the page, write a paragraph or so of text telling people coming to the page the purpose of the brainstorming session—to create a master list of ideas that could be used for delivering to the performance challenge of the team (see Figure 6-2). Then whenever anyone visits the brainstorming page, they will see the specific purpose of the page, and can orient their thoughts and contributions appropriately.

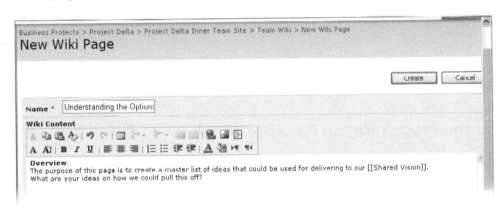

FIGURE 6-2 Create a new wiki page to hold the brainstorming ideas.

Seed the Brainstorming Page with Some Ideas

After you have created the brainstorming page and noted what the brainstorm is all about, seed the page with some ideas (see Figure 6-3). Remember to follow the rules of brainstorming yourself, however, and just write. Don't judge or pre-judge—just get it all out there for others to see.

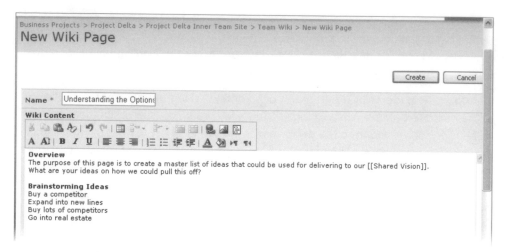

FIGURE 6-3 Seed the brainstorming page with some ideas.

Link the Brainstorming Pages to the Rules of Brainstorming

Before saving the brainstorming page and letting the other team members at it, there is one final thing to do. That is to make it clear at the top of the page that brainstorming rules apply. Because you have created a master page in the SharePoint Team Wiki that lists these brainstorming rules, go up to the top of your master brainstorming page and create a link to that page: as above, you named it [[Brainstorming Rules]]. Therefore, create the text to read something like **Remember that [[Brainstorming Rules]] apply**, right align it, and make it bold, perhaps even the color red to make it really stand out (see Figure 6-4). Now whenever team members open the brainstorming page in the wiki, they will see immediately the rules of conduct that are expected of them.

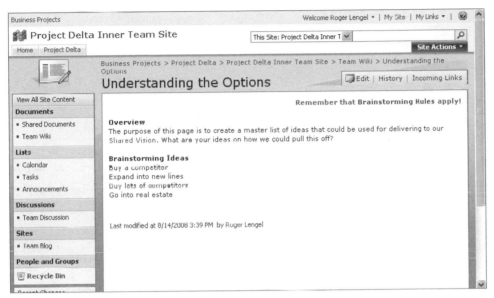

FIGURE 6-4 Link the brainstorming page to the brainstorming rules page.

Create an Announcement Telling the Team That It's Brainstorming Time

With the wiki pages set up for brainstorming, it is time to invite the team members to come and offer their thoughts and ideas. Because this is a matter of coordinating the actions of the whole team and signaling what we want all of the team members to do, create an announcement in the announcements list, with a link back to the brainstorming page in the SharePoint wiki (see Figure 6-5). It's a good idea, too, to note in the announcement that brainstorming rules apply, and to include a link back to those rules in the Team Wiki. Finally, because the brainstorming session will be run in SharePoint for only a few days, include a note to that effect in the text of the announcement, and put an expiration date on the announcement so that everyone knows what to expect.

With everyone signed up to receive a notification by e-mail or RSS whenever a new announcement is created, everyone on the team will quickly know the next thing that they need to do.

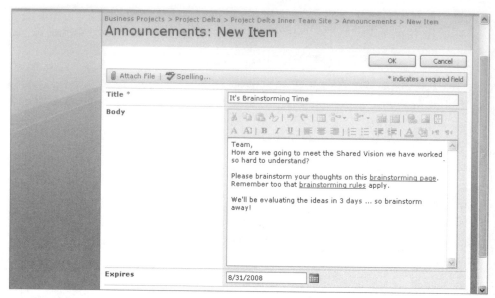

FIGURE 6-5 Write an announcement to invite the team to take part in brainstorming.

Effective Brainstorming in the SharePoint Wiki

When team members come to the page in the SharePoint wiki for brainstorming, what do they do? It's pretty simple really, and the great news is that there are no wrong answers. The idea is to get as many ideas down as possible, and to use the ideas that others have created as a starting place for more ideas. Here are the taks the team members should do:

- Read the overview of the brainstorming challenge at the top of the page. This is a succinct statement of what the brainstorm is all about.

- Scroll down the wiki page, and add your thoughts and ideas to the list of things that others have already written. Type them all in, not just the ones that you think will make the final cut. Stay with the program. Remember that although your ideas may not be brilliant, they may stimulate a brilliant idea in the mind of another person. The objective is a collective breakthrough, not an individual ego stroke. Remember—no pre-judging of what you write; just get it out there.

- After you have exhausted all of your ideas, read back through the list of ideas that your fellow team members have already written down. Some of their ideas will ignite a creative spark in you, and you'll have a series of related ideas. Write those down, too, for everyone to see. Again—don't pre-judge what you think when you see the thoughts and ideas of others, and when you have thoughts and ideas about applicability.

- Keep others accountable for following the rules of brainstorming. If someone has written a judgmental comment next to an idea, it needs to be removed. The person who has set up the brainstorm should be alerted, and should remove the comment and have a private talk to the offender. Remind the offender that brainstorming rules still apply. Perhaps it was simply an unconscious evaluation of the idea, perhaps it was intentional. During an in-person brainstorming session, the facilitator is equally charged with capturing good ideas and preventing people from getting out of brainstorming mode. In a virtual space, the same two charges apply when brainstorming through the SharePoint wiki.

What About Using Another Wiki?

Microsoft added wiki capabilities to SharePoint 2007, but the SharePoint wiki isn't the only option. Your organization may already be using another wiki, so you will need to decide whether you use that one or the SharePoint one. One of the benefits of using the SharePoint wiki is that the wiki pages reside side by side with the other lists and libraries the team is using. This is in comparison to having most of the team's work done in SharePoint and all of the wiki work done elsewhere. If it comes down to that choice, go the SharePoint wiki way.

Some enterprise wikis do not force you to make that decision, however, because they support integration with SharePoint. For example, the Confluence wiki from Atlassian Software Systems offers tight integration between the two products. You can access Confluence pages from directly within a SharePoint team site, and you can view and work with SharePoint lists and libraries from Confluence. Using Confluence rather than the SharePoint wiki means that you have access to some enhanced wiki capabilities:

- Confluence offers richer editing tools, such as page preview, support for minor changes, the ability to compare any two-page versions, and the option to edit wiki pages directly in Word 2007.

- Confluence offers the option of embedding documents and images into wiki pages, including file attachments, video files, and more. This makes for a richer working environment.

- Confluence adds enhanced collaboration capabilities directly within the wiki, such as threaded comments, categories, namespaces, and more.

SEE ALSO   For more information about Confluence wikis, see *www.atlassian.com/ software/confluence*.

WHAT HAPPENS IF TWO PEOPLE EDIT A WIKI PAGE AT THE SAME TIME?

After the announcement of the new brainstorm hits each team member's computer, it is possible that more than one team member will go to the wiki and start entering their ideas into the brainstorm page. If two people open the same SharePoint wiki page in Edit Mode at the same time, when the second person saves the wiki page with his edits, SharePoint alerts him of a save conflict, so there is a built-in safeguard to prevent people from overwriting the work of others. When this happens, the second person needs to re-open the page from the wiki, and enter their comments and changes again.

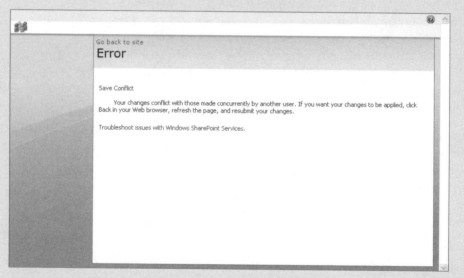

Although this safeguards the work of individuals so as to ensure that no one over-writes what other people are working on, it also means that if you are editing a page in brainstorm mode, you should stay aware of how long you are working in the page, and limit your time to 10–15 minutes so that other people can have a go, too. Get onto the page, make your suggestions, and save the page so others can have their go too. Remember, in a team brainstorm, it's the power of the ideas of the many that are really helpful, and you don't have to do it all. Create time and space for others to have their say, too.

Brainstorming with OneNote 2007

A second approach to brainstorming in virtual teams is to use the capabilities of Microsoft Office OneNote 2007. OneNote is a client application that you install onto your computer, much like Word or Excel. It's not a Web application like SharePoint, but can work together with SharePoint.

Introducing OneNote

OneNote is a software application that creates a digital version of a paper notebook, complete with folders, dividers, and pages (see Figure 6-6). The idea of OneNote is to give people a computer-based way of tracking information in a layout and format that is very familiar to them.

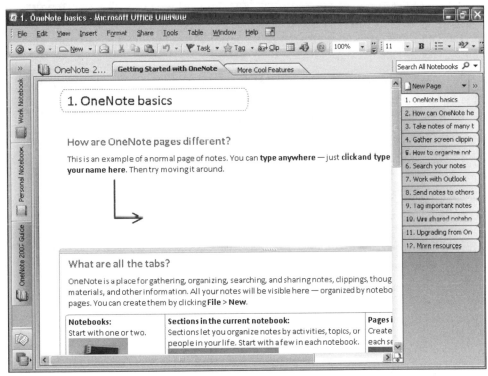

FIGURE 6-6 OneNote is a digital notebook that uses the ideas of a paper notebook.

With OneNote, people can create different "notebooks" for different projects. Tabs in the project separate the major components of the project, and then each tab has pages of information. OneNote is ink-enabled, meaning that someone with a Tablet PC can write directly on a OneNote page, and have what they wrote down in handwriting appear on the page as handwritten text. But OneNote is not just for people with Tablet PCs—anyone with a Windows computer can take advantage of the capabilities of OneNote. Finally, because OneNote can work with multiple notebooks, a person can carry on one computer all of their project work in different notebooks, without the added bulk of many paper notebooks.

With the release of the 2007 edition of OneNote, Microsoft enhanced the ability of OneNote to support sharing of notebooks between team members in various ways, meaning that OneNote 2007 can be used as an alternative for brainstorming in a team project.

Create a Shared OneNote Notebook

OneNote 2007 offers options for multiple people to have a shared notebook. This greatly extends the power of the paper notebook metaphor—not only can OneNote 2007 give you the ability to work within a familiar paradigm, and not only can you carry around multiple OneNote notebooks with you at all times on your computer, but you can also share the complete contents of a OneNote notebook with others and collaborate with them inside of this shared space.

Start by creating the OneNote 2007 notebook that you will be using (click File, click New, and then click Notebook), and give it a name. For Roger's team, the name of the notebook would be something like **Project Delta** (see Figure 6-7).

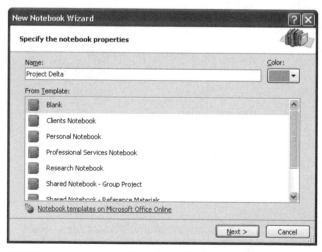

FIGURE 6-7 Start the New Notebook Wizard and give your new OneNote 2007 notebook a name.

When you create a OneNote 2007 notebook, you are presented with three options about sharing: I Will Use It On This Computer, I Will Use It On Multiple Computers, and Multiple People Will Share The Notebook (see Figure 6-8).

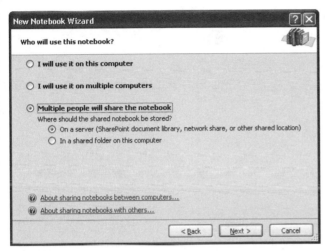

FIGURE 6-8 OneNote 2007 notebooks can be shared in a variety of ways.

The first option when choosing to share your notebook with multiple people is to share it from a server, be that a SharePoint server or a network file server. For teams using SharePoint to collaborate, the best way is to share a OneNote 2007 notebook from a SharePoint site.

A related option is to share it from a file server that everyone can connect to. Generally speaking, this is a fine and adequate approach as long as everyone in your team can access the file server. When you are working with people outside of your firm, it is much less likely that they will be able to get inside your corporate security systems and be able to access internal file servers. Sharing from a file server also means that you will have to set up another place, with the appropriate security permissions for the people involved, for the sharing of a OneNote notebook. And we were trying to get away from having multiple places for sharing information! So, although sharing through a file server is a good option for some teams, there is a better way.

The second main way to share the notebook is from your computer, meaning that anyone who can connect to the name of your computer can share the notebook with you, and can synchronize their changes and updates with your copy. In order for this to work, your computer needs to be accessible on the network. If you frequently travel and are out of the office, sharing in such a peer-to-peer way is not the right way to proceed.

So we will go with the SharePoint approach instead. When you choose the option to share the notebook through SharePoint, you are asked which SharePoint site should host the notebook. Open the home page of the Project Delta Inner Team site and copy its URL to the Clipboard. Paste this into the Path field in the New Notebook Wizard (see Figure 6-9).

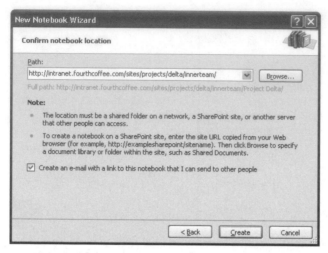

FIGURE 6-9 Tell OneNote 2007 where the new notebook should be created.

Then click the Browse button and choose the document library in which to store the notebook; for example, Shared Documents (see Figure 6-10).

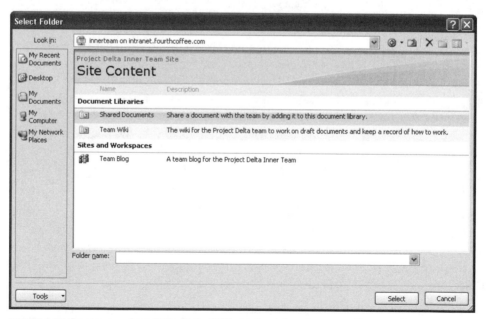

FIGURE 6-10 Create your shared OneNote 2007 notebook in a document library in SharePoint.

Click Select, and then click Create back on the new notebook screen.

After you have chosen the place in SharePoint for sharing the notebook, a folder is created in the document library for storing the notebook. This means that anyone who has access to the document library will be able to access the notebook, unless access rights are set on the folder so that it is only shown to certain people or sub-groups.

Within the folder, each section in the notebook becomes an item in the folder list. So if your notebook has six sections, then there will be six corresponding items in the Document Library folder. Because pages are put into sections in OneNote, this means that each page is not shown in SharePoint; rather the overall section is. Thus, if a section has 10 pages, you won't know that within the SharePoint interface. You will see the section name; not the page count, the list of page names, or anything else about the pages contained within the section.

When someone else needs to access the shared notebook, there are a couple of ways to get there. The first is to navigate to the document library, open the folder that contains the notebook, and click to open one of the sections. Alternatively, you can open the shared notebook directly from OneNote and navigate to your SharePoint site. Either way, the notebook that has been stored in SharePoint will be created within your local copy of OneNote, and will be synchronized for offline access and periodically synchronized between your computer and SharePoint to support the sharing of the latest information with everyone.

After Roger created a OneNote 2007 notebook, he created two sections (Shared Vision and Understanding The Options) to correspond with two phases of the project, and a third section (Team Members) for pages about team members (see Figure 6-11).

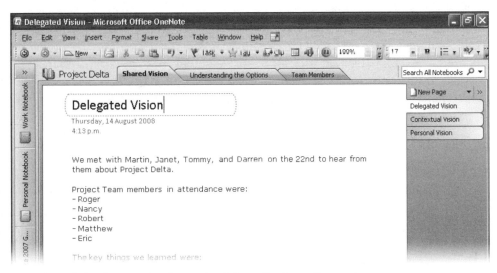

FIGURE 6-11 A OneNote notebook organizes information by sections and pages.

These sections (and the pages within each) have been synchronized with SharePoint, to allow other people on the team to see and access them (see Figure 6-12). If Nancy has OneNote 2007, she can click the OneNote Table Of Contents link or any section heading in SharePoint to open the entire shared notebook in her copy of OneNote 2007.

FIGURE 6-12 SharePoint shows the section names of the notebook.

With the notebook created in your copy of OneNote, and now fully synchronized to SharePoint for sharing with other members on the team, you are ready for the next step.

Create the Brainstorming Rules Page

Regardless of whether you are using a face-to-face meeting, a SharePoint wiki, or a shared OneNote 2007 notebook for brainstorming, it is essential that everyone knows when brainstorming rules apply. So create the page that outlines the rules of brainstorming to summarize this social contract. Either create the brainstorming rules page in the SharePoint wiki—as [[Brainstorming Rules]]—and tell everyone that it's there, or create it as a page in the shared notebook that you are using for the project (see Figure 6-13).

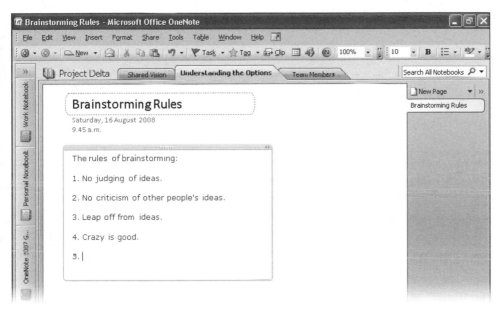

FIGURE 6-13 Create a Brainstorming Rules page in your notebook.

Create the Brainstorming Page in OneNote 2007

To use OneNote 2007 for brainstorming, create a blank page in your shared notebook, and name it **Brainstorming the Options**. As we did when looking at the use of the SharePoint wiki for brainstorming, make a clear statement at the top of the OneNote page about what the purpose of the brainstorming session is (see Figure 6-14). This is the anchor point that will orient the thinking processes of everyone involved.

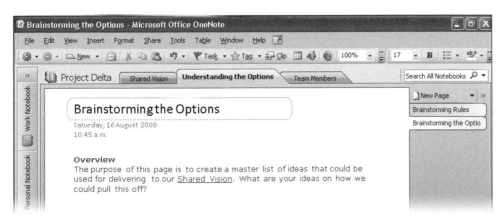

FIGURE 6-14 Create the page for brainstorming, and note its purpose.

Seed the Brainstorming Page with Some Ideas

After you have created the brainstorming page and noted what the brainstorm is all about, seed the page with some ideas (see Figure 6-15). If you have a Tablet PC, start writing with your Tablet pen. If you don't have a Tablet PC, then start typing.

Remember to follow the rules of brainstorming yourself, however, and just write. Don't judge or pre-judge—just get it all out there for others to see.

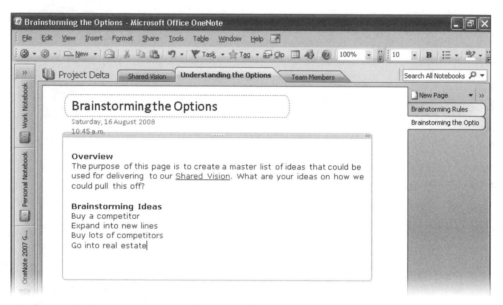

FIGURE 6-15 Seed your new brainstorming page with some ideas.

Link the Brainstorming Pages to the Rules of Brainstorming

Before saving the new brainstorming page with your seed ideas, note at the top of the page that brainstorming rules apply. Get the link to the Brainstorming Rules page by right-clicking on the page name on the left side of the screen, and choosing Copy Hyperlink To This Page. Then highlight the Brainstorming Rules phrase on the brainstorming page, right-click, and click Hyperlink (see Figure 6-16). Paste the link you created, and then click OK.

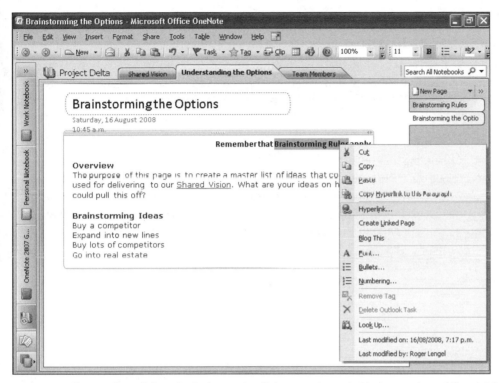

FIGURE 6-16 Create a hyperlink to the Brainstorming Rules page to remind team members of the social contract.

If you have created the list of brainstorming rules in the Team Wiki, include the full URL to get to that. Go to the SharePoint wiki, get the link to the Brainstorming Rules page, and create a hyperlink as you have just done for the OneNote page. It's the same process, but depending on which option you have gone with, will dictate which page gets opened!

Remember that the point of this is to remind everyone of the rules of engagement that apply for the use of the page, so make the statement prominent and bold. Don't skimp on fonts and size (you don't want anyone to miss it), but don't go overboard either!

Create an Announcement Telling the Team That It's Brainstorming Time

With the shared notebook in place, with some seed ideas there to stimulate thinking, and with the rules of engagement clearly and prominently displayed, it's time to invite everyone to open the new notebook and start working. Because what we are interested in is team-level coordination, we create an announcement in the announcements list to advise everyone that there is something new for them to do (see Figure 6-17).

With this being the first time that team members will have used OneNote 2007 as part of the project, we need to tell them a couple of things that we won't need to in future announcements. These include where to find the OneNote 2007 notebook in the Project Delta Inner Team document library, the lead file to choose for opening the shared notebook, and the page in the notebook that is being used for brainstorming.

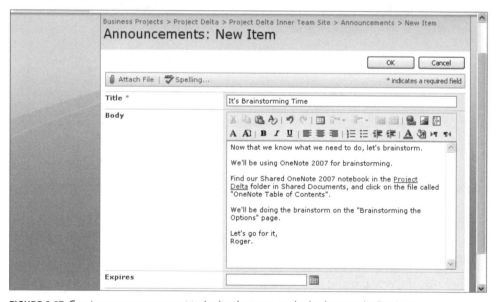

FIGURE 6-17 Create an announcement to invite the team to the brainstorm in OneNote.

Brainstorm in OneNote

And now it's time to brainstorm! Follow the same ideas outlined in the section "Effective Brainstorming in the SharePoint Wiki" earlier in this chapter to undertake brainstorming in OneNote. One major point of difference, however, is that for those users with Tablet PC computers, they will be able to do more of their work with digital ink. This means both the standard work of writing ideas out in digital ink rather than typing them, but also a number of additional things:

- The ability to draw links between ideas, to highlight interconnectivity between different contributions

- The ability to draw pictures and doodles to illustrate ideas, thereby adding richness and another dimension to the sharing of ideas

- The ability to use different colors to highlight certain points with additional insight and commentary

Although you can do all of these things to some degree with typed words, in creative brainstorming sessions, the added capabilities of digital ink can be a real help.

Reflections on Using a Shared OneNote Notebook

We have talked about the process to follow to share a OneNote 2007 notebook in the context of a SharePoint site for the purpose of brainstorming, and we have reviewed some of the added richness that comes to the team when digital ink is used instead of merely typing out the words. Before leaving the topic of OneNote 2007, it is important to ponder whether the use of OneNote is a good addition to the team, or an unnecessary one.

The decision about using OneNote comes down to this: Is SharePoint or a OneNote 2007 notebook the place where team information and data is shared, or are both used for sharing information between team members? If the answer is OneNote 2007, then you wouldn't be reading this book. Therefore this changes the question to: What can OneNote 2007 offer to a team using SharePoint for team collaboration? Is there additional value, or does OneNote merely duplicate what SharePoint has to offer?

I suggest two ways of looking at this. The first is to keep all of your team information in SharePoint, and use OneNote 2007 in an ad-hoc way to support meetings and brainstorming sessions, but don't use OneNote to create another separate place for the storage of information about the project. And definitely don't do things like creating tasks in OneNote and linking them to Outlook, because then you have a separate list of things to do that is separate to the list of tasks in the SharePoint site.

The second way of thinking about the use of OneNote is as a personal productivity tool to support individuals in their day-to-day work. All of the team information is stored in SharePoint—the meetings, the milestones, the documents, the wiki pages—but separately to that, each person uses OneNote 2007 for drafting their work for the project. All of the thinking they have done and are doing, all of the flowcharts, and some of the working out of the direct action points—these things could be drafted out in OneNote 2007 and then the final outputs shared with team members. Remember, there's a delicate balance— anyone working on a virtual team is often working on multiple virtual teams. So in addition to the team work that has to get done (by yourself, but coordinated from the SharePoint site), there's all of your personal work, too. Some of the work that you need to do on your own can be done directly in SharePoint, but you don't have to do everything in there. OneNote provides a place where you can get some of that work done, without going back to the annoyance of paper and pen.

Related to the use of OneNote to support your own work on the many projects that you are involved with, there are ways that you can benefit from OneNote without having to share a notebook. For example, let's say that there is going to be a team meeting, and you are tasked with taking notes about what was discussed and then sharing those notes with everyone else. You can use your OneNote notebook to take the notes and Microsoft SharedView to display them for everyone to see during the meeting. When the meeting is finished, you can save your notes as a Single File Web Page and put them on a meeting-specific page in SharePoint.

> **NOTE**   You can link a meeting that shows in your Outlook 2007 calendar with a page of meeting notes in a OneNote 2007 notebook, and the link is per- petually kept for as long as the meeting is in existence, even if the page is moved around in the OneNote notebook. But note that this link only works for the person creating the link, and if the OneNote notebook is shared, even if the other people sharing the notebook have that same meeting showing in their Outlook 2007 calendar, the link is not and will not be made available for them. It is a person-centric link, not team-centric.

My sense is that, on balance, you are better to not use both OneNote 2007 and SharePoint for the team project, because it will see a separation of materials between the two places. Because OneNote is such a rich environment, it will take a high degree of experience for the people on the team to master how to use it well within the project. If you are currently a OneNote user, and want to use it for your personal planning and contributions within the SharePoint project, by all means do so, and when you are ready, submit the content you have created to SharePoint by using one of the other commands at your disposal. For example, you can work on a page within OneNote, and then when you are done simply click Publish Pages from the File menu to save it to the SharePoint team site as a Web page (see Figure 6-18). The page will retain all of the formatting and layout that you were using in OneNote, thus making it look the same. Or you can use Publish Pages to publish the page as a Microsoft Office Word 2007 document, again to the SharePoint team site (see Figure 6-19). This means the notes can be edited by anyone with Word 2007 at any time.

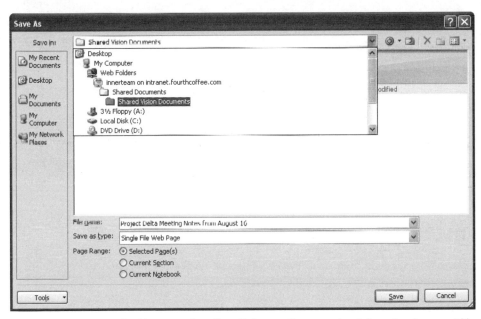

FIGURE 6-18 Save your OneNote page into SharePoint so others can view it from the document library.

There is a subtlety that you need to be aware of. When you publish the page from OneNote 2007 to a SharePoint document library, you break the link between the original page that you authored and the newly published one in the SharePoint team site. If you make another change to the local page, it will not be reflected in the SharePoint edition. There are two separate pages, and there is no ongoing relationship between them. Likewise, if the SharePoint page is changed, then those changes will not flow back to the original content that you created in OneNote. It is a one-way publication of information from OneNote to SharePoint, not a two-way synchronization.

In summary, the key point is to avoid the creation of separate fiefdoms of action points (tasks) and meeting notes in hidden places that are not immediately obvious to people who are joining the team. Or even for those in the team, for that matter.

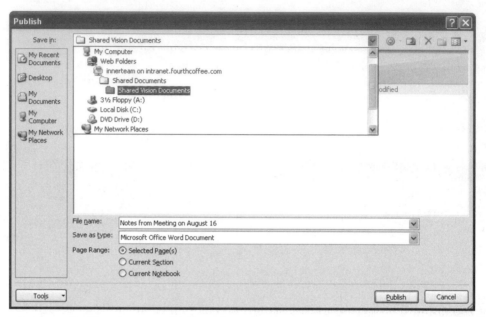

FIGURE 6-19 OneNote pages saved as Word documents to SharePoint can be edited by Word later on.

Brainstorming Through a Conference Call

There is a third way to do brainstorming in a team when the people can't be together, and that's by conference call. The way to do it is not merely to talk on the phone, but to combine the brainstorming talk with a shared screens session, so that everyone has a common visual reference point to what is being discussed. If there is no visual reminder of what has been previously said, then it means that everyone has to carry a greater burden of remembering, and of filtering what they are hearing in the here and now against what they have already heard and said.

The best way to do this is to use digital ink on a Tablet PC in combination with SharedView, and to give one person the job of listening and writing down the ideas as they are said. Text that is handwritten signals to the brain that things are less formed and finalized than typed text does—in a brainstorming session even the little cues count. The use of SharedView means that everyone can see what is being written as it is being said, and if the note taker has written the wrong thing, or misinterpreted what the speaker said, that can be pointed out and corrected immediately.

In terms of logistics for the conference call for a brainstorming session:

- The person organizing the call should check the Common Working Hours page in the wiki, to work out when the best time is to schedule the call based on everyone's availability.

- The upcoming conference call should be created as a meeting in the team calendar, and announced to everyone via an announcement.

- At the start of the call, the conference call leader should remind everyone that it's a brainstorming call, that the rules of brainstorming apply, and that there will be another session another day to look over and evaluate the ideas.

- It is best to separate the brainstorming conference call from the evaluation conference call. This is for two reasons. First, teams with only a small number of hours of overlap in common working hours will feel rushed to get through the brainstorm if they are supposed to be doing both things on the one call. And secondly, it's good to give people a bit of time space between the idea generation part of the process and the idea evaluation part. By focusing the first session on idea generation and then scheduling another conference call for a different day to run the idea evaluation part, everyone can come back to it fresh, with time and space between the idea generation and the need to evaluate the ideas.

Consolidating the List of Ideas

With your brainstorming complete, it's time to look at the ideas that have been generated. You—and often a sub-group from the team working together—now need to go through the list of ideas and get them ready for the next stage, that of analyzing the options.

Preparing for the analysis stage of the team's work involves reviewing the list of ideas, grouping similar ideas together, and eliminating the ideas that are clearly unworkable.

Consolidating the List in the SharePoint Wiki

If the list of brainstormed ideas was created in the SharePoint wiki, then one of the team members opens the wiki page, and removes the text at the top that states that brainstorming rules apply (to signal that these rules don't apply now!). Then the reviewer should work through the list of ideas, looking for similar ideas and concepts that should be grouped together, and looking, too, for ideas that appear to be unworkable.

For the ideas that look to be promising candidates, the reviewer should create a section heading for each of the major ideas, and put any supporting ideas or concepts under each of the section headings (see Figure 6-20). This means that there is some structure beginning to be applied to the ideas, laying the groundwork for the next major piece of work.

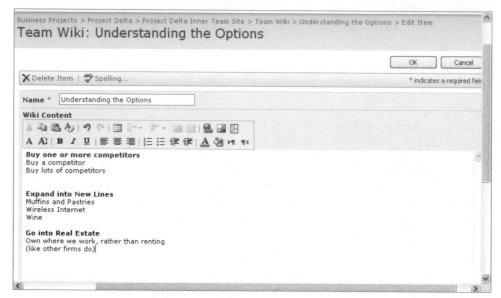

FIGURE 6-20 Group similar ideas together and put supporting information with those ideas.

For the ideas that appear to be unworkable, rather than deleting them from the wiki page all together, move them down to the bottom of the wiki page into a section named **Unworkable Ideas** (see Figure 6-21). This means that other people on the team will still have an opportunity to see all of the ideas, and they will be able to agree or disagree with the assessment of the first person.

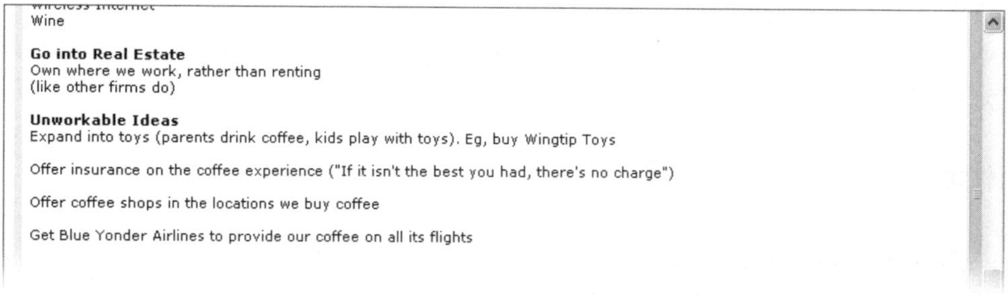

FIGURE 6-21 Don't delete unworkable ideas but do put them in a new section.

After the first person has gone through and re-formed the list into a classified and categorized summary, a couple of other people on the team should be asked to go to the wiki page and do their own review of what the first person has done. These second and third people won't be starting with an unformed list of ideas, but rather with the reviewed and grouped list that the first person has gone through. If they disagree with the placement of some ideas in the Unworkable Ideas section, they should create them as a new section. Or if they find an area of the page where more information would be immediately useful, they should add that in. And finally, if they think that one of the ideas that the first person has seen as being valid and workable is actually unworkable, then they should note that under the appropriate section heading (see Figure 6-22).

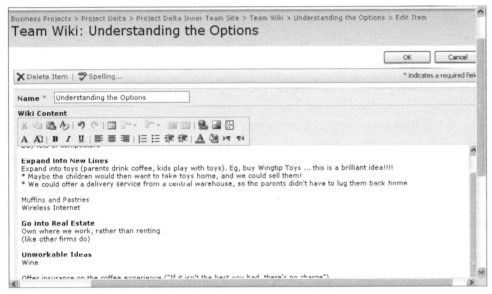

FIGURE 6-22 One or more different team members should do a second review of the list.

Consolidating the List in OneNote

For brainstorming done in OneNote, it's time to take those ideas and create a page in the wiki to capture and synthesize the ideas. By putting it into the wiki, it creates a more easily shared and reviewed consolidated list than if the ideas are kept in OneNote.

After you have created the list in the SharePoint wiki, make a note on the brainstorming page in OneNote that the brainstorming time has now passed, and that the master list of ideas is now in the SharePoint wiki (see Figure 6-23). People can review and read the page in OneNote, but it is not supposed to be an editable page anymore. Its time has passed.

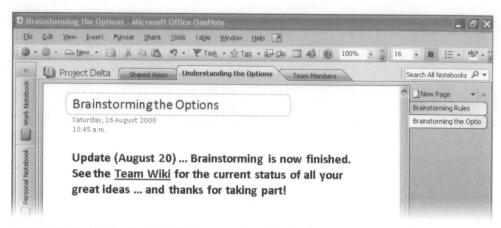

FIGURE 6-23 Update the OneNote 2007 page to signal that brainstorming is now over.

Consolidating the List from a Conference Call

If the brainstorming session was done on a conference call with a SharedView session, it's time to translate the handwritten notes into typed notes in the Team Wiki, and to group the ideas as described for the other two approaches. Ideas that look promising should be categorized separately from ideas that look unworkable, which should be put under the Unworkable Ideas section.

Finally, don't throw away the original page of handwritten notes. If you took your notes in OneNote 2007, publish the page to the team's document library, and include a link to it from the wiki page you have just created. That means that everyone can go back to the original ideas at any time.

CHAPTER 7

Analyzing the Options

ROGER CAST HIS EYES over the collated list of ideas in the SharePoint wiki, and smiled with satisfaction at how far the team had come during the last week. Some of the ideas were still pretty wacky, even after the initial collation exercise by Nancy, Robert, and Shannon—not that he'd say that out loud—but he felt assured that his fellow team members had been unrestrained by convention in suggesting different ways to move toward their great and glorious shared vision.

Now it was time to take the ideas to the next level, and decide which ones warranted more serious investigation. He turned his head and gazed momentarily out the window onto a cold and bleak winter day in New York, and contemplated a three-day intensive meeting in Hawaii with the team, but jolted back to reality as his cell phone rang. As he reached to flick it off his belt, he mumbled under his breath, "It's virtual meeting time, and we have a lot to write before then!"

What Could We "Realistically" Do?

The work of the team in Phase 2, Understanding the Options—was all about being unrestrained by convention and coming up with lots of different ideas on how the shared vision could be achieved. With the focus on *could*, it meant that even potentially crazy ideas were not ruled out too soon in the analysis, and that the team didn't merely fall into the trap of prematurely settling on the first alternative that came to mind—or likewise, prematurely settling on easy and conventional answers.

The next phase of the project, Analyzing the Options, involves changing the rules of engagement again, this time to something more restrictive. With tons of ideas generated, and an initial grouping of those ideas done by two or three members of the team, the task at hand now is to more fully explore the various options and cull from the list the ideas that will not work, for any of the following reasons:

- The idea is too costly.

- The risk is too high.

- The timing is off.

- The organization lacks a strong leader to champion the idea.

What a team needs at the end of the process of Phase 3, nonetheless, is a well-analyzed list of two or three ideas for much further analysis and investigation in Phase 4, Making a Decision. So in order to get there, some ideas are going to have to be eliminated.

Using a Custom List for Team Coordination

Getting from an initially collated list of ideas to a finalized short list requires team members to do more analysis on each of the ideas. Because everyone on the team is not in the same place and can't coordinate their work verbally, they need to use one of the shared tools to support the coordination of this next phase. This brings us to the idea of a custom list in SharePoint.

When Is a Custom List Required?

Many individuals, teams, and groups deal with unique data during their projects. What we're really talking about here is the need to capture data that needs to be tracked, collated, and managed in a certain way, and where the standard libraries and lists in SharePoint will not suffice for the needs at hand. Some things are standard and fit into standard containers within SharePoint—documents go into a document library, tasks go into a task list, events go into a calendar—but other things can require a special type of list, which in SharePoint language is called a *custom list*. The following situations might require a custom list:

- When you want to be able to sort and filter the information based on the data in a certain field; for example, to sort all of the possible locations by city

- When you want to look at the information you have collected, organized, and grouped by one of the data points

- When you want to be able to perform calculations with some of the data that you have collected

In some cases, if the additional fields are few and there's already a list or library in the SharePoint team site that offers 80 to 90 percent of the required functionality, go ahead and customize the existing list or library; rather than creating the whole list from scratch, modify one that you already have.

What About Using Excel 2007 or Access 2007?

Before deciding to create and use a custom list, there are other options that you should consider:

- You could put the data into a wiki document; for example, by creating a table. But then you can't do a lot with it after the fact—it's harder to sort and filter the data on a wiki page; only one person can work with the wiki page at any one time, and not to put too hard a spin on it, the data on a wiki page is "dead text" whereas data in fields in a custom list can be really useful.

- You could put the data into an Excel workbook, but that requires the extra step of opening the Excel workbook, making any required changes, and saving it back into SharePoint. This takes longer, and there are better ways in SharePoint of supporting group and team tracking processes.

- You could put it into a Microsoft Office Access database, but then it's hidden away in Access and is in a separate place from the rest of the work of the team. Again, Access 2007 may have been the way to do it in a previous generation of software, but it's not the ideal way to do it going forward.

Draft a List of the Data Points for Your Custom List

In order to use a custom list to coordinate the analysis work on ideas—or a custom list for any purpose for that matter—the first step is to draft a list of the data elements that will be in your custom list. For our purposes, that draft list would look something like this:

- The name of the idea

- The name of the lead person looking into the idea

- The names of any other people on the team who are contributing to the analysis

- The status of the analysis—with options like Not Started, In Progress, Finalized, Open For Review, and Rejected

- A link to the folder in the team's document library where the actual work is being documented; or if the Team Wiki is being used, a link to the appropriate wiki page

- A notes field for providing a summary of the work

- Depending on the number of ideas being investigated, a number or code for each idea to make identification easier

There's no shortage of fields that you could create—the trick is to go with the minimum number that will permit yourself and others to stay coordinated with who is doing what.

Discuss the Draft List with Your SharePoint Consultant

With the list of data elements drafted, the next step is to talk it over with your SharePoint support person from IT—for Roger, that would be Gareth Chan. The purpose of such a discussion is to ensure that you haven't overlooked anything, and is also intended to give your SharePoint IT professional the ability to point out any other things that you might want to consider.

ROGER TALKS WITH GARETH

Roger looked up from his list of draft data elements, opened his Communicator 2007 instant messaging client, and saw that Gareth Chan from IT was online and available. "You got a few minutes to talk about a custom list?" Roger typed into the chat window. "Yes, sure," came back the reply from Gareth. "Now is good."

Roger copied and pasted his list of data elements into the instant messaging chat window, and then typed away for a couple of lines to tell Gareth what he wanted to do. "Looks like a good list to me," said Gareth. "Just make sure that you choose the right data types for each of the data elements—such as 'Person or Group' wherever you have someone's name, rather than merely a text field."

"Okay, got it," replied Roger, and thanked Gareth for his time and input.

Create the Shell of Your Custom List

If you have permission to create a custom list in your SharePoint team site, it's not a difficult thing to do; it's really just a matter of pointing and clicking in the right places a few times, and typing some text in here and there. If you can use Excel 2007 to create a worksheet with formulas, or Access 2007 to create a database, you can make a custom list!

To start, click Site Actions, and then click Create. On the Create page, click Custom List (see Figure 7-1).

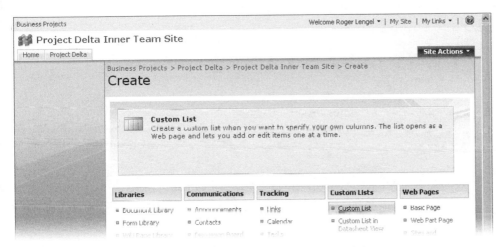

FIGURE 7-1 You can create custom lists in SharePoint, for holding special data.

Give your custom list a name and enter a description, and then select Yes (it should be selected by default, so leave it that way) for displaying your new list on the Quick Launch bar. For our purposes right now, the new list should be named **Analyzing the Options**, and the description should be something like **A list for coordinating who is doing what piece of analysis on the list of options for Project Delta** (see Figure 7-2).

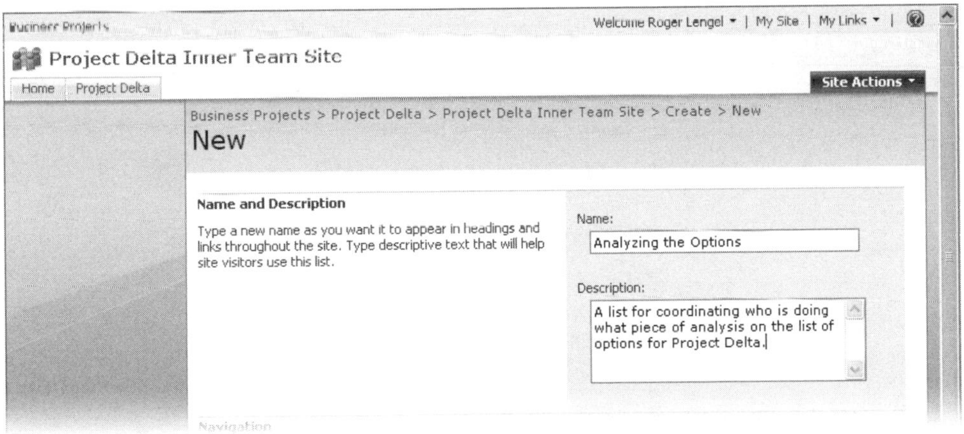

FIGURE 7-2 Enter the details for creating the Analyzing The Options list.

After you are done, click the Create button. SharePoint displays the new empty list (see Figure 7-3). Now you have the shell of your new custom list, or the wrapper of the mini-database that you are creating.

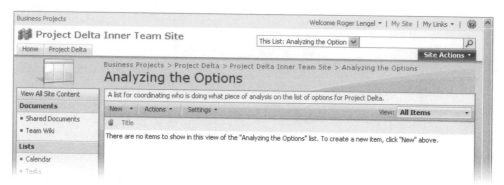

FIGURE 7-3 When a custom list is created, it has only a Title column.

Create Each Data Element as a Column

The next step is to create a column for storing all of the specific data elements you want to capture. The default and automatically created Title field can serve as the place for us to note the "Name of the Idea," but we need to create columns for all the rest. Luckily we have already defined our list of data elements, and so we start by creating the first column. Within your new Analyzing The Options custom list, click Settings, and then click Create Column (see Figure 7-4).

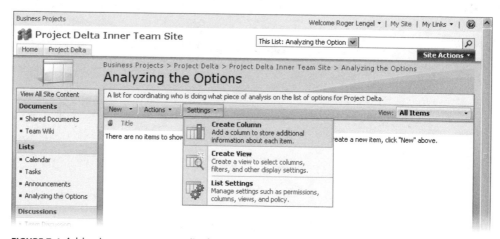

FIGURE 7-4 Add columns to a custom list for storing each data element.

This opens a Web page where you can define one data element (and then you can come back and create all the others one by one). The first one we need to create is the name of the lead analyst, and that is going to be a Person Or Group field (see Figure 7-5).

After you have selected the type of column you are creating, the Additional Column Settings area on the bottom of the page updates to display choices relevant to that type (see Figure 7-6). The page to define all of this is pretty easy to follow, so after all of the information is entered, click OK to create the column.

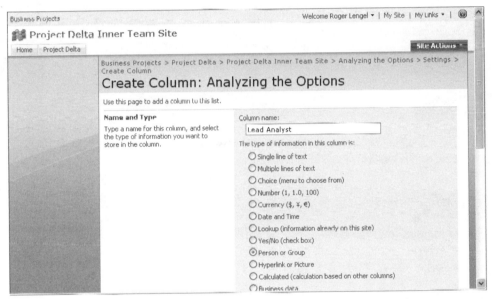

FIGURE 7-5 Create your first column in the custom list—the one for storing a person's name.

You are then taken back to the default All Items view of the list.

You have five more columns (Other Analysts, Status, Document Folder, Notes, ID Number) to create, as described on pages 185–186, so go through the process of defining each of them. Make sure that you choose the right type of data for each element. Once again, remember that as you choose a type in the top half of the page, the options in the bottom half for Additional Column Settings will be dynamically updated to reflect options that are appropriate to the data type.

When it comes time to create the Status column, you know the list of values that will be possible, so you can make the data entry burden on team members lighter by pre-entering the list of valid statuses. To do this, click Choice (Menu To Choose From) in the name and type part of the page (see Figure 7-5), and fill out the additional column settings with the range of options you want presented (see Figure 7-7).

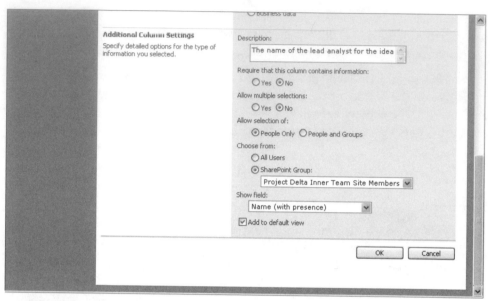

FIGURE 7-6 Fill out the Additional Column Settings area for the lead analyst.

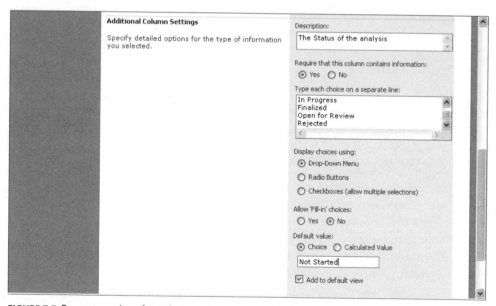

FIGURE 7-7 Pre-enter values for columns where appropriate to standardize data entry.

If you know only the general list of status options, and want people to have the option of entering other values, change the Allow 'Fill-in' Choices option from No to Yes to permit this to happen.

When you create the Notes field, given the volume of information that could be entered in this field, clear the Add To Default View check box. This will prevent the field from being displayed on the default view, even though it will still be viewable after someone opens the actual item.

After you have created all of these columns, you have a perfect list for tracking and coordinating who is doing what on the analysis work. To see what you've just done, click the New button on the view, and fill out the details for the first idea (see Figure 7-8).

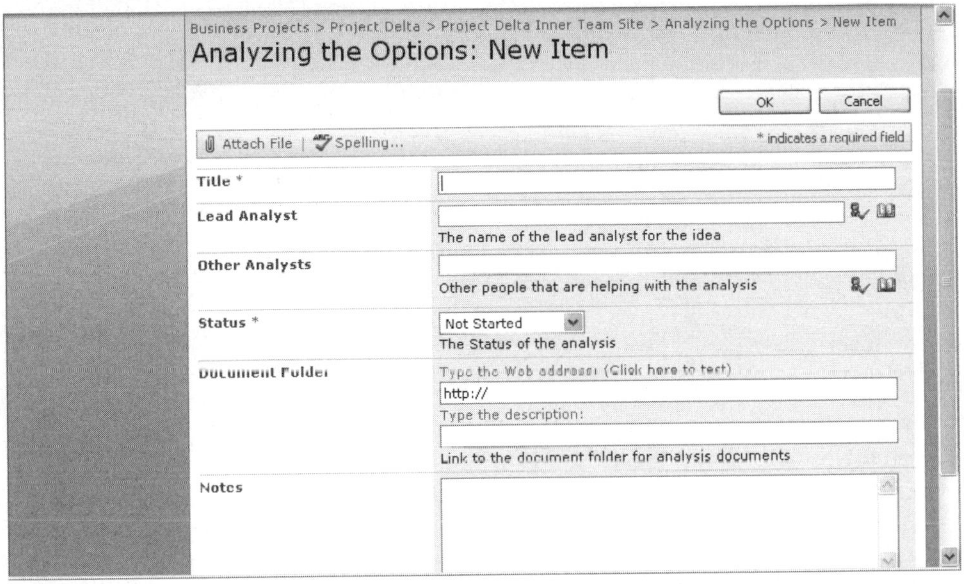

FIGURE 7-8 Add items to your custom list by using your new SharePoint form.

Be sure to test the link to the Document Folder, because the full URL that you copy from the Shared Documents library may be too long for the column here. If it is, trim off the extraneous information, such as anything including and following the URL search string. The URL search string includes the ampersand (&) and anything to its right. You can always ask your SharePoint support person in IT for assistance, too.

After you have entered the details for the first idea, click OK.

Enter the Ideas into the List

With the framework for the coordination list set up, all of the ideas to be considered should now be transferred from the collated page in the SharePoint wiki into the list. Each idea should be entered as a new item, and if there is supporting information on the wiki page about the idea, it should be transferred into the Notes field on the form.

After all of the items have been entered into the Analyzing The Options list, you will be able to see the complete list in the All Items view (see Figure 7-9).

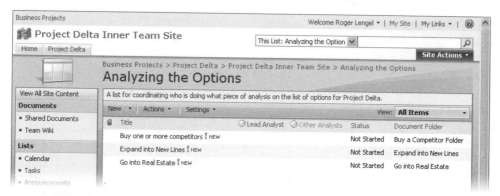

FIGURE 7-9 Add items for each of the ideas to be analyzed in more detail.

Ask People to Review and Volunteer

With the custom list created, and all of the items entered into the list, it's time to ask people on the team to review the list and volunteer to look into one or more of the areas. This is a team coordination issue, so an announcement in the announcements list is the way to go to bring this to the attention of the team.

Here are a couple of guidelines to point out in the announcement:

- Rather than entering their name in the Lead Analyst field, team members should select their own name in the Other Analysts field. This means that everyone who is interested in a certain idea can put their name down, and after it has been noted who is interested, a lead analyst for each idea can be selected.

- For ideas with no voluntary contributors, the project leader will be asking specific people to work on the analysis. Most, if not all, of the ideas will need some analysis done on them.

Keep the List Up to Date

Creating the Analyzing The Options list on day one is one thing, but actually keeping it up to date is something altogether different. If you don't keep it up to date, you are wasting everyone's time.

While you work through the steps involved in gathering the evidence for the ideas that you are responsible for, or contributing to, keep your items in the Analyzing The Options list up to date. This means that if other people make a contribution, add their names to the Other Analysts field. When the status of your work changes—for example, it transitions from Not Started to In Progress to Finalized—open the item and click Finalized in the Status drop-down field.

Being diligent in keeping the list up to date helps everyone stay coordinated about the true current status of the work.

Coauthoring a Document

With all of the ideas set out in the custom list, and now that team members have selected the ideas they will research, it's time to begin the actual analysis. What's needed for each idea is a briefing paper that explores the idea in more detail, outlines the pros and cons of the idea, discusses the supporting arguments, and comes to a conclusion about the risk profile of the idea.

For this type of analysis, there are three main options for the coauthoring piece: using Microsoft Word 2007, using the SharePoint wiki, or using both. Let's examine the three options in turn, and see what is best.

Coauthoring by Using Word 2007

To coauthor one of the analysis documents by using Microsoft Office Word 2007, you open the team's document library and click the arrow on the New button. This shows you a list of the types of documents that can be created directly in the document library, based on a concept named *content types*.

For example, within Project Delta, Fourth Coffee has a specific desired format for the analysis of each idea, so a content type named *Idea Analysis Briefing* has been set up by IT (see Figure 7-10).

After working through the idea analysis document the first time, the team member who started work on the document saves it directly into the SharePoint document library. Other team members working on the document can review what's been written, and make edits and suggested changes based on their expertise and insight. Every time someone on the team is going to work on the document, the team member needs to check out the document (see Figure 7-11).

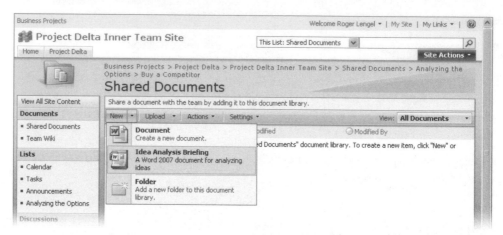

FIGURE 7-10 Content types allow more structured capture of certain types of documents.

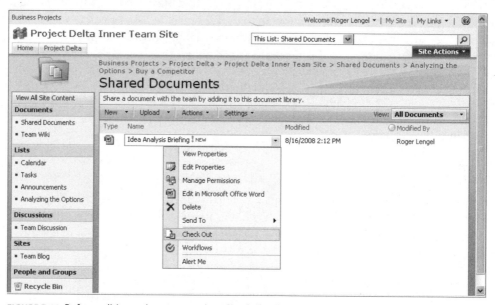

FIGURE 7-11 Before editing a document, select Check Out from the document list so that no one overwrites your edits.

After they have finished their edits, they should check the document back into the document library and leave a comment about what they changed in the document. This provides an at-a-glance summary of what was done in the document.

WHAT'S SO GREAT ABOUT CONTENT TYPES?

SharePoint 2007 introduced a great new idea named *content types*. In essence, these are a description of a certain type of document, along with the document template that should be used for creating the document itself. The template sets the stage, and a document based on the template becomes an example of that template.

So in the case of Project Delta, one of the content types that could be set up is an "Idea Analysis Briefing." A content type has a description, and also has a template associated with it. One of the beautiful things about content types and templates is that SharePoint solves the problem of how to get the most up-to-date copy of a document template out to everyone who needs to use it. With SharePoint, it is a centrally controlled and updated capability, meaning that whenever the document template is updated in one place, every document created based on that template going forward will be based on the latest edition.

Content types and the creation thereof are more of a SharePoint administrator task, rather than a team member or team leader task. So if you think that content types could help streamline your work, talk to your SharePoint consultant in IT.

Coauthoring by Using the SharePoint Wiki

A second option for coauthoring a document is to use the SharePoint wiki. We have already explored the use of a wiki for coauthoring a document—or at least contributing to a list of items (which is really the same thing)—so there's not a lot more to add at this point.

The basic flow for coauthoring a document in the SharePoint wiki is:

- Create a new page from the Analyzing The Options page for each idea to be explored. By doing this from the Analyzing The Options page, all of the different analysis work is linked to from a consistent place.

- Follow a similar structure across the different analysis options, ensuring that consistent information is gathered for each of the ideas. The best way to do this is to create an Idea Analysis Briefing Template page in the wiki, and for the person creating a new page in the wiki to copy and paste the wiki markup from this briefing template page to the new wiki page.

There are two things to note when using the SharePoint wiki to coauthor the idea analysis briefing document. First, you can't use content types with a wiki page, so you have to create your own template page in the wiki. That's not necessarily a bad thing; it's just a different way of getting to the same outcome.

The second thing to note is that some of the idea analysis briefing documents will need to be sent to other people within the firm and external to it. Either you give them access to the wiki, or you put it into a Word 2007 document. The benefit to the team of taking the Word 2007 approach is that you know exactly what you sent out at a certain point in time. This helps with managing the message.

Mix and Match to Use Both Options

The third option is to use both the SharePoint wiki and Word 2007. For example, you might use the wiki first—to create a draft of your ideas, to get input from lots of people in a light way (they don't have to work with Word 2007), and to play around with different orderings of the various parts of the document. After you are happy with the structure and flow in the wiki document, copy and paste it into Word 2007 for wider sharing.

A related way of using the wiki for coauthoring is to get different people to write different sections of the final report, and to do it online so that it is instantly available to everyone else, and offers full version history directly within the browser window. This means that, for each idea, you would first create a page in the wiki for that idea, and then from that page, you would create sub-pages for each major section. Different people on the team would be asked to take the lead on writing one of the sub-pages, and then the other team members would have the freedom to review what had been written and to make suggestions on how to improve the work.

Organize Documents by Metadata or Folders

We really need to look at the next level of detail when talking about creating analysis briefing documents, and that level of detail is about where a sub-team stores its documents and supporting files for each analysis option. Most people are used to using a traditional hierarchical folder structure in Windows Explorer for doing this, and SharePoint supports the continuation of folders for document segregation, but it also offers a newer approach called *metadata*.

The difference between the two is very simple:

- Folders organize information based on *where* something is—it's about location-based storage.

- Metadata organizes information based on *what* something is—it's about meaning.

Which is the right option to use? There are pros and cons to each approach. Let's look at them.

Folders: Organizing Documents Based on Location

Folders are used to store documents in a location. When someone is looking for a particular document, they look in a certain place. Let's consider an analogy:

> Roger has just returned from a trip to Boston for meetings with Nancy Anderson, and when he gets back to the airport at New York, he has to find his car. In the early morning blur of catching his plane on Tuesday, he can't recall where he actually parked the thing. Walking up to the parking building attendant, Roger asks for his car.
>
> "Hi there, I've forgotten where I put my car," Roger said, addressing the parking attendant. "Can you please help me find it, or do I have to walk through all six levels of the building until I stumble across it?"
>
> "I can help you," the attendant replied. "What's the license plate number of your car?"
>
> Roger told him, and the attendant entered the details into his PDA.
>
> "Your car is on the third level, fourth row, and is the sixth car in from the access way," the attendant said, and then looking up with a bright smile, "Our new car search system makes finding cars so much easier!"
>
> Roger thanked the attendant and headed to the stairs.

Roger needed to find his car, and was able to do so based on where it was—its location. The same idea applies for files in folders in SharePoint. What are the benefits of using folders in SharePoint?

Folders are a familiar idea to many computer users. People use them for sorting and storing documents and files in Windows Explorer. People use folders for sorting and retaining e-mail messages in Outlook. People use folders for their own filing needs. When it is time to find something, "I'll look in the folder" is the immediate thought. Because folders are the way that most people work today with information on their local computer, continuing to use them in SharePoint is immediately familiar. And this familiarity really helps with transitioning people from individual work to group work.

Folders in SharePoint help people know what is going on in the project. People can request an e-mail notification for changes in a folder. How do you know that someone else has added a document to a specific folder? With SharePoint, you can get an e-mail alert informing you of that fact. Folder e-mail alerts can be set up for all changes—add, revise, and delete—or just one type of change (see Figure 7-12). Open the folder in which you want to create the alert, click Actions, and then click Alert Me.

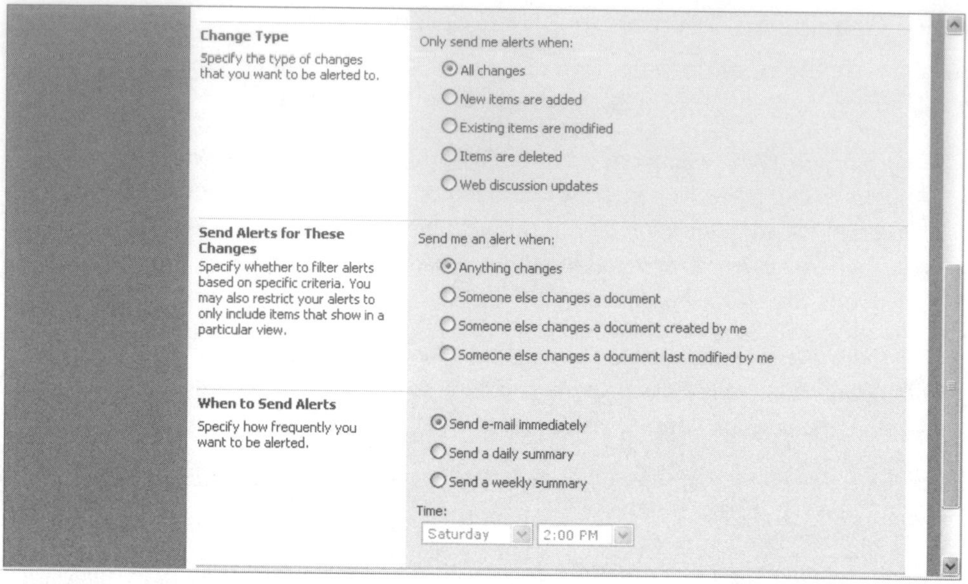

FIGURE 7-12 Create an e-mail alert for folders you are working on, so you don't have to keep checking them.

Thus, there is good capability within SharePoint to tell other team members about the things that are happening in areas of interest to them. People can mosey along with their work on all of the different projects and tasks they have on their To Do lists, and whenever something happens that they should know about, they are told. And because alerts can be set on a folder-by-folder basis, you can filter down to the information that you are interested in and not become overwhelmed by items that are only tangentially interesting.

Another benefit of folders in SharePoint is that you can set access privileges on a folder-by-folder basis. That is, within a document library with three folders, everyone on the team can access the first two folders, but only two of the team members can access the third folder because a specific permissions list has been created. Right-click the name of the folder for which you want to create the unique permissions list, and then click Manage Permissions. After the list of permissions displays, click Actions, and then click Edit Permissions to allow you to change the permissions for this folder. Click OK in the dialog box asking you to confirm, and then add and delete names of people and groups until you have the right subset of people in place (see Figure 7-13).

When Shannon Kempe looks into the *Analyzing the Options* folder in Shared Documents, because she was excluded from seeing the *Buy a Competitor* folder, it does not appear in her list (see Figure 7-14). If she does happen to guess the name of the folder (or click across from the Analyzing The Options custom list), none of the documents in the folder will be displayed.

FIGURE 7-13 Only a couple of people in the group are allowed to access the *Buy a Competitor* folder.

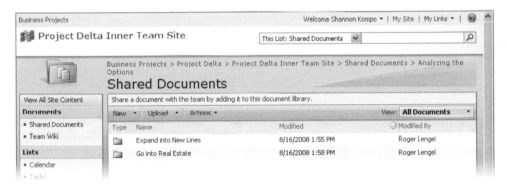

FIGURE 7-14 People without access to a folder are unable to see it listed in the document library.

This could happen when files and documents within a folder are confidential; maybe it's all of the pricing analysis documents for a business project that only two of the people on the team need to see. Different permission lists on folders in a document library mean that all of the team's requirements can be met out of SharePoint; the two who have access to the pricing documents don't have to set up a second and different place to work. When they look at the document library, they see all three of the folders—it just looks normal to them—and when the other people on the team look at the document library, they see only two folders; it just looks normal to them, too.

A final benefit is that folders of documents can be connected to Outlook 2007 so that people can access documents in the SharePoint document library from within Outlook. And the approach for connecting a folder to Outlook 2007 is really neat; you can either synchronize the entire document library by clicking Connect To Outlook when you are at the top level, or you can choose to synchronize only a specific subfolder and all of the folders and documents it contains by going into the desired folder and then clicking Connect To Outlook within there (see Figure 7-15). So it's really flexible based on what individuals within the team want to do, and how they want to work.

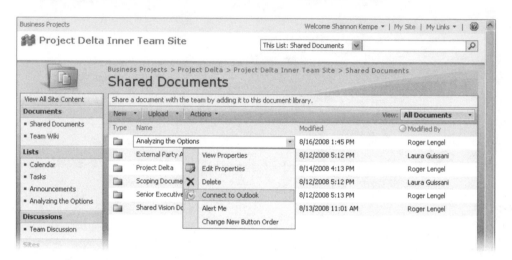

FIGURE 7-15 Right-click a folder name to connect it and its subfolders to Outlook 2007.

There are some downsides, too. First, folders have to be navigated, and that can be a pain if there are a lot of folders in the folder hierarchy. You have to click through the structure to see what's happening, and decide where you want to be.

Another pain is that within the standard look of a SharePoint document library, there is not a list of folders down the left side, as is normal in Windows Explorer. The way to navigate back up to a higher document folder is to use the breadcrumb trail at the top of the page. But then maybe that's not a pain—but it is different.

Metadata: Organizing Documents Based on Meaning

The second of the two options is to use a single folder to store all of the files for the team, but to distinguish between them by what's known as metadata—accurately, "data about data" or the way that the data itself is described. Or you can think about it as the attributes that you use to describe the data.

Assume that both you and I have a car. So far, we have the same thing. But after we start detailing the data about our respective cars, we can start to tell them apart. You have a Ford or a BMW perhaps. I drive a Toyota. If we both drive Toyotas, then we'll need to go to another level of meaning and differentiation in order to distinguish which Toyota is yours and which Toyota is mine.

Thus, the purpose of metadata is to declare information about something that enables it to be quickly differentiated from other things. Let's go back to Roger's arrival back in New York after his visit to Boston, and see how he finds his car in the parking building by using metadata:

> "Hi there, I've forgotten where I put my car," Roger said, addressing the parking attendant. "Can you please help me find it, or do I have to walk through all six levels of the building until I stumble across it?"
>
> "I can help you," the attendant replied. "We have 824 cars parked here at the moment. What is your car like?"
>
> "It's a Toyota," Roger said.
>
> "Neat," replied the attendant. "That narrows it down to 134 different cars. What type of Toyota is it?"
>
> "It's a Toyota Prius," Roger said.
>
> "Wow, one of those new environmentally friendly cars!" the attendant exclaimed. "We are seeing more and more people buying them!" he added. "We have 20 of those in the building. What color is yours?"
>
> "It is navy blue," Roger answered, "with a dual white stripe down both sides."
>
> "Yes, we have it. Your car is on the third level, fourth row, and is the sixth car in from the access way," the attendant said, and then looking up with a bright smile, "Our new car search system makes finding cars so much easier!"
>
> Roger thanked the attendant and headed to the stairs.

Roger needed to find his car, and was able to do so based on what it looks like—its characteristics. He used three items of metadata about his car—manufacturer, model, and color—to help the parking attendant narrow down the search.

The same concept applies for files tagged with metadata in a SharePoint document library. Use metadata to help classify the documents we and others put into the library, to tell them apart. We can write down key describing words or phrases—either free-form words or phrases or selections from a pre-defined list of items—that help us and others to distinguish among all of the documents and files that are put into the library.

By default, the SharePoint document library does not include an area for metadata, so in order to capture metadata, we need to create one by creating the column for capturing metadata values. You already know how to do this, because you did it when we created the custom list earlier in this chapter. In this instance, however, we are modifying an existing list, rather than creating a new one. Click Settings, and then click Create Column. Name the new column **Metadata** and give it a type of Single Line Of Text (see Figure 7-16). Under Additional Column Settings, provide a description and leave Add To All Content Types selected.

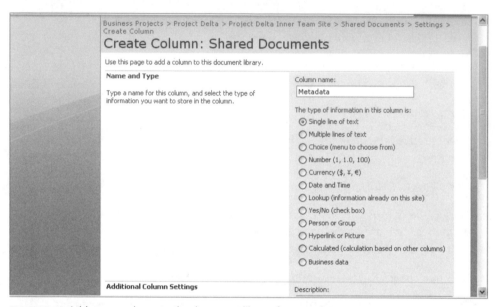

FIGURE 7-16 Add a new column to the document library for metadata.

There are some things that documents and files organized by metadata can't do. Unlike folders, you cannot set an e-mail alert on a certain metadata name or phrase. So if you want to be alerted when a document has been revised, and everything is going into one folder and is being tagged with a metadata value, you will have to find it yourself. You could set up an e-mail alert for changes on the total folder—that may work—it just depends on how many documents are being added. It's a bit of a blunt axe approach, however.

Secondly, you cannot connect a metadata tag to Outlook. In other words, you can't use the Connect To Outlook command to link a certain metadata value with Outlook. You can do it for the complete SharePoint folder, and then create a Search Folder to highlight the metadata items of interest, but you can't only link documents with a certain metadata value to Outlook. So if it's a big folder, you will have lots of unnecessary documents synchronized to Outlook that you don't really need.

Recommendation

Let's come back to the point we've been talking about: How should Roger and his team colleagues organize all of the documents in the Project Delta Team Workings site—by folder or by metadata? On balance, folders are the best way to proceed. SharePoint offers better support for folders than it does for metadata, in terms of the ability to find a document and integration into the current work styles of different team members. For example, the use of folders makes it easier for Roger and his fellow team members to stay abreast of what's happening within the life of the project. In addition, the ability for each team member to connect a certain part of the document library to Outlook, so they can access documents locally and work on them seamlessly when in the office, connected to the network, is a really helpful capability. And finally, the ability to have permission-based access to certain folders within the document library makes sense for supporting many nuances in projects.

Now, let's wrap some additional guidelines around this recommendation to use folders.

First, if your project will result in a small number of documents—for example, 15 to 30—just use a single folder, a descriptive file name, and metadata. Remember, the purpose for using folders or metadata is to enable quick access to a particular document, to differentiate the one from the many. If the number of documents is small to start with, a descriptive file name will suffice, and if that's not enough, add metadata. But for a total of 15 to 30 documents, a folder structure is overkill.

Second, don't go overboard in creating a complex hierarchical folder structure, even if you are dealing with a large number of documents. Have as few levels of folders as possible so that you can easily navigate and find documents. Generally speaking, three levels of folders should be more than enough—anything more than that is a warning sign. After going to three levels of folders, if you are still dealing with a large number of files or documents (more than 50) per folder, and there are clear differences between the documents, then use metadata as well to differentiate among the documents in a folder. But don't go much deeper than three levels.

A Couple of Thoughts on Site Collection Columns

SharePoint is all about flexibility and choice, about making heaps of capabilities available to IT professionals and end users that they can use as they want to achieve the plethora of uses that SharePoint is and can be put to. One of the choices available within SharePoint is the ability to define columns—or *data types*—either within a specific site, or within a collection of sites. If it is defined within a specific site, it can be used only for the needs of that site, and cannot be shared with people and groups using other sites. Think about these types of columns as being ideal for local needs that perfectly match the peculiar needs of a specific team within a site.

On the other hand, there is the idea of a Site Collection Column, where a data type and its constituent elements are described at the level of a site collection. This means that:

- A consistent definition of the data type can be used across all of the sites within the collection.

- A change made to the site collection column will be automatically updated across all of the sites that use that definition.

- The definition can be used by many sites, thus sharing what's been done more widely.

So we have two ideas ... there's the "general" or "wide applicability" way of defining data items, and there's the "local" or "narrow applicability" way of doing the same. And which one you choose really doesn't matter within the life of one specific project, but in terms of the whole organization and making SharePoint work well for everyone, there are some definite benefits to going the more general way at times.

Here's an example. Suppose that within Roger's project, he needs to describe a few metadata fields for documents in the document library: country of applicability, project phase association, and group relationship. On the face of it, should the columns be created as Site Collection Columns or Site Columns?

Country should be a Site Collection Column, because the list of values for that column will be used in many places within the organization, not just for Roger's team. The list of countries is a fairly static list (it doesn't change all that often), but it is a list that can be said to be complete and true at any point in time. Either someone has the authoritative list of countries in their list, or they don't. And you don't want to have end users having to keep a list of countries up to date within the lists and sites they are using. Therefore, on that basis, it should be a definitive column that is created, maintained and administered by the IT group as a Site Collection Column. If it changes, they change it.

Project phase association could be either, depending on how structured a project methodology the organization is using. If there is a standard methodology in use, and the project phases have consistent names—Shared Vision, Understanding The Options, Analyzing The Options, Making A Decision, and Concluding The Project—then the Project Phases column should also be a Site Collection Column. It is unlikely that Roger will be able to create a Site Collection Column—indeed it would be a highly suspect IT group that allowed end users to set up Site Collection Columns! So Roger will need to put in a request for the Project Phases Site Collection Column to be created, or as is more likely the case, the IT group have already set it up, so Roger only needs to add the Site Collection Column to the team's document library.

On the other hand, if the organization doesn't have a standard project methodology, and each project team is free to do what they want and to call the phases within the project whatever they want, then the Column should be set up as a Site Column. Roger goes into the Site Settings area, and creates a Site Column for Project Phase. He defines the names that the project is using for each of the phases.

On the third hand (think General Grievous in *Star Wars*), you can have the situation where there is a generalized piece of data—Country, for example—but some projects that are run on SharePoint sites need access to the complete list of countries, and other projects run on other sites need access to only a subset of the complete country list. What then? Do you give end users the ability to choose from the complete list, and thus give them the ability to choose country names that are not relevant to the work at hand, thus introducing confusion and misunderstandings into the group? Luckily, SharePoint offers flexibility here, too—and not really "luckily" but more "by design"—so that you can take the overall definition of a column from the Site Collection area and then give it a set of local data points. Inherit the general idea, and then make it work locally for the specific project.

The third item of required metadata for Roger's group is Group Relationship, in other words the organizational group or division that a given document should be shared with when the time comes to brief the others about what's going on or coming up. So it's helpful to have this set as a flag, so the list of documents related to a specific group can be quickly identified. Where should this be set: in a Site Collection Column, or just a Site Column? My sense is that it is probably going to be a Site Column, rather than a Site Collection one, because the information is highly specific to the team and the project.

Note, too, that an argument could be made for making it a Site Collection Column, because if the organization has a set project methodology and a requirement for negotiation and communication with certain teams and groups at certain points during the project methodology, then it should also have a standardized list of these groups and divisions for use across the organization. The point is, some of this is highly contextual to other things that the organization has or has not done, and there can't be a general rule because of that contextualization.

I guess the main point to take to heart is that before you go off and create a whole set of site-specific columns, at least:

- Look at the Site Collection Columns that are available.
- Talk to the SharePoint champion or administrator who works with your team to help understand the options and general organizational guidance.

The trick is knowing when to use one or the other—there's a bit of an art to knowing where a Column should be created, and a bit of a science with respect to guidance and theories of good decisions versus bad decisions. When making decisions of this nature, we get into the whole area of information architecture, which although fascinating, can be a huge stop sign for making progress on business projects.

There are some examples and ideas in the previous sections, which we can summarize into the following heuristics:

- If the data that will go into a certain column is data that is generally used, or could be generally used across many projects, make it a Site Collection Column.

- If the data draws from a master database somewhere—for example, a list of customers—in the organization, it should be a Site Collection Column.

- If you need to work with data that is generally held, but only need to use a subset of that information within your project, take the Site Collection Column and change the data values to suit your needs.

- If the IT group at your organization is super-unresponsive and is neither willing to listen nor to quickly deliver some guidance, do your own thing.

If you go through that list and still don't know which way to go, talk to the SharePoint champion for your team or organization, and get some guidance from that person.

Use a Folder to Store Evidence Documents

Assuming that you proceed with the recommendation of using a folder structure in SharePoint, here's one way to set it up for the "Analyzing the Options" phase. Create a top-level folder named **Analyzing the Options** in the team's document library. Below the top-level folder, create a separate folder for each of the ideas to be analyzed. This, actually, is a good place to use the unique code for each idea (assuming you created one), along with a brief extract of the title of the idea. Now when the team members enter the *Analyzing the Options* folder, they will be able to see the complete list of ideas that are being investigated.

Inside each folder should be stored all of the documents and files related to the idea under investigation. This includes:

- Letters to government bodies or other organizations requesting supporting information about the idea

- Financial models in Excel 2007 related to the idea

- Pictures of locations or sites that you are considering for a physical site, if that's appropriate based on the focus of the project

- Anything else that's relevant to the work on the idea at hand—rough notes, mind maps, working documents, research reports, architectural diagrams, test results, and other information

Within the folder for each idea, if the volume of documents that you are creating is large—for example, more than 50—then create another level of folders to help with the differentiation of documents. Do whatever makes sense within the specific context of your project, but because you are working in conjunction with others, talk to them about having a coordinated approach. This means that other people working on other ideas can look at your folder and understand the general structure and layout. This helps with quickly orienting other people from other parts of the team to see what you are working on, and it also makes it easier for new people joining an idea analysis group partway through the process.

Meetings for People Who Can't Be Together

During the process of delivering to the requirements of Phase 3, there will be lots of meetings held between sub-groups of the wider team, as they work through the analysis requirements for doing a great job. When these sub-groups can't be together, how should they meet?

How they should "meet" depends on the type of meeting they are holding; in some cases, the meeting should actually be a blog post read by everyone else. In other cases, the meeting should be a conference call or a screen-sharing session.

Five Reasons to Have Meetings

We hold meetings for different purposes, and some of the meetings that we hold for in-person groups don't make a lot of sense for virtual teams (and often they don't make sense for in-person groups either!). Some of the reasons for holding a meeting when people can meet easily in person are better handled in other ways for virtual teams. The following sections examine five different types of meetings and how they work (or don't) in a virtual team situation.

Information Transfer Meetings

Information transfer meetings provide a place for one person to pass on lots of information to an assembled group of other people. One person talks, everyone else listens. There are times when it makes sense to do this—a hostile bid has just been made for your organization, and the CEO is going to brief the company of the plan of response—but most times the calling of an information transfer meeting strokes one person's ego and wastes everyone else's time. Within virtual teaming situations, given the difficulties of getting everyone together—even for a conference call—keep information transfer meetings to a minimum. Actually, it's better if you don't do them at all. SharePoint provides so many ways of communicating information to others—through an announcement, a blog posting, a document in a document library—that as long as each team member knows where such information will be posted and knows that after it is posted, they are expected to read it, then you can pretty much cut out information transfer meetings all together.

Recommendation: Eliminate information transfer meetings and get the message out using other ways.

Discussion and Decision Meetings

Discussion and decision meetings are for highly interactive conversations and debate about a current pressing matter or a decision that needs to be made (yesterday!). Everyone gathers in a common place or shared virtual space—hopefully with a sense of what is going to be discussed and the ground rules for interaction (for example, critique the idea, not the person)—and then it's a free for all. One person says one thing, another argues the opposite case, a third supports what the first said, the second points the flaws out ... and so on ... until everyone has been heard and all of the ideas have been critiqued and examined. At the end of the meeting, the decision as to "what now?" is made. Either people leave with more work to do—that is, another task or action item—or a decision is suggested and people formally vote or informally agree or disagree. This is the kind of meeting where you want everyone together in one place, and when that's not possible, the second best alternative is a shared virtual space like a conference call with screen sharing or high-definition video conference.

Recommendation: Discussion and decision meetings are the heart of team work, both in person and distributed.

Quick Coordination Meetings

Quick coordination meetings are very helpful for keeping everyone on the same page. At such a meeting, which are ideally held every day at the same time, everyone has 30 seconds to say what they are currently working on and any problems they are up against, and everyone else gets to hear what's happening. This means that a shared cognitive picture of the work of the team or organization builds up over time, and if someone is working on something that piques someone else's interest, an opportunity for spontaneous collaboration and greater value has been created.

Given the difficulties of actually scheduling a regular conference call when everyone can dial in and have this kind of briefing makes it impractical for many virtual teams. And in addition, these meetings work best as forward-looking statements of the work ahead for the day, an idea that doesn't translate across very well to the virtual world where one person's start time is another person's end time. A much better option is for the team to use the blog site in SharePoint, and for everyone on the team to make a blog post each morning about what they are planning on doing that day. Given the ease of subscribing to a SharePoint blog site by e-mail or RSS, everyone else can be kept up to date and reap the same ambient coordination benefits of the in-person variant of this approach within their own work. If people subscribe to the blog site by RSS, for example, every time they go into Outlook 2007 (or another RSS reader), they can see all of the quick status updates from the people on their team. Same benefits, minimal cost.

Recommendation. Use a blog site in SharePoint to provide regular status updates, and track what's going on through RSS.

Social Gatherings

The fourth type of meeting is the social meeting, in which time and space is created for people to share recent experiences, to talk about ideas—in essence, to gather without an agenda but rather a willingness to talk, listen, and see where the conversation meanders. These are really valid meetings to have—people can learn so much and get some great ideas—and they're really easy to do when people work out of the same office. "Coffee, anyone?" is usually all it takes.

Social "catch-up" meetings are much harder to do in a virtual team, but should be done because it can be even more rewarding—people who can't see each other during the work week are able to hear about what's going on, which allows them to form a mental picture about what work is like and the challenges in work for others. This contributes to developing shared understanding, and an empathy for others. Team members who have been keeping track of what others are working on through the blog site in SharePoint can bring up some of those topics, for discussion and dialogue. When it comes time to have the actual social catch-up, use a conference call and a screen sharing tool with the ability to give presenter rights to others if they want to show something from their computer to others.

Recommendation: You'll rarely have time for these meetings in virtual teams, but you have to make the time. They are important.

Collaborative Working Sessions

The fifth and final type of meeting is the collaborative working session, where two or three people get together to actually get work done. In a face-to-face situation, this generally involves sitting around one person's computer, and talking through the work they see on the screen and how to get to a conclusion. This is a bit awkward for people who normally sit alone at their desk—because someone else is there in an area that is built for one person to work—and it's also awkward for others sitting at the desk, because they are out of their normal environment and the computer isn't "theirs." If they want to use it, they have to lean over and take control, which is physically awkward in most cases and socially awkward for the person who "owns" the space.

In an interesting twist, a collaborative working session is easier to do in a virtual team situation than in a face-to-face situation. Both people can work from their standard working environment, have full access to their computer, and not be forced into a socially strange situation with having someone else sit in their work area for a few hours. With the power of screen sharing—the ability for two or three people to work on the same document at the same time and see in real time the changes that others are making—collaborative working sessions can become part of the key delivery strategy of virtual teams.

Recommendation: Shared session–powered collaborative working sessions should become a standard and a no-thinking-required approach to meeting with your team colleagues. Get used to them, and get good at having them.

When Do We Meet? Coordinating Time Zones

Team members will need to find possible times to meet with their colleagues, and because one of the first things that the Project Delta team did was fill out the Common Working Hours page in the Team Wiki, that's the place to start.

Open the page, find the one or two people you need to meet with, and look for overlapping working hours. When you find something that looks like it will work, create the meeting in the team calendar.

Protocols for an Effective Discussion

If team members are going to commit to a real-time meeting with others, then having a good idea of how to have an effective discussion is an essential place to start:

- **Alternatives are identified and explored.** When the purpose of a discussion is to make a decision, it is very good to get all of the alternatives and options on the table quickly. You don't want to prematurely settle on one solution, and thus move ahead on something that is sub-optimal in dealing with all of the evaluation criteria people have. Clearly identifying alternatives through free-flowing brainstorming and mind mapping is critical to effective decision making, and thus to productive decisions. Follow-up conversations can then happen immediately or over time for the intent of exploring alternatives and providing a way for making a decision between competing alternatives.

- **Ideas are critiqued, not people.** Not all ideas are brilliant, but in expressing that view, we need to be careful to critique the idea and not the person who advocated it. If an idea is long-held by someone, that person will become attached to it, and when you call someone's idea "ugly," the person can take offence (and thus reduce further involvement in the discussion). Prefacing your critique with softening words like "I'm so glad that you shared that idea, and here's my different take on it … " can go a long way to smooth human relations. Tone of voice, subsequent words of encouragements, and so on can also help. One of the benefits of separating the idea and alternative generation stage from the critique and evaluation stage is that it can create some social and time distance for the person who proposed the idea/alternative and his hearing of its critique. And, hopefully too, after he has seen the breadth of ideas and alternatives that have been proposed, he will feel less attached to his idea as the sole way of achieving the overall decision and outcome that is desired.

- **A clear decision is made at the end.** At the end of a productive discussion, a clear decision on moving ahead needs to be made. The decision may be made by a leader/manager, or by group consensus. Whatever the approach, a decision is essential for moving forward so that people aren't left hanging.

- **People are willing to discuss again in the future.** A productive discussion should result in two things: (a) a clear decision, and (b) increased capability for the group to discuss things again in the future. If people have been put down, stomped on, and told that their ideas are worthless, although a clear outcome may be reached, their capability and willingness to go through the process again in the future will be much diminished. This is Stephen Covey's "production" vs. "production capacity" idea in action. Encouraging people to go through a process of discussion and evaluation, making it clear through spoken words and non-spoken cues that people are valued even when their ideas don't turn into anything—all these help with getting people to come back to the table for another discussion in the future.

Technology for Virtual Meetings

When people can't be together but need to still work together, you need to create connection points to link up the people. One connection point is an audio channel over the phone or through a Windows Live Messenger call, and a second critical one is shared screens. For the longest time, doing shared screens for ad hoc collaboration has been an expensive proposition, and so most firms have limited the use of screen-sharing services like Live Meeting and WebEx Meeting Center to sales calls where there is a clear return on investment, but this has left project teams out in the cold. With the introduction of some new services, there are a range of free screen-sharing tools available to collaborative project teams. And being free means that there is no hassle with having to get fiscal signoff before using them.

Free Screen Sharing with SharedView

SharedView is a free Web conferencing tool from Microsoft, for up to 15 participants. It enables the creation of a private Web conferencing meeting on the fly with other people. Using SharedView, you can show your whole desktop or just one application, and you can give control to others so that they can work directly with your applications from their computer. After they have taken control (and been granted permission to do so by the meeting convener), they can also change it so that their screen is the one being displayed for everyone to see. Note that SharedView is a Windows-only application, so if you need to work with people on other operating systems, you will have to find something else.

Everyone using SharedView to host a meeting needs to have a Windows Live ID; and if you don't, they are freely available from *home.live.com*. People joining the session do not have to have a Windows Live ID, and they can sign in with any e-mail address. Equally, if they do have a Windows Live ID, they can use that to sign in without entering the password for the session. Regardless of whether the other team members do or do not have a Windows Live ID, the meeting organizer is prompted and asked whether others are allowed to join the session or not.

The term "ad-hoc collaborative meeting" has one particular meaning you need to be aware of. At this time, you cannot schedule meetings in advance and send out invitations. SharedView only works in the moment.

Of course, the huge benefit of having a free screen-sharing tool like SharedView is that you can use it on all of your calls. Make it a part of your day-to-day work. Because you can switch who has control of the screen and who is showing what, you can get a richer insight into what people are thinking about and looking at. Rather than one person saying, "OK, open a browser window and go to this address," because they are in a shared-screen session, it is as easy as clicking to go there. Everyone is immediately on the same page, and can see what the others are looking at.

Screen Sharing with Live Meeting

Live Meeting is a for-fee service for Web conferencing and screen sharing. It is a second option for teams to use, and it can do three key things that the free SharedView tool cannot do:

- Scheduling of calls—that is, the setting up of a meeting and associated screen-sharing session in advance of the actual meeting. You can meet "now" in Live Meeting as you can with SharedView, but Live Meeting 2007 isn't limited to only that.

- Provision of a conference call number, meaning that rather than having people dial each other, everyone can call the conference call number and get into the call directly. In addition to offering standard telephone conference call options, the 2007 edition of Live Meeting also includes voice-over-IP (VoIP) conference calling features, which greatly reduces telephone charges.

- Native support for the Mac platform, meaning the team members on a Mac can join a Live Meeting session—unlike with SharedView.

For people with access to a Live Meeting account—and let's face it, if you are doing a project with a virtual team and thus saving on travel costs and other expenses, then Live Meeting isn't "expensive"—it can meet all of your real-time interaction and meeting requirements.

Note, too, that if your organization is running Office Communications Server 2007, Web conferencing capabilities may be offered directly to you within the firewall. This means that a screen-sharing meeting is only as far away as your Office Communicator 2007 client. If in doubt, talk to your IT people.

What About Meeting Workspaces?

One of the capabilities in SharePoint is the Meeting Workspace; you'll notice it whenever you set up an event in a team calendar, and you'll also notice it as an alternative when you set up a meeting through Outlook 2007. For the Workspace option at the bottom of the page, select the Use A Meeting Workspace check box (see Figure 7-17).

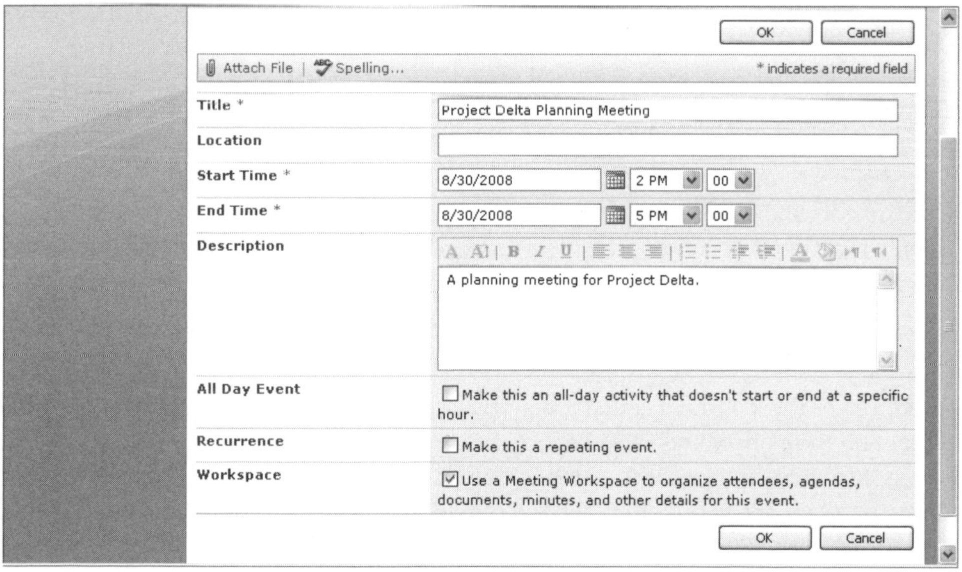

FIGURE 7-17 Meetings can be planned in their own subsites.

Meeting Workspaces are created as subsites within a team site, and in general, there is one Meeting Workspace for every meeting. The point of using a Meeting Workspace is to keep a very tight track on who attended the meeting, the meeting agenda items, and documents relevant to the meeting (see Figure 7-18).

But should you use them in team projects? Here's one way to decide: If the information, artifacts and list items that you want to discuss are already in your team project site, don't bother using a Meeting Workspace. Just set up a standard calendar event entry in the team calendar, and schedule a Web conference to go along with the meeting.

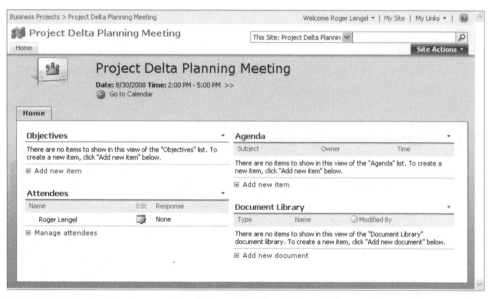

FIGURE 7-18 Meeting Workspaces allow for very tight control over all facets of a meeting.

If the documents and agenda items don't already exist somewhere else in the Inner Team site, then a Meeting Workspace provides a locus of focus to the team meeting. Set up the meeting in the team calendar, and ensure that you choose the option to create a Meeting Workspace for the event. When the group meets, have the Web conferencing tool pointing at the Meeting Workspace.

A second way to think about it is that if the documents that will be discussed during the team meeting have utility and value beyond the meeting—they will be referenced by other people in days and weeks to come—then don't use a Meeting Workspace and lock them up in there. On the other hand, if the documents are transitory documents and have relevance only to a specific meeting, and after that point in time they have no ongoing value, a Meeting Workspace may be the way to do things.

A third way to decide whether the use of a Meeting Workspace makes sense is whether the meeting is part of a series of interconnected meetings, or is a standalone major meeting within the life of the project. If it is part of a series of meetings, then don't use a Meeting Workspace. Use the Team Wiki instead. If it is a major meeting—for example, it is a briefing call with the senior management or a major stakeholder to report back on the progress of the project—then a Meeting Workspace is fine. It provides a focal point for the meeting that others outside of the team will be able to relate to—and remember, they will not have built up your way of working because they are not involved directly in the Inner Team site. The Meeting Workspace provides a common and generally understood layout that can be used in any briefing meeting.

Using the Meeting Workspace During the Meeting

What works really well is when team members have one large monitor that is big enough to have two windows side by side (for example, a 23-inch or larger monitor), or they have two smaller monitors each showing a different window. This means that they can see the team's shared view on one side of the monitor, and the Meeting Workspace on the other.

Here's where you would use both.

The shared view allows the person who is running the meeting to keep everyone focused on the same things.

The personal view on the second monitor allows everyone simultaneously to enter text or make comments. The meeting starts ... and the meeting organizer asks people if there are any other agenda items that they want to see discussed. As each person speaks up and says that they have something they want to see addressed, they are asked to create an Agenda item for that. Over on their personal screen (or the personal side of their large screen), they click to create a new agenda item and save it back into the list. Because everyone on the team is able to add items via their own computers while on the call, the group is not held up by one person having to type and create all of the items.

Agendas are really helpful for setting common expectations about the topics to be discussed, and they are even more helpful when expectations about timing are made explicit, too. The Agenda item form in the Meeting Workspace allows the entry of a time for the specific agenda item, and the list of agenda items can then be sorted for a chronological display of what's coming up.

A Task for Your IT People

The default setup in SharePoint for Meeting Workspaces is that the breadcrumb trail across the top of the Meeting Workspace is not tied to the team site in which the Meeting Workspace is created. In other words, after you are inside a Meeting Workspace, you have no contextualization across the top of which team site it relates to.

There is a setting that can be changed for all team sites in a Site Collection, but this is a change that your central SharePoint people will have to make. Ask them to change the global navigation option for Meeting Workspaces so the same navigation of the parent site is shown in a Meeting Workspace. Hopefully, they've already done so, but if not, you'll have to tell them why.

Pay Attention During Online Meetings

Most people grump and grizzle about the time they spend in meetings for little or no return. "Meetings are the bane of my life, and stop me from getting any real work done" is not an uncommon sentiment. But then the same people who say this tune out during the meetings they do attend or do other unrelated things during meetings—like checking e-mail or reading the news. You can't have it both ways. This means that if you want to get great results from meetings, then you need to become a great contributor to the effectiveness of meetings.

That means:

- Don't do other things during a meeting, whether it is a face-to-face meeting or an online one.

- Ensure that you need to be at the meeting by asking for the agenda in advance. If you have nothing to add, don't go. Pre-eject yourself from meetings that will waste your time.

- Stay engaged in the meetings you do attend. Listen. Contribute. Synthesize. Ask questions. Draw other people out. Be relentless about helping everyone get the most out of meetings.

- If you feel bored and distracted during a meeting, make one of two decisions. Decide to re-engage and be fully present, or get up and leave. On a conference call, say that you have to drop out and do so. Make an adult decision and stop being present in body but absent in every other way.

What all of this means is that if you want other people to respect your scarce time, start respecting theirs.

What About Video Conferencing?

Being able to see the faces of the other people who you are working with in a video conference can sometimes be helpful. At the very least, it is a way to ensure that both you and they stay engaged in the conversation—people are less likely to slack off when you are watching their every move.

I have two observations to make about video conferencing. First, the added cues with video conferencing can be helpful when you are first working with other people, especially other people from other cultures who speak with an accent. Getting the additional visual reading on who they are and what they are saying can go a long way to helping with understanding them.

The second observation is that, for some types of meetings—collaborative working sessions particularly—being able to see their screen and share documents in real time is much more valuable than seeing their face for an hour (hey, don't take it personally!). That's because the focus of the collaborative working session is on a joint work artifact, and having a common visual point of reference for that is much more helpful than staring at them.

Meetings for People Who Arrange to Be Together

Meeting the people who you are working with is a really special thing—there's something about being with the other colleagues that we can't replicate with technology, no matter how great it is. But given the distances at which we live and work from others, there's a huge expense involved in actually getting together. When does it make sense to do this?

The General Rule for Face-to-Face Meetings

As a general rule, meet face to face when:

- There is a lot of intensive work to be done over a short period of time.

- Lots of interactive conversation is required to do so.

One example of when it makes sense is at the very start of the project, particularly when people have not worked together before. Bringing everyone to the same place for a three-day to four-day intensive project workshop enables people to meet and learn a bit about the other people on the team, it gives them the opportunity to see how other people work and how they argue their points, and it enables the quick free-flow of information between everyone at the same time. And it enables focused time and effort, rather than divided time and effort on lots of different aspects of work and living. A team can easily get done in three days of intensive work what could be stretched out over one to two months of back-and-forth communication and miscommunication.

A second time that it makes a lot of sense for an in-person meeting is when there are some big decisions to be made, and especially where people hold very different perspectives on what the decision should be. There will be a lot of interactive debate, arguing, theorizing, and rapid interaction, so trying to get this done over SharePoint is doomed to failure. The tool doesn't fit the work required—that is, what the team needs is not well served by SharePoint. However, SharePoint can be very well used leading up to the in-person meeting, as a place for capturing the agenda of the time together, the main points of agreement and disagreement between the people, and any background reading required for everyone to come to the session ready for a productive time together.

A third time that it makes sense for in-person work is whenever there is an intensive period of co-creation work to be done between two or three people on the team—that is, not the whole team, but a few people who need to do detailed work. So it's very valid for a couple or three people on the team to be put together when they have a major piece of work that has to be finalized within a short period of time. Being together and working intensively together allows for the people to rapidly share ideas, to get feedback live and in real time from others, and to do co-creation that otherwise would be hampered by the technology.

Here's another way of thinking about it. Sometimes the number of time zones being crossed means that there is only one to two hours a day where everyone is actually in the office or online at the same time, and thus available for real-time interaction. And when you have a lot to talk about, even if you cajole the others on the team, they might be able to stretch another hour here or there, but they have commitments outside of the project that are important and that need to be done. You can't expect someone on the other side of the world to suddenly get up at midnight their time for three days in a row in order to hold full-day workshops. You need to get together in person.

What If You Need to Meet Face to Face, But Can't?

As good as this sounds, sometimes there just isn't the budget available for flying people around, and you just can't meet. Or an in-person meeting can't be held due to other project commitments or family responsibilities. So what then? You have to make do, and you have to make do as best you can. Talk frequently—even if it's just one to one. Assign sub-tasks to two or three people, and ask them to work away on a recommendation for tabling with the wider group. Go to the local video conferencing bureau and hire rooms in all of the places where you are, and hold a multi-hour meeting by video conference. Argue to your CFO that you really, really, absolutely need a Cisco TelePresence suite or two at the office. Do whatever it takes to get the job done.

Keep Other Team Members Up to Date with Meeting Happenings

Keeping the other team members informed about the meetings that are happening is a good discipline. The way to do this is through the team blog. You don't have to write a long summary of the meeting, but do write something, such as the following:

- Who attended the face-to-face meeting, and where it was held

- The key topics of conversation from the meeting, and where more information can be found

- If everyone attending the meeting went out for dinner on one of the evenings, a photo from the dinner helps the others to feel that they were there—albeit in a small way, but the sharing of those experiences is good to do

Being disciplined in posting about meeting happenings also means that if other people are working on related issues, they will know that they should be talking to you. This helps with the reduction of duplication within the team, and with the creation of stronger links between people.

Sharing Documents via Groove 2007

One of the capabilities that we touched on briefly in Chapter 4, "Team, Meet SharePoint," was the use of Groove 2007 for sharing documents with external people. Let's talk about that a bit more here. With a document library in SharePoint, anyone who can get to SharePoint can access those documents, assuming they have the right privileges. But what about the external people who cannot?

Groove 2007 can be used to share a document library with external people who cannot access your SharePoint installation. The way this works is that one of the people on the team with access to SharePoint connects the document library to a Groove Shared Space, and then invites other Groove users to access the Groove Shared Space.

This is a powerful capability in a number of situations:

- Where external people don't need access to all of the team coordination work, just some of the documents for a short-term involvement on the project

- Where an external marketing firm or research firm is asked to look at some documents related to the team project, and where rather than sending the documents around via e-mail, they agree to use Groove, with all of the attendant security capabilities therein

- When one person on the team is going to be offline for a few days, and will be unable to access SharePoint, but still wants to work on some of the documents while they are away

To connect a SharePoint document library to Groove 2007, follow the steps in the following sections.

Create a Groove Shared Space for Sharing

The first step is to create a new shared space in Groove 2007. Open Groove 2007, click New Workspace, and give the new workspace a name that ties it visually to your Inner Team site. Use the Standard workspace type (see Figure 7-19). Click OK.

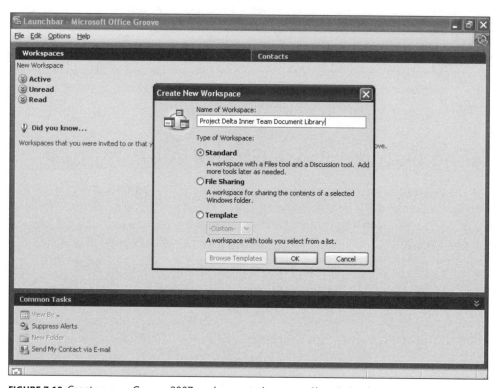

FIGURE 7-19 Create a new Groove 2007 workspace to host your SharePoint document library.

Add a SharePoint Files Tool to Groove

When the new workspace opens, in the Common Tasks pane on the lower-right side of the Groove interface, click Add Tools. From the More Tools dialog box, select the SharePoint Files check box, and then click OK (see Figure 7-20).

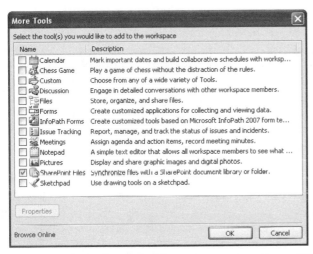

FIGURE 7-20 Add a SharePoint Files tool to your new Groove 2007 shared space.

You now need to connect the SharePoint Files tool to a SharePoint document library or a folder within a document library. Click the Setup button to start (see Figure 7-21).

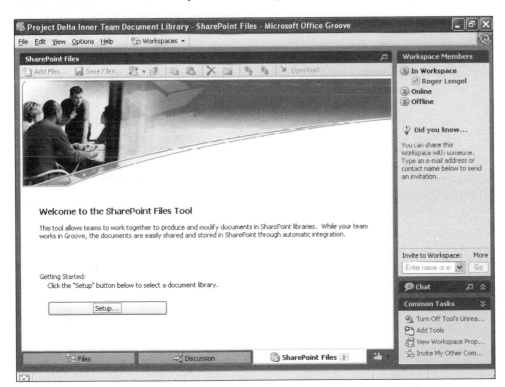

FIGURE 7-21 Click the Setup button to connect Groove to a SharePoint document library.

You are now able to navigate your SharePoint sites, and choose the document library or the folder within the document library that you want to connect. Double-click your way through the document library until you find the folder you want to connect, and then click Select. In Figure 7-22, Roger has selected the whole Shared Documents library rather than just a folder within it.

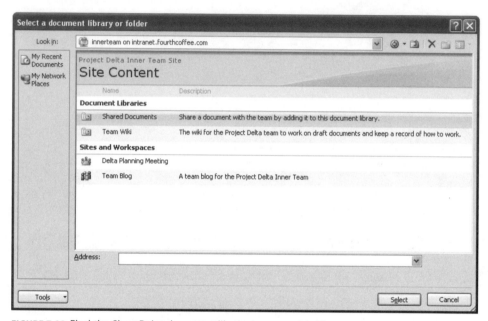

FIGURE 7-22 Find the SharePoint document library to connect to Groove.

Groove 2007 then connects to SharePoint and synchronizes all of the folders and documents in the document library (or sub-folders and documents if only a folder was selected. Groove then keeps its SharePoint Files tool in synchronization with the appropriate document library in SharePoint (see Figure 7-23).

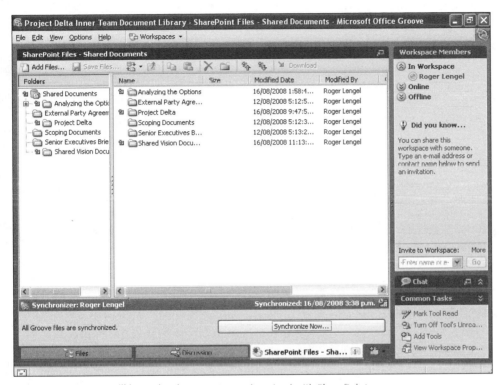

FIGURE 7-23 Groove will keep the documents synchronized with SharePoint.

Invite Other Groove Users to the Shared Space

After you have connected the two together, invite other users to join you in the Groove Workspace, using the More option next to Invite To Workspace. You can enter people's e-mail addresses, or if you know their Groove user names, enter that (see Figure 7-24). After you have entered everyone's name, click OK and you will be prompted for a welcome message for each invitee.

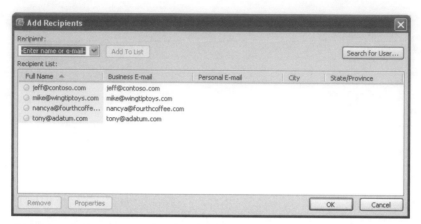

FIGURE 7-24 Invite other people using their e-mail address or Groove user name to join the Groove shared space.

Synchronize Between Groove and SharePoint

With the SharePoint document library connected to Groove, any changes in the documents and files in either place will be synchronized to the other place whenever there's a network connection. In addition, the user who connected Groove to SharePoint can manually initiate a synchronization of the two places at any time.

CHAPTER 8

Making a Decision

WITH THE VARIOUS OPTIONS FULLY ANALYZED, Roger knew that it was decision time. But more than merely making a decision and getting on with it, it was time to make a tentative decision and then to seek input and clarification from the stakeholders and sponsors alike. Roger had been in business for long enough to know that buy-in from the stakeholders was absolutely critical to the eventual success of this initiative, or any initiative for that matter.

Roger pulled out his pad and favorite pen again, and started scribbling down some key ideas. By the end of five minutes, he had drafted a broad framework for this last stage of Project Delta. First, the team needed to come to a common agreement about which option to proceed with. Second, they would need to draft a document encapsulating their chosen recommendation, and then get input and feedback on the recommended direction from the stakeholders and sponsors in Fourth Coffee. And finally, after they had received feedback and additional comments— positive or negative—they would need to work through each of those points and either fully revise their recommendation or merely do some tidying up around the edges.

Roger picked up the phone and dialed Gareth Chan in IT. "Gareth, this is Roger. I need some direction. I need to find out which recom- mendation everyone on the team thinks we should go with. What's the best way to do so, please?" he asked.

"Great question, Roger," Gareth said. "Let's have a talk about surveys."

What "Should" We Do?

The fourth stage of the Five Phases Project Life Cycle Model—and actually the last stage that involves directly working on the content of the project—is making a decision aligned with the shared vision of the project. The team has clarity on what it is working toward, they have brainstormed a plethora of options, some of those options have been fully explored to flesh out consequences and implications, and now it is decision time. What "should" we do becomes the focus of the team—based on all the work that the team has done together leading up to this point.

Making a Decision Within the Team

It's decision time! The team has gone through a lot together already, and the team members have put in time and effort over weeks and months to work effectively, to work collaboratively, and to move toward the shared vision that they collectively and individually embraced. Actually, the team has been making decisions already throughout the whole project—who would talk to what stakeholder, how each would contribute to brainstorming, and the analysis projects that they would work on. So the making of decisions is an essential aspect of team work throughout the life of a team, but this phase is particularly focused on decision making.

Stepping Up

There is a key change that the team has to embrace when it comes time to make a decision: each person has to put aside the feeling of personal ownership for the specific ideas they worked on, and look with new eyes at all of the ideas that were worked on by the team as a whole. The dynamic has to be making the best decision as a team, not about getting your idea across the line in preference to anyone else's ideas.

Pre-Work for Making a Decision

By following the Five Phases Project Life Cycle Model, the team has laid a tremendous foundation for making a decision. They knew what was wanted—the shared vision—and they have talked about, strategized on, and lived out the movement toward that shared vision. After the shared vision was clearly known, no one jumped to an immediate answer—that is, made a quick decision—but rather the whole team shared its ideas through brainstorming all of the options. And then a rigorous process of joint research and analysis was undertaken to fully explore the shape, consequences, and downfalls of each of the options.

The research and analysis for each option is stored in a specific folder in the team's Shared Documents library. This makes it very easy for each team member to access the collective work of the team on all of the options. Equally, because a common approach was taken for analyzing the options—for example, by using the Idea Analysis Briefing template—everyone on the team has a common expectation about what they will find for ideas that they didn't work on personally. With all of the analysis in SharePoint, no documents need to be sent around, because it is all commonly accessible to the team.

The first step in making a final decision is to help everyone in the team become aware of all of the options. The team may have individually worked on one or two or three analysis projects, depending on the number of the options that were explored, but their awareness of and familiarity with the other ideas is likely to be limited. That needs to change, and there a number of ways this can happen:

- Each team member can read through the Idea Analysis Briefing documents for each option.

- The sub-groups that worked on each option can prepare a presentation on the idea and present it to the others (using SharedView or Live Meeting).

- A different sub-group to the one that worked on a given idea can prepare it for presentation to the rest of the team.

Regardless of what strategy is embraced, everyone on the team needs a shared understanding of all of the options.

Getting a Sense of the Decision Through a SharePoint Survey

One of the early things to understand when it is time to make a decision is where the team members are leaning with respect to the draft recommendation. Getting a sense of either the commonality or divergence of opinion is critical to knowing how to make the draft decision:

- If there is a high degree of commonality in opinion, the remainder of the team work can be done without a face-to-face decision meeting.

- If there is a wide variation of opinion, a face-to-face meeting is probably going to be necessary to give team members enough time and space to come to a consensus.

The way to get this sense in SharePoint is to use a team survey. By using the survey and voting capabilities in SharePoint, the people with access to a specific SharePoint site can give their individual input and then see where their input fits in relation to the input of everyone else.

Add a Survey List to SharePoint

The first step to using a survey to get an initial sense of which way the team is leaning is to add a survey list to the Project Delta Inner Team site. Follow the standard approach to do this, clicking Survey on the Create page (see Figure 8-1).

FIGURE 8-1 Add a survey list to the Project Delta Inner Team site.

On the New page, you need to enter the base information for your survey, including its name and description, whether it should display on the Quick Launch bar, whether the survey options should be anonymous, and whether people can fill out the survey more than once (see Figure 8-2). For this survey, results should not be anonymous, and each person should have one vote. When you are done, click Next.

FIGURE 8-2 Give the survey a name and description, and select the base options.

Create the Survey Options

With the shell of the survey created, the next step is to define the question or questions that are asked in the survey itself. You will quickly see the similarity with a custom list in SharePoint—first create the shell of the list, and then create the columns inside the list. It's the same thing with a survey: create the shell of a survey, and then create the questions to ask.

In this case, we have one or two questions that we want to ask:

- What is the best option for meeting the shared vision of our project?

- What is the second best option for meeting the shared vision of our project?

Just like you can choose from many different types of columns to create in a custom list, you can choose from many different types of questions (see Figure 8-3). This means that we can ask a question and predefine how we want to collect the answers—whether as free text for richness of expression and insight, or as a predefined selection to ease collation and analysis.

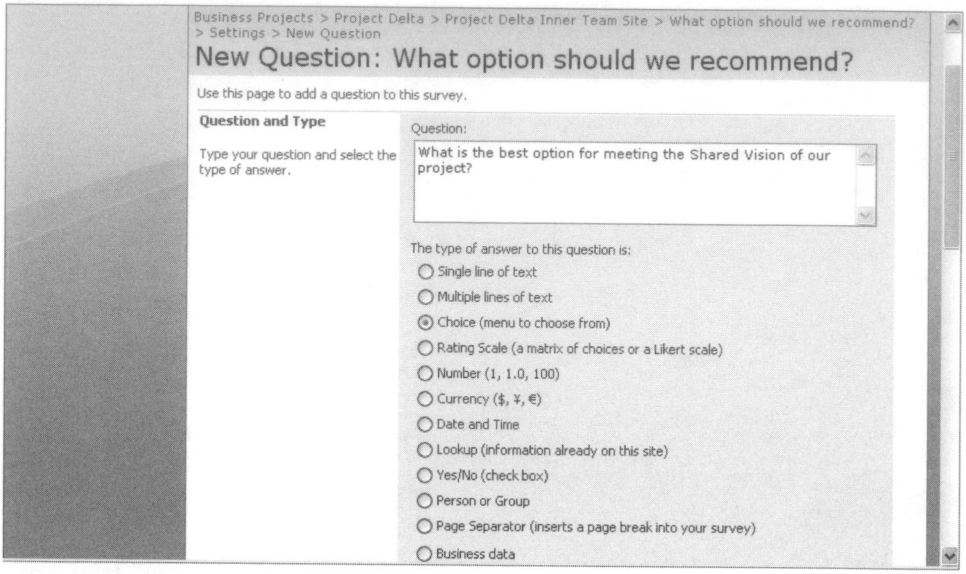

FIGURE 8-3 Questions in surveys have an associated type that specifies how answers are collected.

For the "What's the best option?" question we are asking in this survey, the type could either be Choice (Menu To Choose From) or it could be Lookup (Information Already On This Site). If we choose Choice, then we need to enter the options again. If we choose Lookup, we can tell the question to present a list of options from another list or library in the SharePoint site. Because we already have the list of options noted in the Analyzing The Options custom list, we will look at that.

After you select Lookup as the type, the Additional Question Settings are revised to show the appropriate configuration options. Select Analyzing The Options in the Get Information From list, and select which column from the list should be used to give the options in the survey (see Figure 8-4).

Because we are going to ask for a second-best option, too, click Next Question and set it up in the same way. After you have done so, click Finish.

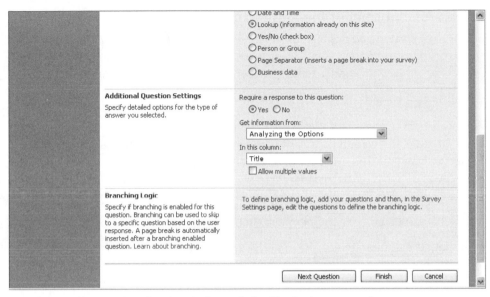

FIGURE 8-4 Look up the list of options in the Analyzing The Options custom list.

Your new survey is added to the Surveys group on the Quick Launch bar, and clicking What Option Should We Recommend? brings up the entry page of the survey (see Figure 8-5).

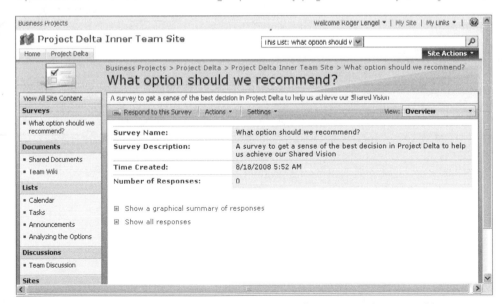

FIGURE 8-5 The home page for the survey shows summary information on the status of the survey.

Create an Announcement Inviting People to Fill Out the Survey

With the survey created and populated with the list of decision candidates, it is time to ask the team to weigh in with their votes. Because we are talking about a coordination issue for the entire team, use an announcement to request each person to fill out the survey.

When you write the announcement, include the following:

- A statement to the effect that the outcome of the survey is not the final decision of the team, but is rather a way of gathering input to help with making the final decision, be that through a conference call or a face-to-face meeting.

- A brief insight into how the survey is set up—in this case, that it has two questions. It's good to let everyone know what to expect, and if the survey is long (unlike this one), how much time team members should set aside for responding.

- A request that people read the underlying documents for each of the options before filling out the survey. If someone just proceeds with an awareness of what they wrote and an ignorance of what everyone else wrote, that is not going to work very well! Everyone needs to be starting from a similar place of prerequisites.

- The link to the survey page, so each person can click from the announcement directly to the survey and fill it out.

With each person having an e-mail alert or RSS feed for the Announcements list, they will be informed of what is required of them in fairly short order.

Fill Out the Survey

When you click within your announcement alert to open the survey, you can click Show A Graphical Summary Of Responses to see the current status of thinking, or you can proceed immediately to fill out the survey. To fill out the survey, click Respond To This Survey. Given the simple nature of our survey, the two questions are shown on one page (see Figure 8-6). Note that the survey does not ask you for your name—SharePoint knows who you are, and will associate your name with your answer in the case of non-anonymous surveys.

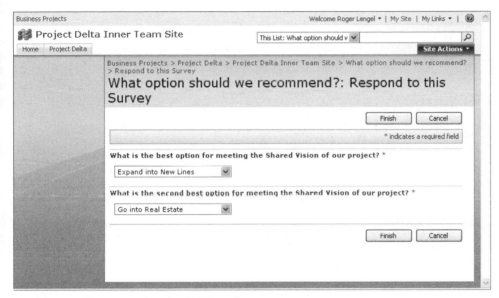

FIGURE 8-6 Each team member should fill out the survey.

When you have filled in your answers, click Finish. If you try to fill out the survey again, SharePoint will tell you that you can't, because the survey was set up to allow only one response per person.

Look at the Completed Survey

After everyone has finished entering their vote for the various options on the survey, you can see a collation of the results across the team. When you open the home page of the survey, SharePoint displays details about the survey (such as its name and the number of responses). It also includes a link to show a graphical summary of the responses (see Figure 8-7 for an example). With a graphical display, team member names are not shown.

To see how each person voted, click Show All Responses on the home page of the survey. This opens a list view of all survey responses, and you can open each response in turn and see the answers of each person (see Figure 8-8).

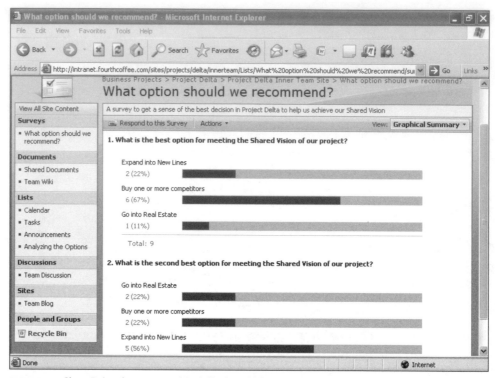

FIGURE 8-7 SharePoint shows a graphical display of all the answers to a survey.

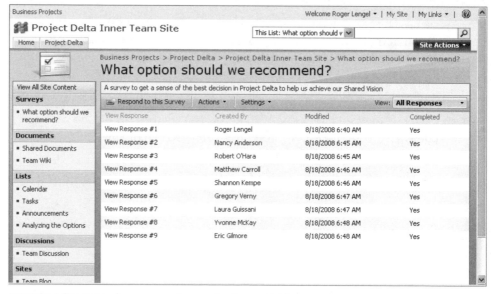

FIGURE 8-8 Team members can see how each other voted for non-anonymous surveys.

Other Uses for Surveys

We have used the survey capability of SharePoint for finding out the degree of alignment between the team members on decision candidates, but there are many other places where surveys can be used with team work—there's enough to explore and understand with surveys that it could be a book just by itself! Here are just three of the many other places where surveys could be used:

- The team could have used a survey in the Shared Vision phase, for getting a sense of where people would like to hold the post-project team celebration.

- The team could have used a survey in the Understanding the Options phase, for voting on whether they wanted to do brainstorming via OneNote, a conference call, or the SharePoint wiki. This would show the summarized preferences of the collective team, and how they want to work.

- The team could have used a survey in the Analyzing the Options phase for narrowing down the wide range of options to a short list of three to five key options for detailed analysis.

Surveys are a good way to quickly get structured feedback from everyone on the team when the survey options are clear. Don't be afraid to use them widely!

Surveys can be used to collect anonymous feedback, too. When you design a survey, you can tie the response to a person (making it open as to who thinks what), or you can make it anonymous (keeping each person's real opinion private and not linked to them). Anonymous surveys are particularly helpful when the subject matter is personally sensitive and the group taking the survey is large and their feelings unknown. In smaller teams, when you have worked alongside other people for weeks or months on a common project, anonymous surveys are less important, because although the survey result will not be tied to someone's name, people can usually guess who has the dissenting opinion. So you don't gain anything by doing an anonymous survey in a small team where strong awareness of each other already exists.

> **SEE ALSO** Given the extensive options available for using surveys, a great reference and training manual is *Microsoft Windows SharePoint Services 3.0 Step by Step*, by Olga Londer, Bill English, Todd Bleeker, and Penelope Coventry (Microsoft Press, 2007).

Making a Decision Through a Conference Call

If the results of the survey show a high degree of alignment and commonality on the decision candidate across the team, then schedule a conference call to thrash out the remaining issues. To find the best meeting time, look at the Common Working Hours page in the Team Wiki in SharePoint. After you have found the best time to meet, create a meeting in the team's SharePoint calendar with the meeting details.

The actual degree of commonality on the decision candidate will dictate how much pre-meeting preparation is required by different members of the team. For example:

- If the vast majority of the team has a common preference for one decision candidate, and one team member has a preference for a second decision candidate, that team member needs to create a presentation outlining the reasons for favoring the second approach. When the conference call is held, the team member should present these reasons by using Live Meeting or SharedView, and then there should be a discussion with the rest of the team in response to the main points.

- If everyone on the team thinks the same thing and has lined up behind one decision candidate, then an agenda of remaining matters for discussion needs to be drawn up. Perhaps the team generally agrees on the decision candidate, but some of the team members have some concerns that they want to discuss more fully. These should be documented in advance of the meeting, so that everyone has a common understanding of the focus of the meeting, and how best to prepare for it.

At the conclusion of the conference call, if a final and shared decision on the decision candidate has been made, the team can proceed to writing the draft recommendation. If no decision has been made, and the team has become stuck, there are two options. One option is for the team leader or a business sponsor to take the input and make a final decision themselves. The second option is to organize a face-to-face meeting where there is more time and space to talk through and debate the options.

Making a Decision Through a Face-to-Face Meeting

In situations where there is a high degree of variance in the survey results on the best way to move forward, a face-to-face meeting is a great way to resolve the variation and come to a consensus. In remote team situations where people work across multiple time zones, finding a common time to meet for longer than an hour or two can be really complex. And when you have a major decision to make—such as how the team should recommend the business or organization to proceed—it's time to pull out the stops and get on those planes.

How do you decide where and when to meet, and even if a face-to-face meeting is most appropriate. Here are the key steps:

- Can the variation be resolved through a conference call, as mentioned previously? If you haven't yet tried to resolve the differences of opinion through a conference call, now is the time to try. Run the meeting, and run a second conference call if required, and if there is still a clear split in the group and no greater common ground has been found, then that's a signal that a face-to-face meeting is required.

- Think about whether everyone needs to meet in person, or just a subset of the wider team. Although it may be nice to have everyone come together, perhaps it is not necessary. For example, if the team is divided into two sub-groups over which decision candidate to embrace, each sub-group could choose a couple of representatives to meet with the others. This would greatly reduce the amount of interruption caused by travel demands, and the amount of money that would need to be spent. After the representatives from both sub-groups meet, they need to report back to the wider team about their findings—either through a follow-up phone call, or a written document.

- Decide the best location to hold the face-to-face meeting. Some cities are really expensive to fly into, and have high accommodation and food costs. Others are not so expensive. When you start to consider the best place to meet, perhaps everyone should travel to a less expensive location, rather than having most people travel to a location that others call home. If the team is crossing country boundaries, maybe meeting in the middle is a more cost effective approach.

- If people are going to travel for a face-to-face meeting, you need to have the expectation that they are traveling for a two- to three-day meeting. It should be a significant period of time, not just a short meeting. Face-to-face meetings cause so much disruption to work life and family life, that is has to be worth it.

You can definitely use tools in SharePoint to support the decision process for deciding where to meet:

- Use an Excel worksheet to calculate meeting costs for different scenarios, and post the worksheet for everyone to read and access in an appropriate subfolder in SharePoint. Hopefully, your organization already has a special Excel template for calculating travel costs, and if it does, it should be linked up as a content type in your team site. If there isn't one, create a worksheet that works for you in this situation, and then ask IT to make it more widely available so everyone in the organization can derive future benefit from your work.

- Use a survey to find out when people are able to travel in the upcoming weeks, or use a page in the wiki to do the same thing. The survey idea is neat because it gives a graphical depiction of where everyone is, and that's easy to understand at a glance. Likewise, the wiki is a neat idea because of its simplicity. Use the option that works best for you and the team.

After the meeting, and especially if there were only some people from the group in attendance, a detailed writeup of the meeting and its outcomes should be prepared. The writeup itself should be uploaded into a folder in the team's document library, with an announcement to tell everyone that it's there and what was agreed.

One final step is required if not everyone was at the meeting: there has to be a follow-up conference call where the two sub-groups can report back about what they discussed, and how they resolved the issues they were facing.

If there is still no common agreement on outcomes, then it's time to do one of the following:

- Bring in a facilitator to help the two sub-groups move toward a resolution.
- Ask the lead sponsor to make a decision that's binding on all parties.

Writing the Draft Recommendation

After the team has come to a conclusion on the best way forward—the team has defined and agreed the best decision candidate—it's time to write up the recommendation so as to communicate the draft recommendation to everyone else. This draft recommendation is going to have some major sections:

- The shared vision of the team's work. You can draw a good summary of this from the Team Wiki, where all of this has already been documented.

- The main options that were considered as possibilities during the project. You can get the list of these from the custom list that was developed for tracking progress on the options.

- The recommendation that the team is making for meeting the shared vision, along with the major reasons and supporting arguments for doing so.

There are two main ways to write the draft recommendation:

- Use the Team Wiki, creating a new wiki page from the team's content page in the wiki. If you want to divide the writing work, create sub-wiki pages from the Draft Recommendation wiki page, so that different people on the team can work on their parts without stepping on the toes of others.

- Use Word 2007 for writing the document, creating it from within the appropriate folder in the team's document library.

Sharing the Draft Recommendation

With the draft recommendation written, you now need to get feedback on the work from the key stakeholders. Where you need to get to is an awareness of how satisfied each stakeholder group is with the draft recommendation, and how willing they will be to support it as a final recommendation. Also, this is a perfect time to discover any requirements that you have overlooked, or downstream implications that the team has not considered. Hopefully, both of these will be minor, but it is much better to find out now than after the final recommendation has been signed off and implementation is underway.

There are seven steps involved in getting feedback from your stakeholders:

1. Make a list of who you need to brief.

2. Decide who is going to brief each group.

3. Determine the best method of briefing them.

4. Assign a weighting as to your expected success in briefing them. Or to put it another way, make it clear within the team who is expected to be easy to brief, and who is expected to be really difficult to brief.

5. Schedule the briefing time.

6. Give the briefing.

7. Capture, document, and share the feedback given by each group.

Deciding Who You Need to Brief

Deciding who you need to brief, who is going to do each briefing, the best way of briefing them, and assessing their brief-ability is a good situation for either a wiki page (where the number of people or groups to be briefed is low, such as four to five groups), or a custom list (where the number is higher).

If you create the list by using a wiki page, create a table in the wiki and get the various fields filled out. You'll need columns for each of the main pieces of information you need to track: name of the group, name of the briefing party, method of briefing, and assessed brief-ability (see Figure 8-9).

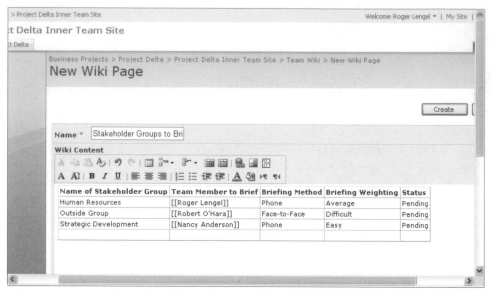

FIGURE 8-9 Create a table in the wiki to track who needs to be briefed.

For situations where more than four or five groups are involved, a custom list could be a better way to go. Remember when we created a custom list for the list of options that we were going to analyze, back in Chapter 7, "Analyzing the Options"? Follow the same process to create a custom list in this situation, for who you need to brief. Here are the columns you need to create, and the type of each column (see Figure 8-10):

- Name of the group to brief (text).

- Name of the person to do the briefing (text).

- The method of briefing each group. Some groups will need a face-to-face meeting, others a conference call, and some will be fine with an e-mail message. So create a choice list, with those three as the options.

- An assessment of brief-ability (choice list, with three options: Easy, Average, or Difficult).

- Status of the briefing (choice list, with Pending, Scheduled, and Completed as the options).

- You could also have a notes field, for people to write any notes or thoughts as they are working through the ideas.

- A place to include the link to the SharePoint Team Wiki where the feedback from the briefing is documented, or to the document in the document library that the group sent in response to the e-mail request.

FIGURE 8-10 Use a custom list to track stakeholder briefings when you have a lot of stakeholders.

After you have created the new list, assemble the list of groups to brief. Draw heavily on the list of groups that were interviewed back at the beginning of the project, when the shared vision was being assembled.

Getting the Critics Involved Early

As you look through the list of groups to brief, some of the groups will be potentially more problematic than others—these are the groups that you and the team have flagged as Difficult. If that's the case, then you need to take extra precautions in briefing them, and take extra time in the due diligence part of getting ready to brief them.

The key question that you need to answer is "Why do we think this group will be difficult to brief?" What is it about the group that you and the team are concerned about? In doing the due diligence in preparation for your briefing with them, you will need a common place to document what you see as being their main concerns, and the strategy that you will follow for dealing with each major concern. Some possible concerns and suggested mitigations are:

- The recommendation that you have developed is not ideal for the group. They would have preferred another recommendation. The mitigation you develop will need to address in extra details why you chose the recommendation you did, along with a comparison chart showing the differences between the recommendation and their preferred option.

- There are personality conflicts between people on your team and people from the other group. These bad feelings threaten to derail implementation of the work. The mitigation you develop will need to downplay individual contributions to the draft recommendation, and emphasize the work of the team as a whole.

- The group has subsequently asserted additional requirements from the work, but it's too late to take these into consideration. The mitigation that you prepare for this situation will depend on the severity of their new requirements, and how much they deviate from the main emphasis of all of your other work to date. If the deviation is large, then you will need to explain that it's too late. Maybe a subsequent project can take into consideration the new requirements, or maybe it's just too late.

Managing Communications with Key Stakeholders

With the list of key groups identified, and mitigations planned for the difficult groups, get the team ready to go with the different briefings. Remember that depending on the group involved, and the relationship that the team has with the group in question, the briefing will take one of three forms: a face-to-face meeting, a conference call, or simply an e-mail message.

How SharePoint Helps with Real-Time Meetings

For the face-to-face meetings and the conference calls, schedule the meetings and note the agreed dates in the team calendar. Each team member running a briefing in person or over the phone needs to keep the briefing table or list up to date, so as to keep everyone in the team current with what's going on. Anytime someone wants to review the status of the briefings, or to see what feedback was given by the different groups, all they need to do is look at the wiki page or view the custom list.

How SharePoint Helps with E-Mail Briefings

For the groups that are being briefed by e-mail, and assuming that there's a lot of them, develop an e-mail template in the Team Wiki. Let one of the team members draft the e-mail cover note for the document in the wiki, and then get other people on the team to review and edit the page. After everyone on the team is happy with the text of the cover note, post the document into the document library in the Sponsors and Stakeholders site, and include a link to the document in the e-mail message.

Using SharePoint Workflow to Collect Feedback

There is another option to sending the document out by e-mail directly, and that is to use the workflow routing capabilities of SharePoint. There are a couple of key benefits to using workflow to distribute the documents, with the main one being trackability in SharePoint of the status of each workflow. In other words, rather than one person sending out the e-mail messages and having to manually communicate response status to everyone else via a SharePoint list or wiki table—or even in response to being asked by phone or e-mail—any team member can see the status of each review.

With Windows SharePoint Services, a couple of sample workflow processes are shipped "out-of-the-box." That means they are available to everyone, and there is no custom development of workflow process charts and rules required. These workflows have already been tested and confirmed by Microsoft, and so are well suited to tasks that align with their design. Luckily for us, one of the workflows is named *Collect Feedback*.

Save the Draft Recommendation in Shared Documents

To start a workflow on your draft recommendation, first ensure that you have the document in a *Shared Documents* folder that the reviewers are able to access. This would be the Shared Documents library in the Sponsors and Stakeholders site.

Click the down arrow next to the document, and then click Workflows (see Figure 8-11).

WHAT HAPPENS IF YOU START THE WORKFLOW IN THE INNER TEAM SITE?

When a workflow task is assigned to someone, the intention is that they will click the alert they receive and be pulled into the site containing the document and the workflow. If they are unable to access the site where the document is stored, they will still be told they have a task to do, but will also be told they can't access it. Talk about frustrating!

So the rule is: When you create a workflow task for someone, make sure they are able to access the required site.

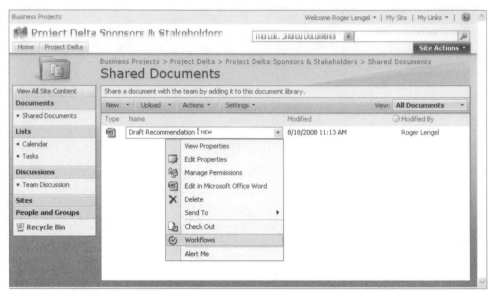

FIGURE 8-11 Select Workflows from the list to start a workflow process on a document.

This opens the Workflows page, and unless your IT department has removed the ability to run the two default workflows, one of the workflows is named *Collect Feedback* (see Figure 8-12).

FIGURE 8-12 The Workflows page for a document showing two out-of-the-box workflows

Start the Collect Feedback Workflow

To start the Collect Feedback workflow, click Collect Feedback on the Workflows page. This opens a new page where you enter the names of the people who you want feedback from, along with the message to be sent with your feedback request (see Figure 8-13). Click the Reviewers button to select reviewers from the directory, and then type an introductory message to the reviewers. Enter a Due Date and, if required, the names of other people who should be notified that this workflow has been started. When you have finished entering the details, click Start.

FIGURE 8-13 Enter the names of the reviewers, an introductory message, and other details for the Collect Feedback workflow.

SharePoint starts the workflow, and displays a "working page" indicating that it is setting up the workflow. It also modifies the document library—adding a Collect Feedback column to the view of documents—to tell you (and everyone else who visits) that the workflow has begun (see Figure 8-14).

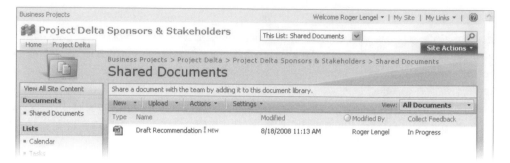

FIGURE 8-14 SharePoint adds a Collect Feedback column to the document library.

View Workflow Status

With the Collect Feedback process underway, you can check on the status of the tasks at any time by clicking Workflows from the drop-down list on a document in the document library. This opens the Workflows page that we used to start the workflow, but now the Collect Feedback workflow has been shifted into the Running Workflows area (see Figure 8-15).

Clicking into the Collect Feedback workflow allows anyone on the team to see the status of the tasks within the workflow, and you can also see a history trail for the workflow (see Figure 8-16).

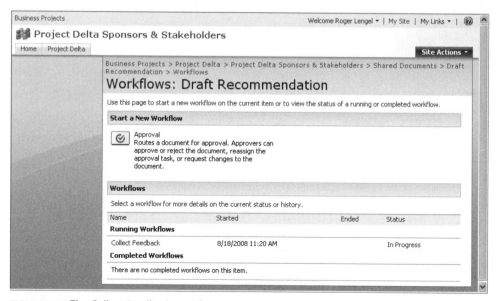

FIGURE 8-15 The Collect Feedback workflow is now running.

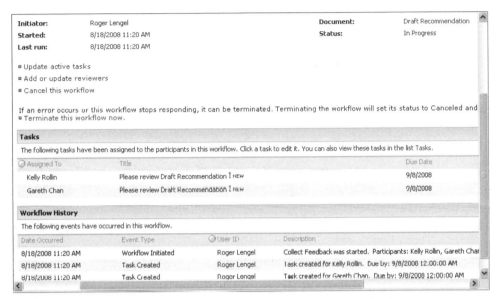

Initiator:	Roger Lengel		Document:	Draft Recommendation
Started:	8/18/2008 11:20 AM		Status:	In Progress
Last run:	8/18/2008 11:20 AM			

▪ Update active tasks
▪ Add or update reviewers
▪ Cancel this workflow

If an error occurs or this workflow stops responding, it can be terminated. Terminating the workflow will set its status to Canceled and
▪ Terminate this workflow now.

Tasks

The following tasks have been assigned to the participants in this workflow. Click a task to edit it. You can also view these tasks in the list Tasks.

Assigned To	Title	Due Date
Kelly Rollin	Please review Draft Recommendation ⁎ NEW	9/8/2008
Gareth Chan	Please review Draft Recommendation ⁎ NEW	9/8/2008

Workflow History

The following events have occurred in this workflow.

Date Occurred	Event Type	User ID	Description
8/18/2008 11:20 AM	Workflow Initiated	Roger Lengel	Collect Feedback was started. Participants: Kelly Rollin, Gareth Chan
8/18/2008 11:20 AM	Task Created	Roger Lengel	Task created for Kelly Rollin. Due by: 9/8/2008 12:00:00 AM
8/18/2008 11:20 AM	Task Created	Roger Lengel	Task created for Gareth Chan. Due by: 9/8/2008 12:00:00 AM

FIGURE 8-16 Open the workflow to see the status of each task and the workflow history.

Provide Feedback on the Workflow

Let's become one of the reviewers and see what happens when we create a workflow
task for them. In this case, we'll become Kelly Rollin, Roger's boss, who was one of the
people who Roger asked to provide feedback on the draft recommendation. Kelly
receives an e-mail message from SharePoint, telling her of the new task that has been
assigned to her, and provides a link to the document and instructions on completing
the task (see Figure 8-17).

When a reviewer clicks the document name in the e-mail alert, the document is opened
directly from SharePoint in Word (if it's a Word document) or whatever other application
is appropriate given the nature of the file. In the dialog box to confirm opening directly
from SharePoint, click Open (see Figure 8-18).

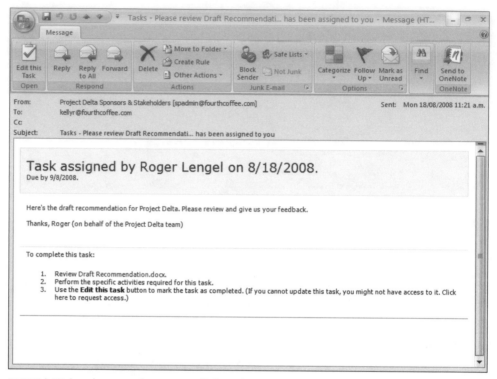

FIGURE 8-17 A reviewer receives an e-mail alert of a new workflow task.

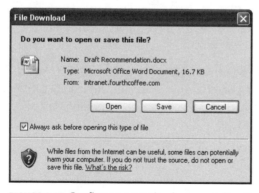

FIGURE 8-18 Confirm to open the document directly from SharePoint.

After the document opens in Word (in this case), there are two notes shown at the top (see Figure 8-19). The first says that it is a server document. To edit it, you need to click the Edit Document button. The second contains the link to the workflow task.

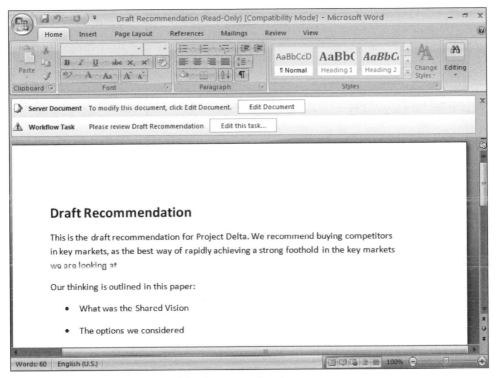

FIGURE 8-19 Two notes at the top of the document alert the user.

Let's assume that Kelly is going to edit the document to add some comments before she completes the workflow task. She clicks Edit Document and makes the changes she wants to make. She then saves the document, which saves it directly back into SharePoint.

In order to complete the workflow task, Kelly then clicks Edit This Task, which opens a dialog box that shows the details of the task: who assigned it, when it is due, the nature of the task, and a space for typing feedback (see Figure 8-20). There are also options for reassigning the task to another person—perhaps they are better qualified to make a judgment call—and the option to request a change, by pushing the task back to the person who kicked it off. For Kelly's purposes, however, she is pretty happy with what the team has pulled together, so enters her feedback and clicks Send Feedback.

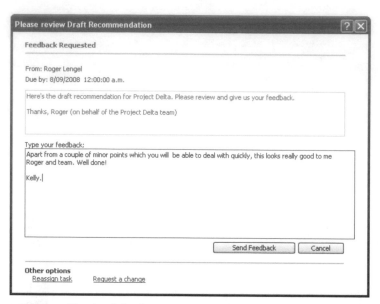

FIGURE 8-20 Use the dialog box to enter your feedback on the document in a Collect Feedback workflow.

With the Send Feedback button clicked, SharePoint is told to update the workflow task to completed (for this reviewer), and Kelly is free to close the document.

Review Feedback on the Document

After all of the people who were asked to take part in the Collect Feedback workflow process have completed their review, the person who started the workflow receives an e-mail alert. The alert advises them that the workflow is now finished, and it lists the feedback that each person gave (see Figure 8-21).

By clicking View The Workflow History at the bottom of the e-mail alert, the user is taken directly to the page in SharePoint where the history (and the current status of the workflow) is displayed (see Figure 8-22).

And even better than having an at-a-glance summary of the complete workflow history—which is great for showing due diligence in key processes and at key stages of the team's work—there is only one copy of the document, and that's stored directly in SharePoint. The lead author of the document—Roger in this case—doesn't now need to merge and integrate multiple editions of the same original document to see what everyone said. Because the Collect Feedback process in SharePoint was used, the team has been able to avoid document chaos.

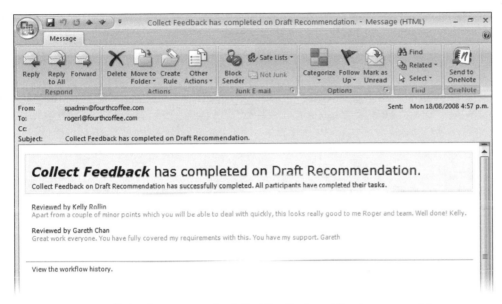

Collect Feedback has completed on Draft Recommendation.

Collect Feedback on Draft Recommendation has successfully completed. All participants have completed their tasks.

Reviewed by Kelly Rollin
Apart from a couple of minor points which you will be able to deal with quickly, this looks really good to me Roger and team. Well done! Kelly.

Reviewed by Gareth Chan
Great work everyone. You have fully covered my requirements with this. You have my support. Gareth

View the workflow history.

FIGURE 8-21 An e-mail alert is sent to say the Collect Feedback workflow is now complete.

Workflow History

The following events have occurred in this workflow.

Date Occurred	Event Type	User ID	Description	Outcome
8/18/2008 11:20 AM	Workflow Initiated	Roger Lengel	Collect Feedback was started. Participants: Kelly Rollin, Gareth Chan	
8/18/2008 11:20 AM	Task Created	Roger Lengel	Task created for Kelly Rollin. Due by: 9/8/2008 12:00:00 AM	
8/18/2008 11:20 AM	Task Created	Roger Lengel	Task created for Gareth Chan. Due by: 9/8/2008 12:00:00 AM	
8/18/2008 4:39 PM	Task Completed	Kelly Rollin	Task assigned to Kelly Rollin was completed by Kelly Rollin. Comments: Apart from a couple of minor points which you will be able to deal with quickly, this looks really good to me Roger and team. Well done! Kelly.	Reviewed by Kelly Rollin
8/18/2008 4:57 PM	Task Completed	Gareth Chan	Task assigned to Gareth Chan was completed by Gareth Chan. Comments: Great work everyone. You have fully covered my requirements with this. You have my support. Gareth	Reviewed by Gareth Chan
8/18/2008 4:57 PM	Workflow Completed	Roger Lengel	Collect Feedback was completed.	Collect Feedback on Draft Recommendation has successfully completed. All participants have completed

FIGURE 8-22 The workflow history lists every action that was made during the Collect Feedback process.

WORKFLOW IN SHAREPOINT: MUCH MORE TO EXPLORE

As with surveys, a whole book could be written on taking the capabilities of workflow in SharePoint and using them effectively. We have touched on one of the out-of-the-box workflow processes available with SharePoint, but Microsoft has made available an entire workflow engine and designer for creating and running ad hoc people processes and document-centric processes. Be aware that in most organizations, the IT department is the group that will actually design workflow processes for your team, so talk to your SharePoint consultant about your ideas.

One final word of advice: keep it simple. Too many workflow systems have been destroyed by unnecessary complexity. Simple is good.

Capturing Feedback from Key Stakeholders

During the conversations with the stakeholders, capture their feedback as a page in the Team Wiki, and create a link between the wiki page and the custom list used for tracking these conversations. For the stakeholders who send their feedback by e-mail or in a document attachment, copy the contents of the e-mail message into a wiki page, and save the document into the team's document library. Create a link between the page or document and the tracking list, marrying the group with their feedback, for ease of review.

Preparing the Final Recommendation

You're almost there! With all of the feedback collected, the team can review what has been passed back, and decide what that means for the draft recommendation. Perhaps it means nothing—the feedback is all positive, and there's nothing to change or tweak. It doesn't often happen, but it could in your project.

A more likely outcome is that a review of the different pieces of feedback will raise challenges to the validity of the draft recommendation, and some additional work is going to need to be done to get to a final recommendation. Do you remember how we handled this in relation to the shared vision? Document the differences in the Team Wiki, and divide the issues into common concerns. Work through and talk through the outstanding items, getting more feedback and input as required from the different groups, and update the final recommendation as appropriate. When you are done, you could use the Approval workflow process on the document.

CHAPTER 9

Concluding the Project

ROGER SLAMMED HIS PALM down on his desk in a sign of triumph. "Done! It's done," he said louder than he intended to speak. He had just received an e-mail message from Kelly Rollin informing him that the recommendations they had put through on Project Delta to the senior management team had been accepted, and that this formally marked the end of Project Delta. And a highly successful end at that, too!

Kelly had also asked Roger if he wanted to run another project like Delta again, but Roger's mind was beginning to form some other ideas that would probably involve a departure from New York. He didn't want to leave Fourth Coffee, but he was finding his thoughts dwelling in the Boston area more and more.

He owed Kelly an answer on that by tomorrow—she had said last Friday that she would need to know by Wednesday this week. But for today, he needed to conclude the formalities of the project with the team, and tidy up the Project Delta site, getting it ready for being archived. He had some great ideas for a team celebration, and was waiting on confirmation from one of the sponsors about a request he had put through.

With respect to the SharePoint team site for Project Delta, Roger had been on a conference call with Gareth Chan from IT on Monday, and Gareth had outlined the key steps involved in tidying up the Inner Team site. It wasn't really a job that Roger wanted to do, but Gareth had rightly pointed out that it had to be done by someone who was intimately involved in the project, and as the project lead, Roger was the man for the job. "Well, let's get it over and done with then," said

Roger. Turning to the SharePoint Project Delta Inner Team site for the last time, he opened the announcement list and found the link that Gareth had created to the Team Wiki with the overview of what he had to do.

"We Did It"

With the acceptance of the recommended decision from the sponsors and stakeholders comes the completion of the team's work. The team has achieved what it set out to achieve, and has provided a way forward for the sponsors and stakeholders. That may have been a recommendation, it may have been a product launch, or it may have to do with changes in a key performance indicator for the organization. Although the project itself may form part of a wider body or program of work, the specific deliverables of the project are now done.

To completely finish the work of the team, there are two remaining actions to be undertaken:

- Celebrate the completion and end the sociology of the team's work.
- Close out the SharePoint site used to facilitate the team's work.

Ending the Formal Work of the Team

Bringing the formal work of the team to an end involves both activities that the team does as a whole, and that individuals do by themselves.

Recognition and Celebration

The various people on the team have worked together over weeks and months to achieve a great performance outcome, and it's time for that work to be recognized. Although the form that such recognition takes should be dictated by the nature of the project, it should happen regardless of whether the project was big or small.

Recognition should include the following:

- Thanks from the lead sponsor for the work done. With many teams made up of distributed workers, getting everyone together for an in-person thank you ceremony is pretty unlikely. But by all means, there should be some other way that the sponsors say thank you. Have the sponsors dial into the last team conference call and verbalize their thanks. If their attendance at a conference call isn't possible, ask them to record an audio file saying thank you, and post it in the SharePoint site. Or for those particularly adept at digital video, get a recording of them saying thank you.

- Given the remote nature of teams, it's pretty hard to have a team meal to celebrate. That doesn't mean that nothing should be done, however! In many cultures, a shared meal is an important event. Give people a budget for having a meal with their family or friends in their location. Or if you have access to the facilities, have a shared meal by telepresence—of course it would be a bit funny, with one group having dinner, another eating lunch, and another having breakfast—but it would be true to life. You can at least try, right?

- Give people a gift voucher if the meal idea is not going to fly. With online retailers selling and shipping to most geographical locations, you are bound to find something that appeals. Books, computer equipment, travel items, stationery... the list is endless.

Finally, with whatever you do, ask the other members of the team to share what they did to celebrate via a photo and blog post. For example, if one person has a meal in London with some friends, request a photo and brief writeup of the celebration. This won't go the full way to creating a shared experience, but it will go some way.

Team Debriefing

With the project at an end, and the realities of project life still fresh in people's minds, schedule a conference call to debrief as a team. There are many questions that can be asked and discussed during a team debriefing, but the three key ones are:

- What was each person's best memory of the project? Perhaps it was a discussion that got very heated, but people stayed in the moment and the outcome was great. Perhaps it was a certain turn of phrase that someone wrote in a document. Perhaps it was a wild and crazy idea that someone came up with during one of the brainstorming sessions. It's good to know these things, and to give people a forum for mentioning them.

- What was the worst thing that happened during the project? This could be a fairly sensitive question to ask, but if there are wounds from careless words or actions, it is better to get them healed now than allow them to fester unattended to. Unresolved offenses will greatly diminish the effectiveness of future collaborative team work, so do whatever it takes to get everyone back to a place of willingness to engage again in the future.

- What would each person do differently if they had to do the project again? This is in the vein of, "If we knew then what we know at the end, what would that mean for us?" Ideas and insights for future improvement of projects and business success can come from these sessions. This discussion can also be had about the use of SharePoint as a way of facilitating the team's work, that being, "How could we have used SharePoint more effectively in this project?"

There are more and less formal ways of undertaking a debriefing of this nature—they become more formal if the notes from the call are written up and distributed, and are less formal if it's just a discussion among peers. You'll have to do what works for the team in your organization and context, but this is, first and foremost, a learning and reflection exercise for the team, and second, of wider value to the organization. Don't compromise the effectiveness of the first by taking a hard-fisted approach to the second.

What Was Your Personal Vision?

Because the work of the team is completed, it's time to revisit your personal vision statement in the Inner Team site. What was it that you wanted to do or get or buy as a result of a successful completion to the project? If the project has been successful for you, and you have fulfilled the requirements you hold yourself to, it's celebration time!

- If you wanted to do something after achieving success on the project, start making plans to do so. By your involvement in the team project, you have demonstrated your capability to plan and deliver. Now it's time to turn those skills to your own celebration.

- If you wanted to get something after finishing the work—say a promotion or something similar—you can't demand it, but think about what you can do now to capitalize on the project's success. In the case of Roger, it could be a discussion with Kelly about where to go from here for that next step up in the organization.

- If you promised yourself that new watch, laptop bag, car, or phone—or something more or less—then it's shopping time. Go for it … you have worked hard; enjoy the fruits of your hard work.

Update Your My Site with Project Details

With the project at an end, now is the right time to update your My Site page in SharePoint, so that other people can stay informed of what's happening in your world. Remember that the My Profile part of My Site—as per our discussion in Chapter 2, "Managing the Project and Finding a Team"—includes a field for listing the projects you have been involved with. Write in the name of the project that you have just completed; in Roger's case, it's Project Delta (see Figure 9-1). With the search capabilities of SharePoint, when other people are looking for those who took part in your project in the years ahead, it will be right there in your My Site page, ready to be found.

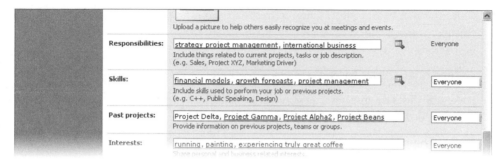

Upload a picture to help others easily recognize you at meetings and events.

Responsibilities:	strategy project management, international business	🔲	Everyone
	Include things related to current projects, tasks or job description. (e.g. Sales, Project XYZ, Marketing Driver)		
Skills:	financial models, growth forecasts, project management	🔲	Everyone
	Include skills used to perform your job or previous projects. (e.g. C++, Public Speaking, Design)		
Past projects:	Project Delta, Project Gamma, Project Alpha2, Project Beans		Everyone
	Provide information on previous projects, teams or groups.		
Interests:	running, painting, experiencing truly great coffee		Everyone
	Share personal and business related interests.		

FIGURE 9-1 Update your My Site page with the name of the project.

Write a Blog Post About the Project

One of the capabilities of My Site that we didn't talk about earlier is the ability to have your own blog. So far, we have concentrated our blogging work within the Inner Team site, but with My Site, you can have a personal blog. If you do have a blog there, go ahead and write a blog post summarizing your work on the project, including the following highlights:

- The role you took within the project

- The names of the other people who you worked with

- The key outcomes of the team's work

- Any key lessons you learned about effective teamwork

Therefore, although your My Profile notes the name of the projects you have been involved with, your blog post goes into more details and gives the human touch. It takes what could be a dull phase and puts a human face on it.

Are You Serious? You Want Me to Do What?

At the conclusion of a team project, someone has to go through and tidy up the documents, files, libraries, and list items within the SharePoint team site. You can't just leave it hanging around forever, because it is information and context that is just not necessary anymore.

Tidying up the SharePoint site for a project like Delta involves the following steps:

1. Publish the final materials and documents into the wider document management system, or on the intranet for everyone to read.

2. Delete the transitory information in the team site that had meaning within the context of the project. With the project finished, this transitory information has no ongoing value.

3. Put in a request to IT for the archival of the Inner Team project site.

4. Delete any lists or libraries that you have added from SharePoint to Outlook 2007, Groove 2007, or Colligo Contributor.

5. Update the general Everyone Else site with the latest information on the project.

And with respect to being serious or not, yes, absolutely. This has got to be done!

Publishing and Sharing the Final Materials

It is time for all of the final recommendation documents and reports from the team site to be published and shared with the rest of the organization. They have been crafted in obscurity, but should now be put out for wider circulation.

Within SharePoint, there are different ways to share the final materials, and you will need to take guidance from your IT people about which method is most appropriate at your organization. For example, the final recommendation document could be published to the document center in SharePoint, or to the intranet as a Web page.

Deleting the Transitory Information

The Inner Team site includes a lot of information that was for the purpose of coordinating team action when coordination of team action was required. With the project finished, this coordination information is no longer useful. It should be deleted. There are three main areas where this information was created:

- The announcements list, for team-wide coordination
- The tasks list, for individual coordination
- The team blog, for contextual coordination

Delete the Announcements and Tasks Lists

You have two choices for deleting the transitory information from the announcements list and the tasks list. Either delete each list entirely from the SharePoint team site, or open each list in turn and go through and see which items should be kept and which should be deleted. For example, to delete the tasks list altogether, open the tasks list, click Settings, click List Settings, and then choose Delete This List (see Figure 9-2).

When you are asked to confirm your deletion, click OK.

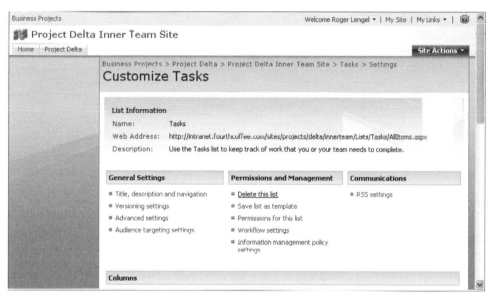

FIGURE 9-2 Delete the Tasks list from the SharePoint site.

To review the items in each list and selectively decide which to delete and which to keep, open the list in datasheet view by clicking Actions, and then clicking Edit In Datasheet. Click and drag your mouse over the items that you want to delete. Right-click and choose Delete Rows (see Figure 9-3). If you use the default view of a SharePoint list, you will have to delete each item in turn by opening it and clicking Delete. That's going to get painful very quickly!

But don't delete the blog! The whole story of the project is in there—you can't delete that!

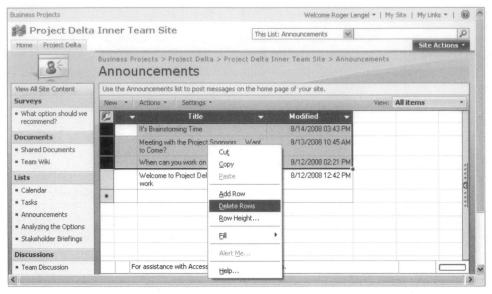

FIGURE 9-3 Select items to delete from the Announcements list.

Delete Unnecessary Document Versions

Another type of transitory information that can be deleted from the team site is the previous document versions. Now that the work of the team is completed, the team site should retain the final versions of all documents, but the intermediate versions can be deleted. Within the Shared Documents library, click the down arrow next to a document, and then click Version History (see Figure 9-4). This opens a page that lists all of the versions for the document. Click Delete All Versions at the top of the page to delete all of the versions of the document, except the latest one.

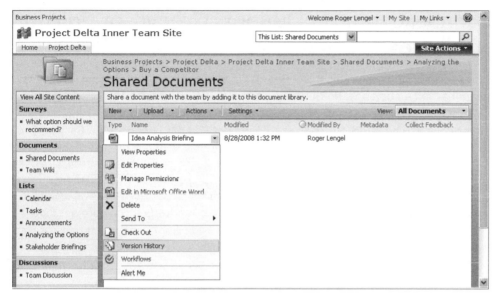

FIGURE 9-4 View Version History for a document and then delete all versions except the final one.

Submitting an Archival Request to IT

With the information in the team site cleaned up and ready for archiving, send a message to your SharePoint consultant in IT and ask the consultant to archive the Inner Team site off the production system. The consultant should have the right workflow tools to enable this movement.

Disconnecting from Outlook, Groove, or Colligo Contributor

With the completion of the project, and the removal of the Inner Team site, everyone on the team has some additional housekeeping to do in any management tools external to SharePoint that were used during the project. Any lists or libraries that were connected to Outlook need to be removed, as do any document libraries connected to Groove, and if the SharePoint site was connected to Colligo Contributor, it needs to be disconnected.

Delete SharePoint Lists in Outlook 2007

In Outlook 2007, find the lists or libraries from the Inner Team site for the project that you have just completed. Right-click the name of the list or library in the left pane of Outlook 2007, and then click Delete (see Figure 9-5). Note that the delete option will include the name of the list or library from SharePoint. When you are asked to confirm that you do want to delete the list or library, click Yes.

FIGURE 9-5 Tidy up Outlook 2007 by removing SharePoint lists and libraries.

Delete Document Libraries from Groove 2007

If you connected the Inner Team site document library to Groove 2007 for offline access to files or for sharing with external third parties, then it is time to delete it from Groove. Open the Groove shared space in which the document library was added, right-click the SharePoint Files Groove tool, and click Delete (see Figure 9-6). When you are asked to confirm that you want to delete the SharePoint Files tool, click Yes.

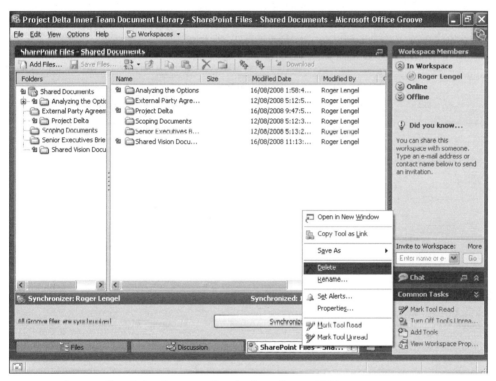

FIGURE 9-6 Remove SharePoint document libraries from Groove 2007.

Remove a Site from Colligo Contributor

If you have used Colligo Contributor to support offline access to the Inner Team site in SharePoint, it's time to remove the site from Colligo. The project work has finished, and you don't need it in Colligo anymore. Open Colligo Contributor, navigate to the site you want to remove, and on the Site menu, click Remove Site (see Figure 9-7). This removes the Inner Team site from your Colligo Contributor client. When you are asked to confirm the removal, click Yes.

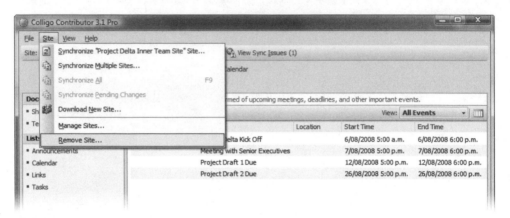

FIGURE 9-7 Remove old SharePoint sites from Colligo Contributor.

Remove RSS Feeds

Any RSS feeds that you have from the Inner Team site should now be removed. With the Inner Team site removed from the production servers, the RSS link that you have been using to access the site will no longer work. So it's time to delete them. The way to do this depends on what you are using for reading RSS feeds:

- With Outlook 2007, expand the RSS Feeds folder, find the folder you created for storing all of the RSS feeds for the project, right-click the folder, and then click Delete (see Figure 9-8). Confirm the deletion when you are prompted.

- Open Microsoft Internet Explorer 7, click Feeds from the Favorites menu, find the feeds from the Inner Team site, and then delete them.

- If you use another product for reading RSS feeds, follow that product's instructions for unsubscribing to a feed.

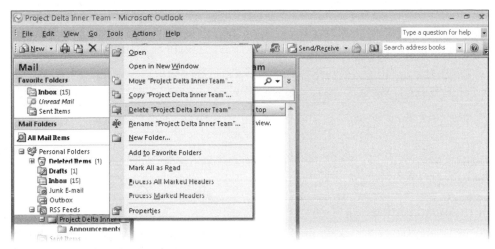

FIGURE 9-8 Delete the RSS feeds from Outlook 2007 for the SharePoint site.

Revamping the Everyone Else Site

With the project completed by the project team, the Everyone Else site needs to be updated to reflect the current and forward-looking nature of the work. During the process of the project, the Everyone Else site needs to reflect "this is what we are doing," but after the work is complete, that emphasis needs to be transformed into both "this is an overview of what we have done" combined with "and this is what's happening now." In other words, this means that the Announcements list in the Everyone Else site needs to be updated to reflect two things:

- What happened in the project
- What's happening now

It also means that the announcements that were previously written, but that are now out of date, need to be deleted or expired. We'll start there.

Delete or Expire the Previous Announcements

The people who visit the Everyone Else site in the future may have no context or background to the project, and so what they find on the Everyone Else site will set the context and background for them. It is very critical, therefore, that what they learn at the Everyone Else site accurately and succinctly states what happened and what's happening, but doesn't mix in previous statements of what happened during the process. This means that the current announcements in the Everyone Else site need to be deleted or expired:

- Deleted announcements are shifted to the Recycle Bin in the Everyone Else site, and no longer show in the Announcements list.

- Expired announcements are noted as being no longer current, but can still be seen in the announcements list if you know where to look.

Taking one approach over the other depends on the record-keeping requirements of your organization.

Delete an Announcement

To delete an announcement, open the Everyone Else site in list view. Open the announcement that you are intending to delete, and click Delete Item (see Figure 9-9). When you are asked to confirm that you really want to delete the announcement, click OK.

Delete all of the announcements that relate to previous stages and phases of the project work, only leaving those that portend to the current reality.

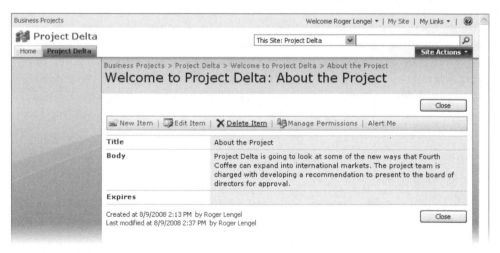

FIGURE 9-9 Delete the old announcements from the list.

Expire an Announcement

When you expire an announcement rather than deleting it, you are signaling that it is no longer a current reflection of reality. An announcement with an expired date that has passed tells the reader that what is stated here was an accurate reflection of reality at some time in the past, but that it is no longer true. An expired announcement no longer shows in the Web Part list of current announcements, but can be accessed by clicking into the Announcements list and viewing all items.

Do three things when expiring an announcement:

- Append (EXPIRED) to the title of the announcement.

- Set the date for expiration.

- Write at the top of the announcement that it is now expired, and note the date of expiration.

To set the date for expiration and make the comment about expiration, open the announcement and put it into Edit Mode. Change the title, set the date to today's date (or a date that is appropriate based on when you are expiring it), and insert the expiration notice at the top of the announcement (see Figure 9-10). If you're feeling particularly colorful, change it to red text to make it leap off the page!

FIGURE 9-10 Expire an announcement that is no longer current.

When you look at the current list of announcements on the main page of the Everyone Else site, you will no longer see the announcements you have just expired. These can be accessed by opening the Announcements list and viewing All Items; the expired announcements clearly state that they have been expired (see Figure 9-11).

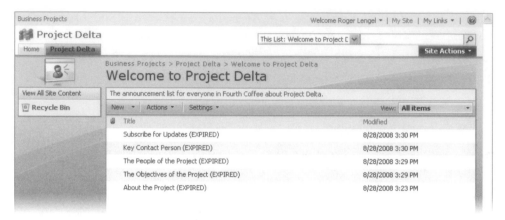

FIGURE 9-11 Expired announcements are clearly marked.

What Happened in the Project?

With the old announcements gone, it's time to create a new set to outline the current reality. There are three key announcements you need to create to talk about what happened in the project:

- An overview of the project
- A list of the people who were involved
- Instructions of where to go for more information

Write the Project Overview

The first announcement to create under the What Happened? category is a summary of the work that was done during the project. This summary needs to include a number of items to give other people an accurate understanding of what happened. For anyone who reads the abstract of the work, it should give keen insight to the context surrounding the work—that is, the factors that described what was going on as the work was being undertaken.

Key areas to note in the abstract of the work are:

- What was the shared vision of the work? Include a brief summary to help people understand the outcomes that were being sought.
- Who were the business sponsors, and at the time of being the business sponsors, what role did they hold in the organization? This signals to future readers the organizational units that were driving the work.
- Who were the stakeholders who were consulted during the project? A brief list of these is sufficient—it shows that you have covered the main people and groups.

- What was the recommended outcome of the work, and where can the key document that summarizes the work be found? If the document is in a document library in another site, include a link to it.

- What were the dates during which the project was worked on? For example, if it ran from August 2007 to July 2008, note that. This helps people in the future who will work with the material to place the work in the organizational context and in the wider marketplace and industry context.

Name this announcement **Project Overview**.

Who Was Involved?

When you review work that has been done by other people, it is helpful to know who was involved. If someone has a good reputation in the organization and has gone on to do great work, that person's presence in a past project sends good signals. If, on the other hand, key players in a project have since been ejected from the organization for negligence or really bad conduct, that calls into question the quality of work they had been involved with.

In making the announcement to outline who was involved, here are some key areas to cover:

- The name of each person, and their organizational role and home (think department or division) at the time of being involved in the project

- For each person, the key expertise that each brought to the project. This signals the type of work that each person did in the context of the project, and where each voice was likely to have been especially strong.

It is too much to expect that you will keep the list of people up to date with their current position in the organization and what they are doing now, but interested readers can start from what you have written, and go from there. Either they will have direct insight into where some of those people are—"Oh wow, Roger's now the Senior VP of International Markets"—or the names will be shrouded in mystery. If the latter, and the mystery needs to be removed, readers can put on their detective hat and make the appropriate inquiries.

Name this announcement **Who Was Involved**.

Where to Go for More Information

The final class of information to include under the What Happened area is where the reader should go for more information. This is important to signal because when people need more information—related to the process, the decisions, the key people—being informed where to go and who to speak with saves them a whole lot of time and effort in trying to figure it out. The team leader and the members of the team know who the best person to speak to will be—they just need to declare that and tell future people who it will be.

So the key information to include when telling people where to go for more information is:

- The name of the key contact person from the team. Ideally there should be a link to the contact's My Site in SharePoint, and at a minimum you should include a current e-mail address and phone number. But the link to My Site would be the perfect thing.

- Where to find the key documents or recommendations coming out of the project. Perhaps those have been published to the intranet, or put into the firm's document management system. For documents published to the intranet, include links. For documents put into the document management system, include links or appropriate references so they can be quickly found.

Name this announcement **For More Information**.

What's Happening Now?

The final announcements to create relate to what's happening now as a result of the project. Knowing where this project fits into the wider fabric of organizational work is helpful for future people, because they are able to track the results of the work and thinking that took place during the project.

Key Projects or Work Coming Out of the Project

The project that you have just finished may be one project in a portfolio of projects related to a common theme. It's important to contextualize this project within that wider work. Do this by including a link to the overall portfolio statement, and to any of the key projects within the portfolio that are able to proceed as a result of this work being completed. Note the dates of the other projects, too, to give a sense of timing to the announcement.

A second way of looking at future projects is that this project could be the seed that started a whole raft of future initiatives. For Roger's project, for example, the strategic recommendations on international expansion will lead to a number of specific projects downstream. You don't have to be exhaustive in including a link to each and every one of these, but you should be at least illustrative. Include links to the key programs of work coming out of your projects, or to the next project in a longer chain of work. Either way, future readers can click through to follow the trail from this project to other things.

Name this announcement **Next Projects**.

Define the Search Terms

The final announcement to create in the Everyone Else site is the one that lists all of the key search terms in the project. Given that the underlying Inner Team site has been removed from circulation through archiving or deletion, the Enterprise Search capabilities in SharePoint will not be able to index the rich corpus of data and documents therein. So you need to make a pretty good attempt at summarizing all of those key words for people who are looking for this project and information related to it in the future.

Create an announcement and enter a free-form list of terms that make sense within the context of the project. You probably don't need to include people's names again, because they are already listed in the Who Was Involved announcement earlier in the announcement list.

Name this announcement **Search Terms**.

Reorder the Announcements

After you have entered all five of the announcements, because the Announcements Web Part orders the announcements by the date and time of last modification, the listing will probably be out of order. We handled this in Chapter 3, "Setting Up SharePoint," by creating the announcements in a certain order, but the other way to do it is to open and resave all of the announcements, starting from the last one to show in the Web Part, and ending with the first one to show in the Web Part.

To resave each announcement, open each one in turn (starting with the Next Projects announcement), click Edit Item, and then click OK. This will save the announcement and put it at the top of the list. Repeat this for each announcement, working backward from what should show at the bottom and ending with what should show at the top. This will take you about 60 seconds for all five announcements.

Remove the Links to the Subsites

With the completion of the project and the archival of the two subsites—the Sponsors and Stakeholders one, and the Inner Team one—comes the need to remove the links to these two sites. Click into the Project Delta Subsites list, and delete the links by clicking the down arrow and then clicking Delete Item (see Figure 9-12). When you are asked to confirm the deletion for each, click OK.

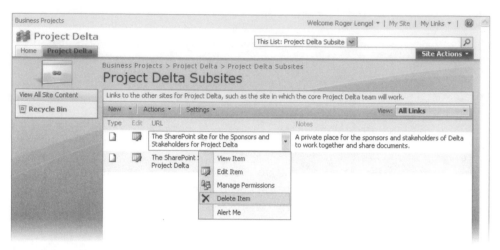

FIGURE 9-12 Delete the two links to the project subsites.

The Revised Everyone Else Team Site

With the old crop of announcements deleted or expired, and the new current and forward-looking ones created, the Everyone Else team site is ready to inform the organization and its people about the project (see Figure 9-13).

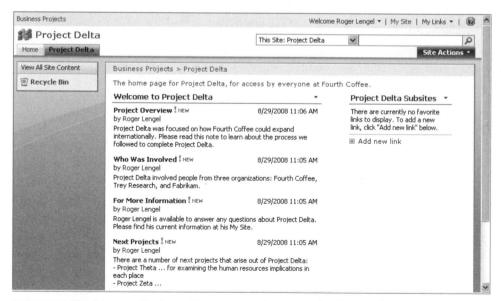

FIGURE 9-13 The Everyone Else team site now shows the correct details going forward.

CHAPTER 10

Winning in the Market

A Year Later ...

ROGER PARKED HIS NEW CAR at his office building in Boston at 7:00 A.M., having breezed through the traffic that morning. He climbed the stairs to his office on the ninth floor, turned on his computer, and looked over his schedule for the day. "Project Delta Team Review Meeting: The 12-Month Milestone" jumped out at him, and he smiled at the recollection of all their work a year earlier. They had done a great job, and today was a day for everyone on the team to meet by audio conference for the annual update and mini-celebration of their work.

The recommendation they had put to the senior executives had been unanimously approved, and high commendations had come back for everyone on the team for the thoroughness and orderliness with which they had carried out the project. The way that Project Delta had been run using SharePoint had become something of a legend in the firm, and a week hadn't gone by since then that Roger wasn't asked to repeat the story and approach to a new team in the firm.

The expansion of Fourth Coffee into the new markets identified by the Project Delta team was progressing beyond expectations—there were already 300 new stores in operation, fully staffed and each turning a profit, and another 300 were in various stages of readiness. That thought brought something to mind, and he fired up Internet Explorer. He opened their latest SharePoint site, the one for tracking the progress of store completions, and was delighted to see that four of the new stores were actually going to open for the first time at 9:00 A.M. today. Indeed, their work had paid off in truckloads, and it had been a great experience for them all.

There had been other changes, too, changes that Roger hadn't anticipated when the project kicked off. He had been living in an apartment in New York, unmarried but hoping to change that. As he had worked with Nancy Anderson more and more closely over the course of Project Delta, and had seen how she worked, and learned first a bit, and then a lot about her interests and goals in life, he had seen a work relationship change into something more personal. They had been married for three months now, and Roger had made the move to Boston and to a suburban home in an upscale area of the city. Truly, life was good!

"It's amazing what can happen in a year," he mused to himself, as he snapped on his headset and dialed into the Project Delta Team Meeting celebration. "Roger here," he said, "It's great to be talking with you all again!"

The Main Tenets of Seamless Teamwork

Our journey to learn how to use SharePoint for collaboration is both at an end and also merely at a beginning. The end—of this book, that is—comes with this chapter, and the ideas and concepts that have been talked through for using SharePoint in teams. The beginning is what happens for you now, for your embrace of the ideas of this book as a set of possibilities for doing your work with others in better and better ways.

So let's recap:

- SharePoint is better for team collaboration than e-mail and network folder shares for quite a few reasons. For example, communicating in SharePoint creates a shared place for teamwork that doesn't suffer from the hazards of e-mail, information management is done right from the beginning, and SharePoint creates opportunities for doing common work practices in better ways than what's possible with e-mail.

- Using SharePoint for team collaboration should be a natural approach to take. Organizations that have set project methodologies can use SharePoint to help run those projects, and for teams that follow the Five Phases Project Life Cycle Model, SharePoint is ideal. SharePoint can help with the entire teaming process, from finding team members, to running the project, and to coordinating the work among a distributed collection of great people.

- SharePoint has to be set up correctly to meet the general needs of the team itself, the wider stakeholders and sponsors of the work, and finally everyone else in the organization who has an interest in what's happening in the project right now, or will have an interest in the future. This calls for a multi-site setup, so all constituencies have their own trusted place to work.

- When a team uses SharePoint for team collaboration, it should be embraced for the three main processes required for a healthy team project: a place for doing the work, an approach for coordinating the work, and a method for sharing the wider context that face-to-face teams get implicitly but which distributed teams usually miss out on.

- The Five Phases Project Life Cycle Model is a common approach taken by teams when working a performance challenge through to completion. Various capabilities in SharePoint can be used to effectively support team collaboration during each part of the process.

- When the performance outcome of the team has been reached, the work of the team needs to be brought to a conclusion. There are people-oriented things to do when a project ends, and there are SharePoint-oriented things, too, such as tidying up the Inner Team site and revising the Everyone Else site.

Doing More with SharePoint

Although this book as an exploration of possibilities with SharePoint is at an end, your exploration should only just be starting. There are many, many capabilities in SharePoint that we didn't even talk about in this book. Some of those will be helpful in your work, and others will not be. Regardless, as you and your team start to use SharePoint more, gaining a deeper appreciation of the whole of SharePoint will arm you with new tools and techniques to bring to your teamwork.

One warning as you start on your own journey of possibilities with SharePoint: as Jessica said in the Foreword, don't let the technology overwhelm the sociology. Just because it is technically possible to do something in SharePoint does not mean that you should do it within your team. By all means try things out and retain what works, but always remember that teamwork requires healthy doses of people stuff on a regular basis. Use SharePoint to support your teamwork, and to put a human face to it, but don't let it become more than it is.

There are many resources available to help you with your ongoing journey of possibilities with SharePoint:

- Numerous bloggers write about SharePoint, albeit many from a technical perspective. There are some gems out there that deal with the user end of SharePoint. Visit *www.seamlessteamwork.com* for a list of the ones I really like.

- Microsoft Press has other books on SharePoint (generally from the technical end). If you can read a technical book on SharePoint and envision the possibilities that it creates for your team, go for it. Visit *www.microsoft.com/learning/ books/default.mspx* to search for other SharePoint books from Microsoft Press.

- There is probably a SharePoint user group in your location. Go along and learn from the experiences of others. If there isn't one, maybe you have just discovered something that you could get involved with.

- There are SharePoint conferences being run around the world every year. Microsoft runs a number, and various conference organizations and Microsoft Business Partners offer others. Search the Web and see what you can find, or talk to your local Microsoft contact about what's coming up. You never know—we might get to meet at such an event!

- Forge a great working relationship with the SharePoint people in your IT organization. Knowledgeable SharePoint consultants are worth their weight in gold, and if they have strong ties with business people and a great awareness of business processes and how to use SharePoint to support teamwork, they are worth 5 to 10 times their weight in gold. If you have such a person at your place, do your bit to building a work relationship with them.

Finally, I have a great interest in learning about your work with SharePoint. I'd love to know about your journey, and how you are applying and modifying the ideas of Seamless Teamwork in your teams. Send me a message at *michael@michaelsampson.net* or contact me through my Web site at *co.michaelsampson.net/contact.html*.

Finding Chapter 11

The focus of this book was on using SharePoint effectively for team collaboration. Although we set up a SharePoint site for the sponsors and stakeholders, we didn't really talk about how they could use that site for their work. In Chapter 8, "Making a Decision," Roger used it to share the draft recommendation with stakeholders by using the Collect Feedback workflow process, but there's much more that can and should be done.

For that, there is Chapter 11, "How to Use the Sponsors and Stakeholders Site." It is an online-only chapter that extends the ideas of Seamless Teamwork to the Sponsors and Stakeholders site, talking about how these groups use the site that has been set up for them.

Given that you own a copy of this book, you can download your free individual copy of Chapter 11 from *www.seamlessteamwork.com*. Use the coupon code "IHAVETHEBOOK" to remove the online price that is shown for the chapter.

Finding Chapter 12

What is written in *Seamless Teamwork* is true and valid within certain parameters: people working on one project, with a small project team, and following the Five Phases Project Life Cycle Model. That is what *Seamless Teamwork* is designed to do, but clearly those parameters are somewhat limited. When you step outside those parameters, do the ideas of *Seamless Teamwork* still apply? Yes, but ....

The "but" is that there are a number of vital governance issues to address when SharePoint is used for collaboration in an enterprise context. And if you don't deal with those issues, bad things are going to happen. Those issues include dealing with larger collaborative projects, avoiding information chaos and anarchy, facilitating adoption and change, the fit between collaborative work and the wider enterprise content strategy, and more. Clearly, these are important issues—and if you and I were discussing SharePoint at your firm, these are the issues we would be discussing—but they are beyond the scope of *Seamless Teamwork* itself.

To introduce these governance issues and to ensure adequate attention is paid to them right from the beginning, there is Chapter 12, "Beyond Seamless Teamwork." It is an online-only chapter that introduces the main governance issues to be considered and agreed upon when embracing SharePoint for collaboration in the enterprise.

As with Chapter 11, you can download your free individual copy of Chapter 12 from *www.seamlessteamwork.com*. Use the coupon code "IHAVETHEBOOK" to remove the online price that is shown for the chapter.

Index

A

B

C

What do you think of this book?

We want to hear from you!

Your feedback will help us continually improve our books and learning resources for you. To participate in a brief online survey, please visit:

microsoft.com/learning/booksurvey

...and enter this book's ISBN-10 or ISBN-13 number (appears above barcode on back cover). As a thank-you to survey participants in the U.S. and Canada, each month we'll randomly select five respondents to win one of five $100 gift certificates from a leading online merchant. At the conclusion of the survey, you can enter the drawing by providing your e-mail address, which will be used for prize notification only.*

Thank you in advance for your input!

Where to find the ISBN on back cover

Example only. Each book has unique ISBN.

Stay in touch!

To subscribe to the *Microsoft Press* *Book Connection Newsletter*—for news on upcoming books, events, and special offers—please visit:

microsoft.com/learning/books/newsletter